The Myth of Morality

In *The Myth of Morality*, Richard Joyce argues that moral discourse is hopelessly flawed. At the heart of ordinary moral judgments is a notion of moral inescapability, or practical authority, which, upon investigation, cannot be reasonably defended. Joyce argues that natural selection is to blame, in that it has provided us with a tendency to invest the world with values that it does not contain, and demands that it does not make. Should we therefore do away with morality, as we did away with other faulty notions such as phlogiston or witches? Possibly not. We may be able to carry on with morality as a "useful fiction" – allowing it to have a regulative influence on our lives and decisions, perhaps even playing a central role – while not committing ourselves to believing or asserting falsehoods, and thus not being subject to accusations of "error."

RICHARD JOYCE is Lecturer in Philosophy at the University of Sheffield. He has published a number of articles in journals including *Journal of Value Inquiry*, *Phronesis*, *Journal of the History of Philosophy*, and *Biology and Philosophy*.

T0381704

The Myth of Morality

Richard Joyce
University of Sheffield

CAMBRIDGE UNIVERSITY PRESS
Cambridge, New York, Melbourne, Madrid, Cape Town, Singapore, São Paulo

Cambridge University Press
The Edinburgh Building, Cambridge CB2 8RU, UK

Published in the United States of America by Cambridge University Press, New York

www.cambridge.org
Information on this title: www.cambridge.org/9780521808064

First published 2001
This digitally printed version 2007

A catalogue record for this publication is available from the British Library

Library of Congress Cataloguing in Publication data
Joyce, Richard, 1966–
The myth of morality / Richard Joyce.
p.   cm.
Includes bibliographical references and index.
ISBN 0 521 80806 5
1. Ethics.   I. Title.
BJ1012 .J69 2001
170–dc21   2001025740

ISBN 978-0-521-80806-4 hardback
ISBN 978-0-521-03625-2 paperback

Wretched virtue! Thou art a mere name,
but I did practice thee as real!

Unknown; cited by Plutarch
"De superstitione," *Moralia*

Contents

Preface

This book attempts to accomplish two tasks. The first part of the book examines moral discourse with a critical eye, and finds the discourse fundamentally flawed. Just what it means for a discourse to be "flawed" will need to be carefully discussed. For the moment, it will do to compare the situation with that of *phlogiston* discourse. Through the sixteenth and seventeenth centuries, the dominant theory for explaining a variety of phenomena – most notably combustion – was to posit a kind of invisible substance in the world: phlogiston. The theory allowed for various chemists, such as Stahl and Priestley, to employ what might be called "phlogiston discourse" – they asserted things like "Phlogiston is lighter than air," "Soot is made up largely of phlogiston," etc. In the eighteenth century Lavoisier showed that this discourse was utterly mistaken: there simply was no such stuff as phlogiston. I wish to argue that our moral discourse is mistaken in an analogous way. We assert things like "Generally speaking, you mustn't tell lies" and "Cloning humans is a terrible thing and mustn't be permitted," and these assertions fail to be true. They fail to be true not because lying or cloning are really okay, but because they employ predicates like ". . . is forbidden" and ". . . is morally good" which are (in senses to be explored) vacuous. Roughly, when one reflects carefully on what it would take for an action to instantiate a property like *being morally forbidden*, one sees that too much is being asked of the world – there is simply nothing that is forbidden in the specifically moral sense of the word. The thought that morality is a fiction in this way is hardly an original thought, enjoying a long history that can be traced back through Camus, Wittgenstein, Russell, Nietzsche, Hume, Mandeville, Hobbes, and all the way to Antiphon and characters like Callicles and Thrasymachus.

Many pieces of our moral vocabulary, of course, have non-moral uses (moving one's rook diagonally in chess is *forbidden*); this non-moral language is not under attack. A further part of the project will be to argue that the obvious response of simply "asking *less* of the world" – that is, of defining or redefining our moral language in such a way that it matches the "unproblematic" evaluative language – is to strip the discourse of its very purpose. The whole point of a moral discourse is to evaluate actions and persons with a particular force, and it is exactly this notion of force which turns out to be so deeply troublesome. To push the analogy: if Lavoisier's concept *oxygen* is theoretically successful, then why could we not redefine "phlogiston" so that it means the same thing as "oxygen," thus rescuing phlogiston discourse from its error? The answer is that when Stahl, etc., asserted things like "Phlogiston plays a central role in calcification," he meant something quite specific by "phlogiston" – the whole point of talking about phlogiston was to make reference to a substance that is *released* during combustion. To use the word "phlogiston" to refer to oxygen – a substance that is *consumed* during combustion – is to undermine the very heart of phlogiston discourse. Likewise, to use the words "morally forbidden" to refer to an "unproblematic" notion of impermissibility – perhaps one with the same logic as "You mustn't move your rook diagonally," or "You ought not stay up so late" – is to undermine the very heart of moral discourse.

Suppose that this first part of the project is correct. One question that it prompts is "Why have we made such a mistake?" – something I spend a chapter addressing in a discussion of the evolutionary origins of a "moral sense." Another question that it raises, the answering of which can be considered the second task of this book, is the practical query: "What, then, ought we to do?" Finding the fatal flaws in phlogiston theory posed no practical problems: we simply did away with that discourse, and it is now only of historical or philosophical interest. Could we really do the same with our *moral* discourse? And if we could, *should* we? Moral discourse, after all, seems terribly important to us in an intimate, potent way. Important decisions – at the level of individual, institution, and state – purport to be sensitive to moral issues. The mere fact that somebody who argues that morality is a "myth" is seen frequently as maintaining not merely a counter-intuitive position, but a *pernicious* or *dangerous* position, reveals that something precious and consequential is at stake.

I wish to argue that morality *is* precious and consequential, but is no less flawed for that. What we *do* with our moral discourse, once we see its flaws, is a pragmatic issue, to be resolved by reference to what is the optimal practical outcome. If morality is useful, then doing away with it incurs a cost. On the other hand, keeping a flawed discourse – one that appears to commit us to holding untrue beliefs and making untrue assertions – also comes at a price, for truth is a very valuable commodity. The latter part of this book is devoted to exploring a means of resolving this tension – a stance which I will call "fictionalism." To take a fictionalist stance towards a discourse is to carry on using it, but in a way that does not commit one to error. One employs the discourse, but does not believe, nor assert, its propositions. Merely in order to gain an initial impression of what I mean, think of a story-teller. The story-teller utters sentences that are false – "Once upon a time there lived a dragon," etc. – but we do not accuse her of lying, error, self-deception, cognitive dissonance, bad faith, or any other dramatic failing. This is because she does not believe the proposition in question, and utters it without assertoric force.

It is not being claimed that our present attitude towards morality is anything like a story-teller's attitude towards her fictional tale. Rather, the attitude is being suggested as something a group might adopt once it has become convinced by arguments for a moral error theory. As such, fictionalism must be seen a piece of advice, not as a "truth." For it to count as good advice, it must win a certain cost-benefit contest. First, we must attempt to ascertain the costs and benefits of doing away with morality altogether. Then we must surmise the costs and benefits of believing (and promulgating belief in) a theory evidence of whose falsehood is available. Lastly, we must examine the costs and benefits of the fictionalist option – the possibility of maintaining the discourse but taking an attitude other than belief towards it (uttering it without assertoric force). I will argue that it is plausible that the third option promises the better results. Examining costs and benefits is, of course, an empirical matter, and the above comparison involves far-fetched and complex counterfactuals. I am sympathetic to anyone who thinks that it is no job for a philosopher to be confidently adjudicating such things, and I make no claims about having a special insight for making such a calculation. My primary task is to ensure that the avenue is properly mapped out, that we at least understand what is involved in taking a fictionalist stance towards a problematic subject matter. Whether it is the stance we *ought* to take towards morality is not something I pretend to assert with any assurance, though I will certainly offer considerations to that conclusion.

My calling morality a "myth" has both a less interesting and a more interesting connotation. The less interesting interpretation is simply that I think morality is a fiction, that it embodies falsehood; in the same way one might speak of "the myth of phlogiston." But "myth" also has a more complex implication, when it signals a false narrative which is important to us – which, perhaps, underlies or regulates many of our actions – a set of images or narratives which we *employ*. This is the view championed by the anthropologist Malinowski, who writes that myth is "a vital ingredient of human civilization; it is not an idle tale, but a hard-worked active force; it is not an intellectual explanation or an artistic imagery, but a pragmatic charter."[1] What particularly interests me is the possibility that myths are frequently identified *as such* by the culture employing them – they are not treated as history or cosmology in any straightforward sense; in other words, those who appeal to the myth realize that they are doing something other than describing the world in a conventional way. The Dorze of Ethiopia, for example, take it that leopards are Christian animals which observe the fast days of the Ethiopian Orthodox Church.[2] This is not a metaphor, for metaphors are something they understand perfectly well, and they do not treat this claim about leopards as one. Nevertheless, a Dorze is no less vigilant in guarding his livestock from leopards on fast days than on any other days. We may simply ascribe to the Dorze inconsistent beliefs on the matter, but the more intriguing possibility is that their attitude towards the proposition "Leopards observe fast days" is a kind of acceptance – one that may modify their behavior in certain circumstances – but is something other than belief.

Whether a particular claim like this will stand up as descriptive psychology is not something that I am qualified to judge, but it does serve as an illustration of the stance that is being suggested for our moral discourse. We may be able to carry on endorsing moral claims, allow them to have a regulative influence on our lives and decisions, perhaps even playing a central role – all the while not committing ourselves to believing or asserting falsehoods, and thus not being subject to accusations of "error." This is, no doubt, all more suggestive than edifying, but at this stage I am just outlining the program in a rough-handed way. The following chapters will attempt to clarify these claims, marshal arguments, and address the obvious criticisms.

This book began life as a Ph.D. dissertation at the Princeton philosophy department, written under the supervision of Gil Harman and Gideon Rosen through late 1996 and early 1997. Without their early support and advice, I doubt that the project would ever have gotten off the ground. Paul Benacerraf, Sarah Broadie, and Harry Frankfurt all contributed productive

---

[1] B. Malinowski, *Myth in Primitive Psychology* (London: Kegan Paul, 1926), p. 23.

[2] This example is from Dan Sperber, *Rethinking Symbolism* (Cambridge: Cambridge University Press, 1984), pp. 93–5.

feedback (the latter being the first person to encourage me to turn it into a book). In the following years the project was intermittently worked and reworked, until it bore little resemblance to my first attempt. During that time several elements have appeared as journal articles: "The Fugitive Thought," *Journal of Value Inquiry* 34 (2000), pp. 463–78; "Rational Fear of Monsters," *British Journal of Aesthetics* 40 (2000), pp. 209–24; "Darwinian Ethics and Error," *Biology and Philosophy* 15 (2000), pp. 713–32. I thank the editors concerned for providing useful criticism. J. E. J. Altham, David Lewis, Michael Smith, and R. Jay Wallace read penultimate drafts of the manuscript and gave invaluable comments. (They did their best, and any foolishness that remains is entirely my own.) I should like, finally, to thank my wife, Wendy, whose faith in the project was invariably there when my own flagged.

1

Error theory and motivation

1.0 FAULTY FRAMEWORKS

When European explorers first interacted with cultures of the South Pacific, they found the islanders employing an unfamiliar concept: a type of forbiddenness called "tapu." Europeans developed this into the familiar English term "taboo," but what we mean by "taboo" is quite unlike what the Polynesians meant. (It is to signal this difference that I have chosen the Maori word "tapu" over "taboo.") It is not the case, for instance, that "tapu" may be translated into "morally forbidden," with accompanying understanding that the Polynesians have different beliefs from Europeans concerning which actions are forbidden. "Tapu" centrally implicates a kind of uncleanliness or pollution that may reside in objects, may pass to humans through contact, may be then transmitted to others like a contagion, and which may be canceled through certain ritual activities, usually involving washing. This is not a concept that we employ, though one may find something similar in ancient Roman and Greek texts.[1]

If one of the European explorers had a penchant for metaethics, what would he say about the Polynesians' discourse? He would naturally take them to have a *defective* concept; no judgment of the form "ϕ is tapu" is ever true (so long as "ϕ" names an actual action[2]) because there simply isn't anything that's tapu. Saying this implies nothing about how tolerant in

---

[1] The Roman term is "sacer" and the Greek "agos." Cf. S. Freud, *Totem and Taboo* [1913] (London: Routledge & Kegan Paul, 1950), p. 18. Whatever ancient European equivalents there may have been to the Polynesian concept, they belonged to a bygone era by the time Maimonides (twelfth century) was trying to explain away the somewhat embarrassing references to "abominations" in Leviticus. I should say that my selection of "taboo" as an illustration is inspired by comments by Alasdair MacIntyre, *After Virtue* (Notre Dame, Ind.: University of Notre Dame Press, 1984), pp. 111–13.

[2] Throughout this book, the symbols "ϕ" and "ψ" generally stand for actions. However, sometimes they stand in for verbs ("ϕing is good," "I want you to ϕ") and sometimes they do the work of nouns ("The action ϕ"). I find this convenient and not noticeably jarring.

The myth of morality

attitude the explorer would be of the Polynesians' discourse; his identifying their discourse as "defective" is consistent with recognizing that it serves them well, and choosing not to point out to them their error. It is also consistent with his electing to employ the concept in sincere assertions of the form "ϕ is tapu," but only when this is an anthropological judgment, elliptical for "For the islanders, ϕ is considered tapu." It would be strange for him to make non-elliptical judgments of the form "ϕ is tapu" if he thought, as he naturally would, of the whole framework as mistaken. And in all of this the explorer would be quite correct: "tapu" is certainly not a term that I apply (non-elliptically), and the reason I don't is that reflection on the kind of "metaphysical uncleanliness" that a literal application of the term presupposes leads to recognition that *nothing* is tapu. I treat the Polynesians' discourse – with all due cultural respect – as systematically mistaken.[3]

But how could it be that a discourse that is familiar to a group of perfectly intelligent people – one that they employ every day without running into any trouble or confusion – is so mistaken? After all, the users of the term unanimously apply it to certain types of action, unanimously withhold it from other actions, and perhaps even agree on a range of types of action which count as a "gray area." Doesn't all this amount to the predicate ". . . is tapu" having a non-empty extension? To see that the answer is "No" we might reflect again on the European explorer's own defective concept: *phlogiston* (we'll assume that his travels predated Lavoisier). The chemists Stahl, Priestley, *et al.*, were equally able to agree on the extension of their favored predicate. Indeed, they were able ostensively to pick out paradigm examples of phlogiston: they could point to any flame and say "*There* is the phlogiston escaping!" And yet for all that they were failing to state truths, for there wasn't any phlogiston. Clearly, when speakers used the predicate ". . . is phlogiston" something more was going on than merely applying it to objects. What sentenced the predicate to emptiness, despite its ostensive paradigms, was that users of the term (considered collectively) thought and said certain things *about* phlogiston such as "It is that stuff stored in bodies," "It is that stuff that is released during combustion" and

---

[3] Cf. the anthropologist E. E. Evans-Pritchard, who, in his influential study of the Azande people, writes of their belief in witchcraft that they display "patterns of thought that attribute to phenomena supra-sensible qualities which . . . they do not possess"; that "witches, as the Azande conceive them, cannot exist". *Witchcraft, Oracles and Magic among the Azande* [1937] (Oxford: Clarendon Press, 1965), pp. 12, 63.

"Soot is made up almost entirely of it," and these concomitant statements are false.[4] It's not that any competent user of the word "phlogiston" was disposed to make these statements – our Pacific explorer, for example, may have had only a rudimentary grasp of the theory, despite being considered perfectly competent with the term. But he would have been willing to defer to the firm opinions of the experts in chemistry of the day, and *they* would have said these things.

Let us say that the above three propositions concerning phlogiston were firmly held by the experts. Let us pretend, further, that these three propositions have a kind of "non-negotiable" status. What I mean by this is the following: Imagine that we were to encounter a population speaking a quite different language to our own, most of which we have translated and tested to our satisfaction, and we find that they have a concept that appears rather like our concept of *phlogiston* (say, it plays a central role in explaining combustion and calcification) – call their term "schmogiston" – but we also find that they don't endorse one of the three propositions about schmogiston. If that would be sufficient for us to decide *not* to translate "schmogiston" into "phlogiston," then the proposition in question must be a non-negotiable part of our concept *phlogiston*. It may not be that any *one* proposition is non-negotiable: perhaps we would be content with the translation if any two of the "schmogiston"-propositions were dissented from, but if the speakers dissented from all three (i.e., they said "No" to "Is schmogiston released during combustion?", "Is schmogiston stored in bodies?", and "Is soot made up of schmogiston?") then we would resist the translation – we would conclude that they weren't talking about *phlogiston* at all. In such a case we might call the disjunction of the three propositions "non-negotiable."

This translation test gives us a way of conceptualizing what we mean by a "non-negotiable" proposition, though I don't pretend that it gives us a widely usable decision procedure (involving, as it does, a complex counterfactual about when we would or wouldn't accept a translation scheme). The point is to make sense of a distinction. On the one hand, we might have a discourse that centers on a predicate "... is P," involving the assertion of a variety of propositions – "*a* is P," "*b* is not-P," "For any *x*, if *x*

---

[4] My rudimentary knowledge of phlogiston theory is derived from F. L. Holmes, *Lavoisier and the Chemistry of Life* (Madison, Wisc.: University of Wisconsin Press, 1987), and J. R. Partington and D. McKie, *Historical Studies on the Phlogiston Theory* (New York: Arno Press, 1981).

is P, then *x* is Q," etc. – and when we discover that we're *mistaken* about one or more of these things – e.g., we discover that some things that are P are not Q – we don't decide that the whole "P discourse" has been a disastrous mistake; we simply change our minds about one aspect of it: we stop making the conditional claim and carry on much as before. On the other hand, there are some discourses regarding which the discovery that one or more of the things we've been assenting to is mistaken leads us to throw in the towel – to stop using the discourse altogether. The latter describes what happened in the phlogiston case: the discovery that we had been wrong in thinking that there is a stuff stored in combustible bodies and released during burning was sufficient for us to decide that there is no phlogiston at all. When Lavoisier gave us the concept *oxygen*, it wasn't available for Stahl to say "Well, this stuff that Lavoisier is calling 'oxygen' just *is* what I've been calling 'phlogiston' all along – I was just mistaken about its being stored and released during combustion." The belief that phlogiston is stored and released was a *non-negotiable* part of phlogiston discourse – the falsity of this belief was sufficient to sink the whole theory.

Now we can see how a smooth-running, useful and familiar discourse, apparently with clear paradigms and foils, could be systematically flawed. The users of the target predicate (or the experts to whom most users firmly defer) assent to a number of non-negotiable propositions – propositions which would play a determinative role in deciding whether or not a translation goes through – and a critical number of these non-negotiable propositions are, in fact, false. This might be how our explorer-cum-metaethicist conceives of the concept *tapu*. If the Polynesians had merely used "tapu" as a kind of strong proscription, and thought, say, that public nudity is *not* tapu but burying the dead is, then (*ceteris paribus*) this would not have prevented the explorer from translating "tapu" into "morally forbidden" while ascribing to the Polynesians some different beliefs about which actions are morally forbidden. But given the kind of robust metaphysics surrounding the notion of tapu – centrally involving supernatural and magical forces – no obvious translation (along with the ascription of different beliefs) was available. The explorer doesn't just attribute to the Polynesians a set of false beliefs – he attributes to them a faulty *framework*. (I don't intend this to sound culturally critical – the eighteenth-century European is certainly no better off with his concept *phlogiston*, and nor, I will argue, are we with our familiar moral concepts.)

4

The terminology introduced by John Mackie to describe this situation is that the European explorer holds an *error theory* regarding the historical Polynesians' "tapu discourse," just as we now hold an error theory with respect to phlogiston theory (for shorthand we can say that we are "error theorists about phlogiston").[5] We don't hold an error theory about *any* discourse involving the term "phlogiston," of course. People continue to talk about phlogiston long after Lavoisier's discoveries – saying things like "Georg Stahl believed in phlogiston," "Phlogiston doesn't exist" – and *that* phlogiston discourse is just fine. What we don't do is assert judgments of the form "*a* is phlogiston" (or make assertions that imply it). It is only a discourse that made such assertions, such as the one existing through the seventeenth century, regarding which we are error theorists.

An error theory, as we have seen, involves two steps of argumentation. First, it involves ascertaining just what a term *means*. I have tried to explicate this in terms of "non-negotiability," which in turn I understood in terms of a translation test (but there may be other, and better, ways of understanding the notion). So, in artificially simple terms, the first step gives us something roughly of the form "For any x, Fx if and only if Px and Qx and Rx." We can call this step *conceptual*. The second step is to ascertain whether the following is true: "There exists an x, such that Px and Qx and Rx." If not, then there is nothing that satisfies "… is F."[6] Call this step *ontological* or *substantive*. The concept of *phlogiston* – with its commitment to a stuff that is stored in bodies and released during combustion – and the concept of *tapu* – with its commitment to a kind of contagious pollution – do not pass the test.

[5] J. L. Mackie, *Ethics: Inventing Right and Wrong* (New York: Penguin Books, 1977). All textual page references to Mackie are to this work. See also his "A Refutation of Morals," *Australasian Journal of Philosophy* 24 (1946), pp. 77–90.

[6] This way of representing the problem is known as giving a "Ramsey sentence" of a term. See F. Ramsey, "Theories," in D. H. Mellor (ed.), *Philosophical Papers* (Cambridge: Cambridge University Press, 1990), pp. 112–36. See also M. Smith, *The Moral Problem* (Oxford: Blackwell, 1994); D. Lewis, "How to Define Theoretical Terms," *Journal of Philosophy* 67 (1970), pp. 427–46, and *idem*, "Dispositional Theories of Value," *Proceedings of the Aristotelian Society*, supplementary volume 72 (1989), pp. 113–37. Those familiar with Lewis's work will know that satisfying the Ramsey sentence does not require finding something that "exactly fits," but something "close enough" will often suffice. The way that I have presented the matter, however, propositions are "weighted" (in a desirably vague manner) *before* the Ramsey sentence is constructed; i.e., a vagueness is intended to be respected in the procedure whereby we establish "non-negotiability." The end result, I take it, is the same. That is, there is no difference between (i) putting forward the Ramsey sentence "$\exists x$ (Fx & Gx & Hx)" and claiming that the sentence is satisfied so long as two of the three conjuncts are satisfied by some object, and (ii) putting forward the sentence "$\exists x$ (Two out of three of the following: $\{Fx, Gx, Hx\}$)."

1.1 THE SEMANTICS OF AN ERROR THEORY

Before proceeding, we shall consider what might be said, semantically, about such an erroneous discourse. It has been claimed that an error theory is the view that all the judgments that comprise the discourse are false.[7] This seems unlikely. For a start, within, say, phlogiston discourse – even that employed by Stahl – there would be a smattering of true claims: he may assert things like "Priestly also believes in phlogiston," "If we were to burn X and phlogiston were to escape, then X would get slightly heavier" (sometimes phlogiston was considered lighter than air). One might try to define "discourse" more carefully, so as to rule out these embedded claims – claiming, perhaps, that they are not *central* to the discourse – but I don't know how that might be done in a systematic way, and I see no reason why such a claim might not be a central one.

A different worry would be that some of the claims might best be considered neither true nor false, especially if we take on board certain views from philosophy of language. Peter Strawson argued that an utterance of "The present king of France is wise" is neither true nor false (if uttered in the present), due to the referential failure of the subject-term of the sentence.[8] Earlier I had Stahl making claims of the form "*a* is phlogiston," but this was rather artificial – surely he also made numerous claims of the form "Phlogiston is F." It would appear then, that if Strawson is correct, the latter kind of judgment ought to be considered neither true nor false. We can take this even further. Frank Ramsey argued that in a sentence of the form "*a* is F," which element is the subject and which element the predicate is entirely arbitrary.[9] For any such sentence we may nominalize the predicate (provide a name for the property) and make *it* the subject of the sentence, and thereby express the same proposition. So "Socrates is wise" becomes "Wisdom is had by Socrates"; "*a* is phlogiston" becomes (less elegantly) "Phlogistonness is had by *a*"; "Mary is next to John" becomes (I suppose) "The relational property of *being next to* is had by the pair <Mary, John>." If we combine Strawson and Ramsey's views, we get

---

[7] For example, by G. Sayre-McCord, "The Many Moral Realisms," in *The Spindel Conference: The Southern Journal of Philosophy*, supplementary volume 24 (1986), pp. 1–22.
[8] P. F. Strawson, "On Referring," in A. Flew (ed.), *Essays in Conceptual Analysis* (London: Macmillan & Co. Ltd., 1956), pp. 21–52.
[9] F. P. Ramsey, "Universals" [1926], in D. H. Mellor (ed.), *Philosophical Papers*, pp. 8–30. For a much more recent discussion of the same idea, see A. Oliver, "The Metaphysics of Properties," *Mind* 105 (1996), pp. 61–8. For defense of Ramsey see L. Nemirow, "No Argument Against Ramsey," *Analysis* 39 (1979), pp. 201–09, and M. C. Bradley, "Geach and Strawson on Negating Names," *Philosophical Quarterly* 36 (1986), pp. 16–28.

the interesting result that if "Fness" fails to refer, then an assertion of the form "*a* is F" ought to be considered neither true nor false.

Just how far this takes us is difficult to say without embarking on a detailed course of metaphysics, for it is not clear what an abstract singular term like "Fness" refers to – what *kind* of thing is a property? I will not advance an answer to this question, but will indulge in a couple of suggestive comments. Nominalizing predicates may smack of Platonistic tendencies, but this appraisal would be unfair. Whatever account we give of *satisfying a predicate* – however metaphysically austere our preference – we can give a matching account of property names. Quine, for example, understands having properties in terms of class membership; the nominalized predicate would then be a name for the class.[10] Referential failure for the class name would require the non-existence of the class, but, since classes are usually thought of as abstract entities, it is hard to know what this would amount to.

One thing it might amount to is this: if the predicate "... is F" has an empty extension across all possible worlds, then "Fness" fails to refer. Typically, concepts that we think of as defective will not satisfy this criterion. For example, the natural thing to say about "... is phlogiston" is that it has an empty extension in the actual world, but has a non-empty extension in other possible worlds: phlogiston theory is false, but only contingently so. In other words, there *is* a property which "phlogistonness" denotes, it is just that nothing in the actual world has this property. It is possible, however, that a predicate might suffer a more serious kind of defect: if it were in some manner self-contradictory, or if it entailed a strong modal claim which turned out to be false, then we might conclude that its extension is empty in all possible worlds. (Later I will discuss concrete cases for which this might be argued.) I am suggesting, though not arguing, that this may be sufficient for the conclusion not merely that nothing has the property in question, but that there simply is no property at all.

Whether we accept the latter unusual view is a matter of how we choose to theorize about properties, which in turn is dependent on weighing the theoretical costs and benefits of various contending positions, and none of this is attempted here, bar one comment. An obvious rejoinder from the Quinean is that property names *do* succeed in referring even when they have empty extensions over all possible worlds – they refer to the null set.

---

[10] See W. V. Quine, *Mathematical Logic* (Cambridge, Mass.: Harvard University Press, 1951); *idem, Methods of Logic* (London: Routledge & Kegan Paul, 1952); *idem, Theories and Things* (Cambridge, Mass.: Harvard University Press, 1981).

A consequence of this is that all such property names would refer to the same entity, so that "Round squareness is purplish yellowness" would be a necessary (and *a priori*) truth. This is such a counter-intuitive result that it must be classed as a theoretical cost.[11]

The above comments are not put forward with any rigor, and are intended primarily to undermine the claim that an error theory holds that the judgments of a discourse are *all false*. Putting aside the complex question of property names, the same point may be made employing only Strawson's familiar (though by no means uncontested) views. We can conceive of a discourse revolving around a normal singular term, like "Elizabeth I," and if we were to discover (bizarrely) that our Tudor history has been the subject of a monstrous hoax, and in fact the name "Elizabeth I" fails to denote anybody, then a Strawsonian would conclude that large tracts of our "Tudor discourse" are neither true nor false. (This might be what we choose to say about the failure of ancient Greek polytheistic discourse – with all those empty names like "Zeus," "Aphrodite," etc.) This conclusion would be properly classed as an *error theory*.

To some readers, this may seem like a surprising taxonomy. The view that our moral judgments are neither true nor false is often equated with the metaethical position known as "noncognitivism," but the noncognitivist and error theoretic positions are distinct. However, I prefer to understand noncognitivism not in terms of truth values, but in terms of assertion. Assertion is not a semantic category; it is, rather, a purpose to which a sentence may be put: one and the same sentence may on some occasions be asserted, on other occasions not asserted. The question then is not whether "*a* is F" *is* an assertion, but whether it is typically used assertorically. The noncognitivist says "No": the sentence "*a* is F" is typically used to express approval, or as a disguised command.

A moral cognitivist will, by contrast, hold that sentences of the form under discussion are usually used assertorically. But this is not to say that the cognitivist holds that moral sentences are usually either true or false, for (some have argued) there can be assertions that are neither. Strawsonian presupposition failure is one example. According to some views,

---

[11] An insistence that such terms refer to the null set might be accused of being a philosophically motivated attempt to provide a term with a referent at all costs (a "shadowy entity" as Quine called it in *Methods of Logic*, p. 198) – a strategy widely, though not universally, rejected for empty ordinary singular terms like "Zeus," "the present king of France," etc. For proponents of *the null individual*, see R. Carnap, *Meaning and Necessity* (Chicago: University of Chicago Press, 1956), pp. 36–8; R. M. Martin, "Of Time and the Null Individual," *Journal of Philosophy* 62 (1965), pp. 723–36.

the assignment of certain vague predicates to "gray area" objects will also result in assertions that are neither true nor false. The difference is brought out by imagining a conversation in which one person utters "The present king of France is wise" and her companion responds "Say that again." A Strawsonian would hold that neither utterance is true or false, but it would be an odd view that held that the former utterance is not asserted (and an odd view that held that the latter utterance *is* asserted). We might say that the former utterance was "in the market for truth," whereas "Say that again," being a command, is never in that market, and is therefore automatically neither true nor false.

An error theory, then, may be characterized as the position that holds that a discourse typically is used in an assertoric manner, but those assertions by and large fail to state truths. (These qualifications of vagueness should not cause concern; to expect more precision than this would be unrealistic.) This is clearly the correct stance to take towards phlogiston discourse. The view that seventeenth-century speakers typically spoke without assertoric force when they uttered sentences of the form "*a* is phlogiston" may be rejected. And such judgments were not true. (Presumably they were simply false, though we've left open the door for an argument to the conclusion that they were neither true nor false.) However, when it comes to our other model – "tapu discourse" – noncognitivism raises its seasoned head.

1.2 NONCOGNITIVISM

A noncognitivist of the classic stripe might claim that when a Polynesian utters the sentence "ϕ is tapu" she is doing nothing more than evincing her disapproval; she is really saying something equivalent to "ϕ: boo!" Charles Stevenson claimed something more complex (about "morally bad" rather than "tapu") – that the utterer is both asserting something about herself *and* issuing a command: "I disapprove of ϕ; do so as well!"[12] If either version is correct, the error theoretic stance dissolves: regardless of what kind of properties there are or are not in the world, the speaker is not reporting them – and *a fortiori* is not mistakenly reporting them. (I'm putting aside the self-describing element of Stevenson's account, since one is hardly usually going to be in error regarding oneself.) If one employs a faulty theory – astrology, say – but withholds assertoric force from the propositions in

---

[12] C. L. Stevenson, "The Emotive Meaning of Ethical Terms," *Mind* 46 (1937) pp. 14–31; *idem*, *Ethics and Language* (New Haven: Yale University Press, 1944).

question – for example, if one says "As a Cancer, I'm inclined towards domestic pursuits and sentimentality" as part of telling a story, or a joke – then (despite the falsity of the *sentence*) one has not made a mistake. Should there be a discourse comprised of such utterances, the error theoretic stance would be inappropriate.

Noncognitivism is often naively presented in terms of "When people say X all they are really saying is Y." This relation of "all they are really saying," "all they really mean," is quite puzzling. There are two ways of understanding the relation: as a semantic or as a pragmatic relation. Early noncognitivists, it would appear, read it as a semantic relation. When a person says "ϕ is good" what the sentence *means* is "ϕ: hurray!" (or whatever). In a much-quoted passage, A. J. Ayer claims that a moral judgment like "Stealing is wrong" lacks "factual meaning." If I utter it, I "express no proposition which can be either true or false. It is as if I had written "Stealing money!!" – where the shape and thickness of the exclamation marks show, by a suitable convention, that a special sort of moral disapproval is the feeling which is being expressed. It is clear that there is nothing said which can be true or false."[13] This is, on the face of it, an odd claim. Why would we clothe our emotive expressions in the form of sentences generally used to report facts, when we have at our disposal a perfectly good means for expressing them without going to the trouble? If all we're saying is "Do ϕ!" then why don't we just *say* "Do ϕ!"? The fact is, if someone participating in a serious moral discussion chose to express herself explicitly in the "uncooked" manner – imagine a member of a hospital ethics committee expressing her judgments as a series of "Hurray!"'s and grunts of disapproval – we would be appalled. This is quite telling against the noncognitivist: it is implausible that two types of sentence could *mean the same* if we would treat discourse conducted in terms of one as sober and serious, and reject discourse conducted in terms of the other not merely as inappropriate, but as utterly mystifying. This kind of semantic noncognitivism, furthermore, is notoriously subject to a powerful criticism known as the "Frege–Geach problem."[14] This objection states that utterances like "Hurray!" and "Do ϕ!" do not behave *logically* like their supposed counterparts of the indicative mood. You cannot sensibly put "ϕ: Boo!" into the antecedent slot of a conditional (whereas you can plug in "ϕ is tapu"); nor could it appear as the minor premise of a valid piece of *modus ponens* reasoning

[13] A. J. Ayer, *Language, Truth and Logic* [1936] (Harmondsworth: Penguin, 1971), p. 110.
[14] See P. T. Geach, "Ascriptivism," *Philosophical Review* 69 (1960), pp. 221–5; *idem*, "Assertion," *Philosophical Review* 74 (1965), pp. 449–65.

(since validity is defined in terms of the *truth* of the premises guaranteeing the truth of the conclusion).

A noncognitivist fares better if he proposes the relation of "what they really mean" as a pragmatic one. This is how the theory was presented above, and is, apparently, how Stevenson understands things when he claims that the "major *use* [of ethical judgments] is not to indicate facts, but to create an influence."[15] This need not be a claim about meaning, but a claim about how we employ our moral language (thus "what they really mean" is roughly equivalent to "what they really intend"). One advantage of this version is that the noncognitivist can at least point to areas of our non-moral vocabulary for which noncognitivism is a highly plausible option. A useful case to think about is that presented by John Austin.[16] According to Austin (and I've never found reason to doubt it), someone who utters the sentence "I name this ship *The Beagle*," when in the orthodox circumstances involving cheering crowds, a bottle of champagne, etc., is not asserting anything, despite the indicative mood. She is not *describing*, or *reporting* the fact that she names the ship – the uttering of the sentence *is* the naming of the ship. Another example is that of an actor: someone playing the part of Hamlet on the stage would at some point utter "The air bites shrewdly," but would not be asserting this fact. A third example is sarcasm: if one were to utter the sentence "That dinner party was fun" in a tone dripping with sarcasm, one would not thereby be asserting that the event was fun.

Now the noncognitivist might present her position along similar lines: although we frequently render our moral judgments in the indicative mood, we are (generally) not asserting them; rather, we are expressing emotions, issuing commands, etc. Such a noncognitivist could claim immunity from the Frege–Geach problem. If it were pointed out to Austin that the following is a valid instance of *modus ponens*, it would hardly cause concern for his theory of performatives:

1. I name this ship *The Beagle*
2. If I name this ship *The Beagle*, then I must have the authority to do so
3. Therefore, I must have the authority to do so

The fact that the sentence "I name this ship *The Beagle*" is usually, or even always, used in a non-assertoric manner does not mean that it cannot

---

[15] Stevenson, "Emotive Meaning," p. 18 (italicization altered).
[16] J. L. Austin, *How to do Things with Words* (Oxford: Oxford University Press, 1962).

function perfectly legitimately in logically complex contexts; it does not follow that the sentence *means* anything other than what it appears to mean.

So the noncognitivist who claims that moral judgments (or tapu judgments) are not assertions can at least locate some partners in innocence. But despite this it is highly implausible that moral discourse is non-assertoric. Let us say that to assert that p is to express the belief that p.[17] It does not follow that the speaker need have the belief: a liar may express a belief that she doesn't have (a lie being a species of assertion). The pertinent relation of "expression" here denotes an expectation of what the utterance accomplishes, which is determined by a set of linguistic conventions. For example, if the utterance is preceded by "Once upon a time," then convention stipulates that the speaker may not believe what follows, and is not putting it forward for others to believe. (Similarly if it is uttered in an overtly sarcastic manner.) Linguistic conventions are not maintained through mind-reading – they are taught, learned, and communicated – and we should therefore be able to determine whether a fragment of language is assertoric.[18] What is required is an investigation of the ways moral language is used, in order to determine whether it bears any features indicative of the withdrawal of assertoric force.

Peter Glassen, in his 1959 paper, argued that whether an utterance is an assertion depends upon the intentions of the speaker.[19] I do not think this is quite correct, since a person may misunderstand the linguistic conventions to such an extent that despite a sincere intention to assert something, she fails to. (I once saw a comedy sketch in which an unfortunate person was doomed to utter everything in a sarcastic tone of voice.) Nevertheless, Glassen's way of arguing against noncognitivism is along the right lines. He asks "What would count as evidence of a person's intentions when he uses moral language?" – and he answers that since we are fallible with respect to reporting our own intentions, the best one could do is look at how a person does in fact use moral judgments. "We must observe the way he utters them, what else he says in relation to them, how others interpret them, and so on; in short, we must observe the characteristic

---

[17] The account of "assertoric force" appealed to throughout this book is intended to be that put forward by Austin, *How to do Things with Words*, and developed by J. R. Searle, *Speech Acts* (Cambridge: Cambridge University Press, 1969). Assertion is discussed in greater length in Chapter 7, below.

[18] By "linguistic conventions" here I do not mean to include the grammatical features of language, for which, of course, there is excellent evidence of their being innate.

[19] P. Glassen, "The Cognitivity of Moral Judgments," *Mind* 68 (1959), pp. 57–72.

features of moral discourse, and see how they compare with the characteristic features of discourse already known or, at any rate, believed to be cognitive" (pp. 61-2). Glassen's point is that if all the evidence suggests that we intend to use our moral language in an assertoric manner, then all the evidence suggests that our moral language *is* assertoric, for assertion is entirely a matter of our intentions. The evidence that Glassen assembles I would employ to a slightly different end: as confirmation that the linguistic conventions that govern moral discourse are those of assertions. Here is Glassen's list (which we can feel confident in assuming holds for historical Polynesian "tapu discourse," too):

1. They (moral utterances) are expressed in the indicative mood
2. They can be transformed into interrogative sentences
3. They appear embedded in propositional attitude contexts
4. They are considered true or false, correct or mistaken
5. They are considered to have an impersonal, objective character
6. The putative moral predicates can be transformed into abstract singular terms (e.g., "goodness"), suggesting they are intended to pick out properties
7. They are subject to debate which bears all the hallmarks of factual disagreement

We can add to this list the two related characteristics highlighted by Peter Geach.[20]

8. They appear in logically complex contexts (e.g., as the antecedents of conditionals)
9. They appear as premises in arguments considered valid

The noncognitivist Rudolf Carnap wrote "Most philosophers have been deceived [by syntactic structure] into thinking that a value statement is really an assertive proposition . . . But actually a value statement is nothing else than a command in a misleading grammatical form . . . It does not assert anything."[21] Given Glassen's evidence, Carnap's claim that *philosophers* have been misled into thinking moral utterances are assertoric is surely too weak – rather, it would seem that we are *all* misled. But it simply will not do for the noncognitivist to claim that we are all misled or mistaken in

---

[20] P. Geach "Assertion." See also C. Wellman, "Emotivism and Ethical Objectivity," *American Philosophical Quarterly* 5 (1968), pp. 90–9.
[21] R. Carnap, *Philosophy and Logical Syntax* (London: Kegan Paul, Trench, Trubner & Co. Ltd., 1935), pp. 24–5.

participating in the above practices, for it is exactly our participation in these practices that provides the best evidence as to the truth of the matter.

There is one kind of *non*-assertoric discourse that bears many of the above features, and that is fictive discourse. This is so because fictive discourse by its very nature mimics ordinary discourse – it is the job of make-believe to copy. But fictive discourse is still, in a wider context, distinguishable from assertoric discourse, for we are disposed to "step out" of make-believe when pressed. If someone says in the appropriate tone of voice "But you don't *really* believe in Sherlock Holmes, do you?", the story-teller (despite having just uttered a series of indicative, logically complex sentences involving "Holmes") answers "No, of course not." We find no such widespread tendency concerning moral discourse.

In the absence of an explanation of *why* we would have a non-assertoric discourse bearing all the hallmarks of an assertoric one – in the absence of an explanation of why, if we already have perfectly good linguistic devices for expressing commands (imperatives) we should choose to cloak them systematically in indicative form – we must assume that if something walks and talks like a bunch of assertions, it's highly likely that it *is* a bunch of assertions. Stevenson attempted to provide such an explanation when he claimed that moral language is largely a manipulative device: "When you tell a man that he oughtn't to steal . . . [you are attempting] to get him to disapprove of it. Your ethical judgment has a quasi-imperative force which, operating through suggestion, and intensified by your tone of voice, readily permits you to begin to influence, to modify, his interests."[22] I find Stevenson's explanation, however, curiously self-undermining.

If I want James to ϕ, and I am going to attempt to satisfy this desire using language, I have a choice of how to proceed. I might say to James "Do ϕ!" Or I might say "I very much want you to ϕ." Or I might say "You must ϕ; ϕing is obligatory." Stevenson says that moral language (the third option) evolved because it is the most effective. Whence its extra rhetorical force? Presumably, the thought of an action being *required* carries more influence than a mere order or statement of desire. By merely barking an order to James, I can expect a request for a reason, and that reason may be only the statement that I have a desire to see ϕing done. But just telling James that I want to see him ϕ wears its "escapability" on its sleeve: if James has no interest in satisfying my desires, then he has been provided with no reason to ϕ. If, however, I say that ϕing is *morally required*, then it would

[22] Stevenson, "Emotive Meaning," p. 19 (italicization altered).

seem that I have provided James with a reason: morality demands ϕing, and James, like everyone else, is bound by the prescriptions of morality. If I can promulgate to my fellows that there is a set of rules which binds us all, then I have created a framework within which I can express my "will to power" most effectively – all I need do is persuasively claim of any action which I desire to see done that the set of rules demands it.

Suppose this Stevensonian picture, with its manipulative view of moral interaction laid bare, were correct. Then, when I say "ϕing is obligatory" what is the function of my utterance? We can agree with Stevenson that the utterance is a tool by which I hope to see my desires satisfied. But how does the tool work? It's a tool which makes reference to certain properties had by certain actions (even potential actions): "obligatoriness." It is in virtue of making reference to these properties that the utterance has more rhetorical influence than "I want you to ϕ" or "I approve of ϕing; do so as well." If I am clear-headed about my manipulative behavior, then I do not really believe that there is any such property – I am making reference to it merely in the hope that my audience is gullible. In such a case I am lying: I am trying to get my audience to form beliefs that I don't have. Chances are, few of us are so scheming in our expressions of will to power; rather, we have been subject to the manipulative behaviors of others, and thus have bought into the whole "must-be-doneness" framework. So when I really want to see ϕing done, I may well *believe* that it instantiates this property; thus my utterance is no lie, it's an expression of a belief. But either way – whether we are clear-headed about our manipulative ways or not – moral utterances turn out to be *assertions*. The fact that I say something in order to satisfy a desire to see James ϕ does not make that utterance a command, any more than my saying to a student "Descartes was French" is a command in virtue of the fact that ultimately I hope to influence the student to write true things rather than false things in the exam.

In light of these problems for the noncognitivist, I will proceed under the natural assumption that our moral language is used largely in an assertoric manner. Noncognitivism is implausible as a description of our own moral language, just as it is implausible as an account of serious judgments of the form "ϕ is tapu." Of course, there is much moral language that is clearly not assertoric ("Don't do that!" etc.), but it bears a vital relation to the assertoric portion: if one were not willing to assert "ϕing is morally forbidden" one would not be willing to press the moral injunction "Don't ϕ!" Were the assertoric language shown to be hopelessly flawed – based on a mistake about the nature of agency, or the nature of the world – then the imperatival portion of the language would not remain unscathed.[23]

Now we know what an error theory in general looks like, we can turn to the case that interests us: the possibility that it is the appropriate stance to take towards our own familiar moral discourse. In this section I have argued that moral discourse is assertoric; it remains to be argued that these assertions are *untrue*. The argument is most usefully approached via a discussion of Mackie's original version.

1.3 MACKIE'S ERROR THEORY

John Mackie's argument for a moral error theory embodies two steps. First he attempts to establish a conceptual relation – that is, he looks for what a moral use of the predicate "... is good" *means*. He then embarks on the substantive step, showing that the meaning in question is not satisfied by the world. Concerning the former, Mackie thinks that all uses of the word "good" boil down to "*such as to satisfy the requirements of the kind in question.*" The "requirements in question" could involve the use to which we put cars (allowing us to speak of "a good car"), the end of winning a game of chess ("a good move"), or the fulfilling of a social role ("a good quarterback"), etc. These are all, in one way or another, requirements which *we* impose upon the world. When we use "good" with moral strength, however, we advert to requirements which are "just there" – in the nature of things. All non-moral uses of "good" involve requirements for which there is, roughly speaking, a "requirer"; but when we up-the-ante to a moral "good," we are implicitly referring to requirements for which there is no requirer – laws for which there is no law-maker. Non-moral uses of "good" are what we might call "subjectively prescriptive" (they are prescriptive ultimately in virtue of our desires, intentions, beliefs, etc.), but moral uses of "good" are "objectively prescriptive." That's the conceptual step. The substantive step of Mackie's argument is to argue that there *are no* "objective prescriptions": the universe, without our impositions upon it, simply does not make requirements. Thus judgments of the form "ϕ is morally good" are never true (when ϕ takes an actual value).

One may attempt to block the two-step operation at either stage. One class of critics agrees that "objective prescriptions" are completely bizarre, but they deny that our moral discourse ever commits us to anything so

---

[23] I discuss noncognitivism in more detail in "Noncognitivism, Motivation, and Assertion" (forthcoming).

strange. Another class is inclined to agree that our moral discourse does embody a commitment to objective prescriptions, but denies that they are particularly odd – properly understood, the universe does make requirements of us. Strategically, it is available to the error theorist to play off the two types of critic against each other. That critic who finds "objective prescriptivity" sustainable will generally also want to argue that we *are* committed to it (for it would be an unusual view that held that objective prescriptions are defensible but the truth of nothing we say requires their defense). From this critic's latter arguments the error theorist may draw adventitious support against her other type of opponent.

Sketched in the above terms, Mackie's notion of "objective prescriptivity" is too blunt for a proper argument to be conducted; in what follows I shall attempt to nail down what it might mean in more precise terms. Whether my claims ultimately are convincing as illuminations of Mackie is not important. What matters is that I utilize the same form of argument: first to find some thesis T to which our ordinary moral discourse is committed (a "non-negotiable" element), then to argue that T is false. The latter step promises to be the more straightforward: the annals of philosophy are strewn with arguments exposing faulty theses. This is not to say it is easy – but at least we know the nature of the sport. But to make a case that a discourse is "committed to some thesis" is an altogether more elusive game. In §1.0 I suggested a way of conceptualizing the issue – in terms of when we would or wouldn't accept a translation – but this was not intended as a decision procedure.

I will examine two broad interpretations of "objective prescriptivity." The first occupies the remainder of this chapter. The reader ought to be warned that I do not take this argument to be very convincing, and so the chapter ends on rather an unsatisfactory note. The intention is, first, to pursue an argument which is interesting even if not altogether persuasive, and, second, to gain insight into how an argument for a moral error theory might operate. Perhaps it is best if the rest of this chapter is seen as a warm-up exercise for a much stronger argument – the second interpretation of "objective prescriptivity" – which will occupy later chapters.

1.4 INTERNALISM ABOUT MOTIVATION

There is a thesis which I will call "internalism about motivation" which has been thought (i) to be a non-negotiable commitment of moral discourse, and (ii) to be false.

MI: It is necessary and *a priori* that any agent who judges that one of his available actions is morally obligatory will have some (defeasible) motivation to perform that action.

Advocates of (i) tend to reject (ii), and proponents of (ii) tend to reject (i), and thus most followers of either (i) or (ii) avoid an error theory. David Brink appears to interpret Mackie's error theory as consisting of the endorsement of (i) and (ii).[24] Understandably so: reading *Ethics: Inventing Right and Wrong*, it certainly seems as if the flaws of moral discourse have *something* to do with motivation. "Objective prescriptivity" is compared with Platonism, whereby knowing that something is good "will not merely tell men what to do but will ensure that they do it" (*Ethics*, p. 23), and will provide the knower "with both a direction and an overriding motive" (p. 40). The argument that Brink finds in Mackie presumably goes like this:

"Mackie's Argument":

　　1. MI is false
　　2. Morality is committed to MI
∴. 3. Morality is flawed (i.e., a moral error theory)

Brink goes on to argue that MI is false. But in the context of reading Mackie as above, while trying to resist the conclusion, this seems an odd strategic move. Perhaps Brink is arguing as follows:

"Brink's Argument":

　　1. MI is false
∴. 2. Morality was never committed to MI in the first place
∴. 3. "Mackie's Argument" is unsound

However, the move from premise (1) to (2) in "Brink's Argument" is simply question-begging against the moral error theorist.

　　At any rate, if MI is so fantastic, it is curious that it finds so many staunch defenders. Hume wrote: "Morals excite passions, and produce or prevent actions. Reason of itself is utterly impotent in this particular."[25] In a similar vein, W. Frankena writes that "it would seem paradoxical if one were to say 'X is good' or 'Y is right' but be absolutely indifferent to its being

---

[24] D. Brink, "Moral Realism and the Skeptical Arguments from Disagreement and Queerness," *Australasian Journal of Philosophy* 62 (1984), pp. 111–25; *idem*, "Externalist Moral Realism," *Southern Journal of Philosophy*, supplementary volume 24 (1986), pp. 23–41.

[25] D. Hume, *A Treatise of Human Nature* [1739], book 3, part 1, section 1, ed. L. A. Selby-Bigge (Oxford: Clarendon Press, 1978), p. 457. The noncognitivist conclusion that Hume immediately draws is that the "rules of morality, therefore, are not conclusions of our reason."

done or sought by himself or anyone else. If he were indifferent in this way, we would take him to mean that it is generally regarded as good or right, but that he did not so regard it himself."[26] The latter quote, focusing on the possibility or impossibility of a type of agent – one who makes sincere moral judgments but is left motivationally inert – draws the battle lines for debating MI: if such an agent is possible, then MI is false; if not, then it is true. I agree with Brink that MI is false, and will present my reasons in a moment. I must admit, however, to being somewhat half-hearted about the task, since I have doubts about the second step of the argument: that our moral discourse is committed to MI.

Debate has focused on the *amoral* agent: a stipulated form of amoralism that consists precisely of making sincere moral judgments but having no motivation. We are invited to imagine a thoroughly depressed person – utterly unmoved yet still making moral judgments.[27] The motivation internalist will try to deny the case: perhaps the person is not really making a moral judgment, but rather saying something "in quote marks." "Although I know that fulfilling my promises is correct, I just feel unmoved" becomes "Although I know that most people think that my fulfilling my promises is correct, I just feel unmoved." The latter claim is not a moral judgment; it is a non-moral judgment about what other people's moral judgments are. This is a useful rejoinder for the motivation internalist. It is a response that can be used again and again because we are considering an agent who *ex hypothesi* is motivationally inert, and therefore our only grounds for holding that she makes a moral judgment is that she *says so*; but given people's notorious unreliability at reporting their own states, the evidence for the occurrence of a sincere moral judgment is always going to be vulnerable to reinterpretation. It would be better if we could locate an agent for whom there is some feature that is *explained* by her having made a sincere moral judgment. The best contender for the role of counter-example to MI, therefore, is not the amoral agent but the thoroughly *evil* agent – the agent whose moral judgments do not leave him motivationally cold, but which provide the reason for his diabolical actions. (This is not to deny that depressed agents may well *be* counter-examples to MI, it is just that it is difficult to establish the fact.[28])

[26] W. K. Frankena, *Ethics* (Englewood Cliffs, NJ: Prentice-Hall, Inc., 1973), p. 100.
[27] See Brink, "Moral Realism"; Smith, *Moral Problem*; R. D. Milo, "Moral Indifference," *The Monist* 64 (1981), pp. 373–93.
[28] See M. Stocker, "Desiring the Bad: An Essay in Moral Psychology," *Journal of Philosophy* 76 (1979), pp. 738–53.

1.5 PURE EVIL

Few cases from history and literature of what we would usually call "evil" will satisfy this criterion. One of the internalist's standard rejoinders – that the agent is akratic, or acts badly so as to attain some end (and therefore is not doing evil *for evil's sake*), or has just rejected the whole realm of morality – will probably be highly plausible and not *ad hoc*. Occasionally, though, we run into an evil character who is really interested in morality itself, and with whom we must credit genuine moral judgments in order to explain his or her behavior. Some of the villains from the Marquis de Sade's work, for example, are not just interested in hedonism and sadism – they appear to be self-consciously pursuing whatever they consider to be *bad*.[29] If they judged excessive, sadistic hedonism to be morally acceptable, then we naturally think of them as ceasing to pursue it. Shakespeare's despicable Aaron, from *Titus Andronicus*, goes to his death with the words "If one good deed in all my life I did, I do repent it from my very soul." Or consider the following from Edgar Allen Poe:

> Who has not, a hundred times, found himself committing a vile or a silly action, for no other reason than because he knows he should *not*? Have we not a perpetual inclination, in the teeth of our best judgment, to violate that which is *Law*, merely because we understand it to be such? This spirit of perverseness, I say, came to my overthrow. It was this unfathomable longing of the soul *to vex itself* – to offer violence to its own nature – to do wrong for the wrong's sake only – that urged me to continue and finally to consummate the injury I had inflicted upon the unoffending brute.[30]

The upholder of MI will have to deny that Poe's character, taken at face value, is possible. But this denial, if pursued, becomes implausible. Before proceeding though, let me make a brief aside to head off some potential misunderstanding. The "big picture" that we are considering is that moral discourse is committed to MI, and MI is false (hence, an error theory). However, we are now attacking MI, and our means for doing so is to

---

[29] Marquis de Sade, *The Complete Justine, Philosophy in the Bedroom, and other Writings*, trans. and ed. R. Seaver and A. Wainhouse (New York: Grove Press, 1965); *The Misfortunes of Virtue, and other Early Tales*, trans. D. Coward (Oxford: Oxford University Press, 1992). My discussion of de Sade is greatly indebted to G. Rosen's "Internalism and Common Sense: A Philosophical Lesson from *Philosophie dans le boudoir*" (unpublished manuscript, 1989). Though Rosen draws conclusions from the philosophical lesson very different from my own, the major arguments that I employ here, and the example of Eugenie, are his.

[30] Edgar Allen Poe, "The Black Cat" [1843], *Selected Writings* (Harmondsworth: Penguin, 1985), p. 322.

attempt to establish the possibility of evil agents. Isn't this perplexing? – How can the existence of *evil* entail a moral error theory?! Well, there's evil and then there's *evil*. About a certain kind of agent – which for convenience I'll call "purely evil" – one must be a success theorist. This agent is defined entirely in terms of her intentions and motivations. But "pure evil" is a term of art. The kind of evil agent we more familiarly speak of not only has bad intentions, but acts, or intends to act, in ways *she must not* (where this is interpreted *de re*). A full-blooded *moral* assertion of "S is evil," in other words, holds (i) there are things that S must not do, and (ii) S intentionally does (or at least is motivated to do) these things. We might add for certain agents: (iii) S does them *because* S judges them forbidden.[31] The purely evil agent, by contrast, is under a misapprehension: she believes that there are things she must not do, and she is motivated to do them, but her belief is mistaken. The error theorist need not deny the existence of the purely evil agent, but does deny the "ordinary" evil agent captured by (i)–(iii). (End of aside.)

The important thing about pure evil is that it supports certain counter-factuals. Let us describe one of Sade's characters, Eugenie, who starts out life as innocent and morally upstanding, only to be utterly corrupted by a couple of typical Sadistic libertines. Eugenie is, before her downfall, competent with moral predicates – indeed, she has been well brought up, and has a particularly sensitive moral sense. After her conversion at the hands of the diabolical Mme. de Saint-Ange, Eugenie applies those predicates as before: she calls acts of charity "good," acts of licentiousness "wicked." But her motivation has shifted: what she calls "good" repels her and what she calls "wicked" attracts her. This much is uncontroversial.

Is it plausible that her putative moral judgments are somehow in quote marks – that is, is it plausible that she wants to do what *others* judge as wicked, perhaps in order to shock or titillate? Let us say "No," via stipulating certain counterfactuals to hold. Eugenie knows, let's imagine, that she was raised to be particularly morally sensitive, and knows herself to be a more reliable judge than those around her, so even if everybody else in the world were to judge that some act of hedonism is permissible, if Eugenie judges herself to know better, then she would still want to perform

---

[31] See I. Kant, *Lectures on Philosophical Theology*, ed. A. W. Wood and G. M. Clark (Ithaca: Cornell University Press, 1978), p. 22: "When we think of evil as the *highest degree* of evil, we think of it as the immediate inclination to take satisfaction in evil merely *because it is evil*, with neither remorse nor enticement and with no consideration for profit or advantage."

that act. Similarly, if the world were to judge some type of action to be dreadful, but Eugenie judges that really it's quite acceptable, then she would be motivated to refrain from performing it. (Of course, she might not want her refraining to be public knowledge, since to be seen to refrain from acts widely considered to be wicked might *itself* be a good act, and Eugenie wants to avoid *that*. But this is an unnecessary complication: imagine the action in question to be hidden from all eyes . . . except those, perhaps, of her victim.) If the counterfactuals make sense, then the internalist's standard defense – that Eugenie is motivated to do what others regard as bad, and not what she sincerely believes to be bad – is thwarted. This internalist defense, furthermore, leaves an explanatory gap. Eugenie is interpreted as motivated to do what the local community, or Christians, or some group or other, regard as wrong, while she does not share their judgments. But why would she want to do that, as opposed to doing what the Buddhists or Muslims regard as wrong? One could no doubt invent a history that would answer this, but if we interpret her just as being motivated to do what *she* judges to be wrong, then the extra explanation isn't necessary: moral value is something which *she* believes in, and is deeply and personally interested in. We can see why her wicked projects are important to her, and we can understand perfectly why violating the norms peculiar to, say, Islam, does not interest her – it's not the moral system in which she believes.

Some might object that the version of internalism that I have chosen is too strong. Michael Smith, for example, argues that the thesis to which morality is committed is not MI, but rather the following:[32]

MI*: It is necessary and *a priori* that any agent who judges that one of his available actions is morally obligatory *either* will have some motivation to perform that action *or* is practically irrational.

MI, it is held, cannot account for weakness of will, and therefore is not a serious contender. It is worth noting that it is only a very strong form of weakness of will that MI cannot allow: one where the motive to do what one judges to be correct is completely *extinguished*. The more usual case – where the motivation to do what is judged correct is merely *defeated* by a contrary motive – is perfectly compatible with MI. But in any case, the move to MI* does not affect my argument. It is simply implausible to insist that Eugenie is practically irrational or weak of will. She has set herself certain ends, and she acts smoothly in ways conducive to those ends. One

---

[32] Smith, *Moral Problem*, p. 61. See also Christine Korsgaard, "Skepticism About Practical Reason," *Journal of Philosophy* 83 (1986), pp. 5–25.

of the most chilling things about Sadean villains is exactly their calmness and *lack* of internal conflict. Whatever test for strength of will one cares to put forward, Eugenie passes it. Smith would have Eugenie *trying* to make moral judgments but failing, and when our example is the amoral agent this can look feasible; but when we move to the purely evil agent, it founders. Eugenie's wicked actions are *explained* by the fact that she has succeeded in making a moral judgment. In what sense has her judgment failed? To say that she fails because she has the wrong motivation is to beg the question. (This is further discussed in §3.4 below.)

One might complain that examples of pure evil drawn from fiction no more prove its possibility than *Dr Who* demonstrates the possibility of time travel. But the object isn't to *prove* anything possible, only to establish who bears the burden of proof. Assertions of impossibility need to be explained, not merely insisted upon. ("Consider things possible until they are shown otherwise" seems a perfectly unobjectionable principle.) One can quickly expose the troubling paradoxes of time travel, thus showing *Dr Who* to be incoherent, and in doing so one would reveal what the viewer needs to ignore in order to enter imaginatively into that fictional world. But the internalist has provided no analogous exposure of the "paradoxes" of purely evil characters, beyond a question-begging reiteration of internalism. When one enters imaginatively into, say, Shakespeare's *Titus Andronicus*, it is clear that one ignores or suppresses various beliefs (those concerning the utter implausibility of the plot, for example, or those concerning the fact that it is a stage with actors upon it that one is watching), but it does not seem that one suppresses any beliefs about the *impossibility* of Aaron's character (nor does one assume him to be lying or self-deceived about his self-descriptions). For all that, it *might* be an impossible character who is being described, but it is up to the internalist to explain, in a non-question-begging way, in what that impossibility consists.

1.6 MOTIVATION INTERNALISM AS A COMMITMENT OF MORAL DISCOURSE

Let us say, anyhow, that MI has been shown to be false. What of it? To use this result in favor of a moral error theory it will be necessary to show that MI is a non-negotiable aspect of our moral discourse. It might be objected that the very fact that we will, if forced, recognize the falsity of MI (i.e., recognize the possibility of Eugenie), shows that we were never committed to MI. If we were really committed to MI, then we simply would not admit the possibility. But I do not see why this must be so. There is no reason why we might not ordinarily employ a discourse that embodies certain commitments, but when forced carefully to consider a type of unusual case, we see that those commitments are mistaken. In recognizing that the commitment is mistaken – in acknowledging the counter-example – we will need to "step out" of the ordinary discourse, to stop using its terms. Again, one might find this last admission self-undermining. How is it that we can step outside moral discourse and yet continue to recognize a case of somebody judging that some action is *good*? – isn't to recognize a case of somebody judging something to be *good* to participate in moral discourse?

No, it is not. Suppose I had some reason to think a predicate ("... is F") flawed in some respect: I see that all statements of the form "ϕ is F" are false, or neither true nor false, or perhaps even, in some sense of the word, "nonsensical." Still, I might overhear Mary talking about her conviction that "ϕ is certainly F." I know Mary to be foolish, so I have no reason to change my mind and endorse "ϕ is F," yet I would not hesitate in assenting to "Mary believes that ϕ is F." (A Strawsonian would, I imagine, say the same about "John believes that the present king of France is wise.") Whatever kind of defect "... is F" may suffer from, it does not infect the whole sentence when embedded in a propositional attitude context.[33] The same is true of the error theorist's capacity to describe the purely evil agent. An error theorist may well hold that all assertions of the form "ϕ is morally good" are untrue, but need not baulk at ascribing to others the belief that things are morally good. To "step out" of moral discourse, upon seeing its central notions as flawed, is to cease to make assertions of the form "ϕ is good [evil, obligatory, etc.]"; it is consistent with continuing to recognize pure evil (in the special way that it has been here defined).[34]

---

[33] One might think there's a problem here. Can Strawson, for example, hold that "The present king of France is wise" is neither true nor false while holding that "Mary believes that the present king of France is wise" is true? Wouldn't the latter go the same way as the former, due to its equivalence to "The present king of France is such that Mary believes him to be wise"? I resist this equivalence, and my earlier acceptance of converting predicates into names, Ramsey-style, doesn't commit me to its validity. The sentence "Mary believes that ϕ is F" can be rendered as containing either a two-place or one-place predicate: either "The property of *believing* is had by the pair <Mary, 'ϕ is F'>" or "The property of *having-the-belief-that-ϕ-is-F* is had by Mary." However, the opacity of the propositional attitude context precludes the extraction and nominalization of a predicate contained *within* the believed proposition In other words, "The property of *Fness* is such that Mary believes ϕ to have it" is excluded.

[34] But (the point may be pressed) what of the purely evil agent's own moral judgments? Surely she can see that motivation internalism is false – she only need look at herself – so surely

So there is nothing *in principle* problematic or incoherent about our moral discourse being committed to MI but MI being false. Still, the case that it *is* so committed has not been made. I have already admitted that I do not think the case can be made with strength, but let us muster what we can. If there were a familiar discourse that was committed to some thesis T, and T were false, then what might we safely predict about the case? First, we would expect that T is not *obviously* false; if it is to be shown false by the provision of a counter-example, then the counter-example must be rarely encountered (or at least not readily recognizable *as* a counter-example). Common discourses evolve in the practical world, and are tested in day-to-day life. If the counter-example were constantly encountered and obvious, then the question "Why would this discourse have made such a glaring error?" would be very telling. If, on the other hand, the counter-example were truly unusual, or perhaps something which we would countenance only in extraordinary imaginary situations, then the fact that a common way of looking at the world failed to accommodate it would be no surprise. Second, we might expect our confrontation with the counter-example to be characterized by puzzlement and discomfort. The counter-intuitiveness will go beyond being unexpected or unusual; it will, rather, "seem paradoxical" and smack of incoherence. In so far as we are participants in a common discourse, we struggle to explain the putative counter-example away. In so far as we are able to step outside of the discourse, and are able to reject its precepts, we will recognize that the counter-example is a true one.

Whatever else we might conclude, it is at least safe to say that the internalist debate manifests both of these characteristics. First, the counter-example, when properly construed, is very rare – or, speaking more carefully, the conditions under which we will recognize the counter-example *as* a counter-example are very rare. Even the standard villains of art and folklore can seldom be so-described. Much more often than not, the characters we usually describe as "evil" have rejected the whole realm of morality altogether, and are not making moral judgments at all. The villain

---

she isn't committed to MI when she sincerely uses predicates like "... is good"? How strong this objection is (and it is potentially troublesome) depends on how we understand the notion of "commitment." As I argued regarding "phlogiston," the commitment in virtue of which a discourse may fail need not be something to which any competent user of the term is disposed to assent. The purely evil agent may indeed be disposed to *deny* MI; nevertheless, her participation in a linguistic community of users of the term "good" may still be sufficient to establish that when she asserts things of the form "ϕ is good" she is committed to MI. Meanings, as the slogan goes, ain't in the head.

who appears to do evil for evil's sake is, on reflection, hard to locate – usually the baddies are motivated by some other end, like world-domination. And when we find a character who does appear to take an active interest in evil, more often than not his interest seems to be in doing what others believe to be morally despicable. If his victims and the outraged public were to alter their views about what was morally acceptable, we imagine the evil character altering his behavior accordingly (for really he wants to shock and outrage and make people unhappy). The wicked character who would stand firm to his moral beliefs, even in the face of widespread disagreement, is scarce.

Second, when the possibility of amoralism or pure evil is faced, we feel confusion and temptation in different directions. Even by many of its critics, it is admitted that internalism holds the intuitive ground: R. Milo writes "although I shall argue that the thesis of internalism is false, I do not wish to deny that it has strong intuitive appeal. There does appear to be *something* paradoxical about supposing that a person believes that some act is wrong . . . and yet has no con-attitude whatsoever towards it."[35] This phrase "seems paradoxical" pops up several times – we've already seen Frankena use it, and W. Falk, in the paper that initiated the debate, chooses exactly the same words.[36] Although one wouldn't want to make too much of this, it is, I'm suggesting, an expression of exactly the kind of attitude that we should expect: as participants in moral discourse, we cannot recognize the coherence of the counter-example, but if we "step out" of the discourse we are able to acknowledge its possibility. The overall impression would be that the case tastes of paradox – that there must be a subtle misdescription – but we cannot say exactly where.

This is all a long way from being clinching, of course; it is merely some oblique evidence. We can conceptualize the issue via imagining a piece of translation. Suppose we have undertaken a radical translation of the language of an alien community very like our own, and we have translated nearly all of it to our satisfaction, except for a few normative expressions.

---

[35] Milo, "Moral Indifference," p. 375.
[36] W. D. Falk, "'Ought' and Motivation," *Proceedings of the Aristotelian Society* 48 (1948), pp. 121–2: "It seems paradoxical that moral conduct should require more than one kind of justification: that having first convinced someone that regardless of cost to himself he was morally bound to do some act we should then be called upon to convince him as well that he had some sufficiently strong reason for doing this same act. 'You have made me realize that I ought, now convince me that I really need to' seems a spurious request, inviting the retort 'if you really were convinced of the first, you would not seriously doubt the second'".

They have some words that operate rather like our moral terms "good," "obligatory," etc. (call their words "schmood," "schmobligatory," etc.). If something is schmood then it is thought probably to promote or sustain alien well-being. Schmood acts are expressive of concern and respect. Schmood things are considered important. People considered schmood are praised, an absence of schmoodness is disciplined. And so on. Yet we find that this population has an aberrant twist: when someone is considered to have judged an action ϕ to be schmood, this is not considered to have bearing on whether that person is motivated to see ϕ done. The agent who has convinced us that he sincerely judges ϕ to be schmood (and judges no other available action to be schmood), and yet, calmly and with no explanation, feels utterly unmotivated in favor of ϕ, raises no eyebrow, produces no puzzlement in this society. To judge something schmood, in short, is not necessarily to be in favor of it.

I cannot argue that we *would not* translate "schmood" into the English "good"; at best I can say that there seems something troubling in the prospect. It seems as if something important would be lost in translation, and, once we had learned each others' languages, we could anticipate many puzzling and exasperating conversations. But again, this is hardly convincing. If someone were simply to claim that they have no qualms about the translation – that they do not think that it would even require us ascribing to the aliens a false belief about the good – then I have nothing persuasive to say. There *is* a counterfactual truth about what we would decide, as a community – perhaps with a degree of debate and mutual adjustment of beliefs – were we ever faced with such a predicament, and it is with this counterfactual – untested and, to all intents and purposes, untestable – that the fact of the matter lies.

1.7 IMPASSE

This avenue, then, leads to an impasse – at least as far as I can see at present. Out of interest, it is worth noting that if some of the above arguments *could* be brought home, there is space for a novel result. MI is a modal thesis; if it is false at all, then it is false at every possible world: even at worlds where all agents manifest a reliable connection between moral judgment and motivation it will be false that such a connection is *necessary*. If, then, the truth of MI is a precondition for the truth of a basic moral sentence – say, "ϕ is obligatory" – then the predicate ". . . is obligatory" will have an empty extension not just in the actual world but

27

across all possible worlds. Earlier I sketched an avenue for arguing that this is sufficient for the referential failure of the property name "obligatoriness." A Strawsonian would then be in a position to argue that "Obligatoriness is had by ϕ" is neither true nor false, and by nominalizing the predicate, Ramsey-style, we could conclude that ordinary moral judgments of the form "ϕ is obligatory" are neither true nor false. Since none of this would be to concede that ordinary moral judgments are used non-assertorically, it would not collapse into noncognitivism – it would properly be classed as a type of error theory.

I present the outline of the argument not in anticipation of making it stick (there are far too many "if"'s along the way for me to want to embark on that project), but as a piece of humble taxonomy. There may well be other arguments that construe our moral discourse as assertoric but neither true nor false, and we should class these as error theories. We might, for example, decide not that moral discourse is committed to some false thesis, but that it is just so nebulous and fragmented that its judgments do not fulfill the minimal criteria for being accorded truth value. Lavoisier leveled an analogous accusation at his rivals: "[C]hemists have made phlogiston a vague principle which is not strictly defined and which consequently fits all the explanations required of it; . . . It is a veritable Proteus that changes form every instant."[37] His complaint, in the hands of a philosopher, might well be forged into the position that the predicate ". . . is phlogiston" is so vague – contains so many contradictions, even in the mouths of the "experts" – that one who asserts "*a* is phlogiston" is approaching nonsense. Wittgenstein expressed a view on moral judgments that construed them as nonsensical – nonsensicality being "their very essence."[38] One might worry about how this fits with my claim that such judgments might still count as assertions – if something like "moral goodness" is, at bottom, just a crazy idea, then just what are we *thinking* when we employ it in assertions? Wittgenstein claims that when we employ moral language we are constantly using similes, but "as soon as we try to drop the simile and simply state the facts which stand behind it, we find there are no such facts. And so, what at first appeared to be a simile now seems to be mere nonsense." To understand what might be meant by "similes" we might think about Bentham's slightly bizarre attempt to analyze the idea behind *obligation*: "the emblematical, or archetypical image, is that of a man

---

[37] A. Lavoisier, *Réflexions sur le Phlogistique* [1783], quoted in D. McKie, *Antoine Lavoisier* (Philadelphia: J. B. Lippincott Company, 1936), p. 230.

[38] L. Wittgenstein, "Lecture on Ethics," *Philosophical Review* 74 (1965), pp. 3–12.

lying down with a heavy body pressing upon him,"[39] or Mackie's talk of obligation being an "invisible cord" and a demand for payment being an "immaterial suction-pipe" dredging for the owed money.[40] Bentham's and Mackie's images are attempts to catch the "feel" of obligation, and perhaps all we need is a shared *feel* in order to communicate successfully, to have mental states that are best described as *beliefs*, to perform linguistic tasks that are best described as *assertions*. If this is correct, then there need be nothing philosophically troubling about the idea of our believing and asserting impossible things.

But so much for taxonomy. The more important point is that we haven't been able to make a secure case for an error theory that turns on motivation internalism. Thus the argument which has been under consideration may be considered something of a false start, but it is intended to be instructively so. Though reaching no conclusion, we have gained an insight into how, in general terms, an argument for a moral error theory might proceed – the argumentative framework that is to be used. In the next chapter I will deploy what I take to be a much more robust and cogent set of considerations that favor a moral error theory.

---

[39] J. Bentham, "Essay on Logic," in *Collected Works*, vol. 8 (Edinburgh: William Tait, 1843), p. 247.
[40] Mackie, *Ethics*, p. 74.

2

Error theory and reasons

2.0 MORAL INESCAPABILITY

Despite Mackie's references to motivation, it is doubtful that the argument of the previous chapter lies at the heart of his "objective prescriptivity." His complaint about objective prescriptivity is that it would be a "queer" property: one that finds no place in our considered world view – "value-entities or value-features of a quite different order from anything else with which we are acquainted" (*Ethics*, p. 40). Suppose that the queerness of morality were to reside in its "intrinsically motivating" qualities. Clearly, the mere fact that something is obligatory does not mean that people *are* automatically motivated to pursue it – we are all familiar with people not being motivated to pursue the good, if only because they are ignorant of what is good. What seems troubling is not somebody's being unmotivated to pursue what *is* good, but being unmotivated to pursue what she *judges to be* good. So if MI were the mistake that moral discourse makes, then it would be more natural to describe it as a mistake about what moral agents are like, not what moral properties are like. This being the case, if Mackie thought that MI were the culprit, it would be odd for him to expend time arguing about our attributing to the world queer properties (wondering how we would recognize the presence of such properties, etc.). Furthermore, the falsity of MI provides grounds for holding that moral predicates have empty extensions over all possible worlds, yet if one thought that a property is uninstantiated throughout the modal universe, it would be a misplaced strategy to argue that it doesn't fit within the received view of what our world is like.

Brink's interpretation of a queerness that hinges on MI has been persuasively criticized by Richard Garner, who holds that the putative queerness of moral properties lies not with MI, but with the notion of moral *bindingness.*[1] Put in simplest terms, it is the idea that there are actions which we "have to do, regardless" that underlies the claims of objective prescriptivity. The problem of ordinary moral discourse is not a matter of what motivations accompany our moral judgments – it is, rather, that we think that people are "bound" even if they make no moral judgments at all. Even the person who has rejected that whole realm we still think of as being under the jurisdiction of morality. It is this *moral inescapability* that Garner thinks powers the argument from queerness. Not only do I agree that this is a much more persuasive reading of Mackie, I think it provides a compelling argument for a moral error theory.

Moral inescapability is an elusive notion. Imagine the child asking why he mustn't pinch his play mate. The parent replies "Because it's wrong." The child continues "But why mustn't I do what's wrong?" The parent might give an exasperated "Because you mustn't!" It is the attempt to clarify the inadequate parental response that is the task of this chapter. Of course, there are all sorts of kinds of reasons that the parent might give: "If you pinch Violet Elizabeth, then she might pinch you back" or ". . . then she won't play with you" or ". . . then you'll be sent to your room." All good (and possibly effective) *prudential* reasons. But prudence, I shall argue, is not what underwrites *moral* prescriptivity. Regarding any type of prescription which can be justified on prudential grounds, we can always imagine an unusually situated or unusually constituted agent who "escapes" the prescription. Perhaps the child doesn't want Violet Elizabeth as his friend, perhaps he doesn't mind being pinched or being sent to his room. Or perhaps these costly consequences are things he has the power to avoid. In such a case what becomes of the injunction against pinching? On prudential grounds, it must evaporate. But *moral* proscriptions do not evaporate, regardless of how we imagine the agent situated. If it is not pinching, but *torturing* that is at stake, then there is no escaping. But the thought that torturing is always proscribed on prudential grounds is just silly. That it always is *as a matter of fact* is a case that might be made – but that it *must be*, even in situations where the philosopher gets to stipulate the costs and benefits (let's say without breaking any laws of nature) is nothing but groundless optimism. (Morality as a kind of prudence is discussed further in later chapters: §3.2 and §7.1.)

---

[1] R. T. Garner, "On the Genuine Queerness of Moral Properties and Facts," *Australasian Journal of Philosophy* 68 (1990), pp. 137–46.

As in so many things, it was Plato who first presented the issue with clarity. In the *Republic* we are told the story of a Lydian shepherd, Gyges, who comes across a ring of invisibility, which he uses in morally objectionable ways to gain whatever he wishes – ultimately setting himself up as king.[2] And why shouldn't he? It is not enough to say "Well, it's just a fairy tale, so we needn't worry about it." Plato saw that answering the question is important, precisely because we employ a notion of what "must be done" with which we purport to transcend the contingent circumstances or constitution of those to whom we apply it.

Suppose we have caught a criminal who stands before us in the dock. There is no question about his guilt – he admits it freely. What is curious about this criminal is that he is utterly unrepentant: he tells us that he desired to kill the person, and that the killing did not frustrate any of his desires (we imagine that he even wanted to be caught and punished). Such criminals with such desires may be statistically rare, but they are surely possible. Imagine that the criminal is quite convincing in relating all this to us. Are we in any way moved to retract our judgment that the criminal did something that he morally ought not to have done? Does our moral condemnation of him depend upon ascertaining or assuming that he has statistically normal desires and interests (or that he is not about to produce a ring of invisibility)? Of course not. Certainly desires can *sometimes* constitute mitigating circumstances, but not for, say, torture. (I choose an extreme example to avoid getting distracted by the details of a more moderate wrong.) When we morally condemn a criminal, we do so with a force that implies "regardless of whether it suits you." When we judge that torture is morally wrong, the force of our prohibition does not depend on prudential considerations of potential self-harm; the strength of the condemnation is "Even if you had a ring of invisibility and stood to gain from the action, it would still be wrong for you to do that."

Despite this, a standard strategy for trying to make sense of our moral denunciation even of Gyges is to attempt to uncover a form of self-harm. An obvious framework to appeal to is a supernatural one, wherein all actions are observed, and rewards and punishments doled out accordingly. Centuries before Plato, Hesiod imagined that thousands of invisible observers pass among us:

> Clothed in a mist, they visit every land
> And keep a watch on law-suits and on crimes.

[2] See Plato, *The Republic*, 360b–c (Harmondsworth: Penguin, 1974).

> One of them is the virgin, born of Zeus,
> *Justice*, revered by all the Olympian gods.
> Whenever she is hurt by perjurers,
> Straightaway she sits beside her father Zeus,
> And tells him of the unjust hearts of men,
> Until the city suffers

In case we missed the moral, Hesiod tells us straight: "He hurts himself who hurts another man, and evil planning harms the planner most."[3] But this, eloquent though it is, is merely an appeal to magic. In the *Republic*, Plato sees the inadequacy of appealing to the wrath and rewards of the gods, though his preferred explanation of self-harm turns on an utterly implausible isomorphism between the structure of the state – which requires the harmonious functioning of its internal elements (i.e., justice) in order to flourish – and the individual – who allegedly also requires internal harmony (i.e., justice, i.e., goodness) in order to flourish. Yet right at the end of the *Republic*, Plato cannot resist appealing to a supernatural supplement to the main argument, involving a metaphysics of post-mortem reward for the good soul while the wicked souls are cast into Tartarus. This is no better than Hesiod's magical hypothesis of an anthropomorphized Justice who runs weeping to Zeus.

Hume, on the other hand, would have us believe that the shepherd must sacrifice "inward peace of mind, consciousness of integrity, a satisfactory review of [his] own conduct" – that despite avoiding the more tangible costs of law-breaking, he still incurs the important loss of *fellowship* (for the shallow gains of "feverish, empty amusements of luxury").[4] This is a more promising argument, but it has inevitable limits. Our stipulated criminal participates in a sincere and caring manner in his *local* community, and wouldn't dream of cheating his friends. It is only upon a neighboring community that his harmful activities are visited.

Looking to self-harm to underwrite moral injunctions is an odd enterprise. Is that really why the Nazis were morally wrong in building their death-camps? – that in doing so they harmed *themselves*?! And if that were the case, why would we then harm them more by punishing them? Deterrence and self-defense are two answers, of course, but those are not

---

[3] Hesiod, *Works and Days*, 252–266, trans. Dorothea Wender (Harmondsworth: Penguin, 1976).

[4] Conclusion of *Enquiry Concerning the Principles of Morals* [1751] (Cambridge: Hackett Publishing Company, 1983), p. 82. Here Hume is putting forward considerations with which we might *persuade* a wrong-doer, which is different from saying that the wrong-doing consists in self-harm.

the reasons we actually use. We punished the Nazi leaders because they deserved it, an answer that makes little sense when the wrong is understood as self-harm. In my opinion, philosophers have attempted to found moral injunctions on self-harm – willfully overlooking the implications – precisely because it is difficult to know where else to turn. What else *could* we mean when we tell the criminal that he "ought not have done it"? One thing we surely don't mean is merely "These are the laws that we've decided upon, and you have broken them; prepare to be punished." Morality is not just a list of *Do*s and *Don't*s backed with punishment. We think that a person is bound by those rules whether he accepts them or not – that the rules are, in some sense, *his* rules whether he accepts them or not. But what could it mean for the rules to be "*his* rules" even if he explicitly rejects them? Let me try to come at this by describing the contrasting case, where rules apply to a person even though they clearly are not "*his* rules."

2.1 INSTITUTIONAL "OUGHT"S

Consider Celadus the Thracian, an unwilling gladiator: he's dragged off the street, buckled into armor, and thrust into the arena.[5] Despite his protestations, he is now a gladiator (I take it that *being a gladiator* is rather like *being a shark attack victim* – something that can be forced upon one very unwillingly). Let's imagine that there are various rules of gladiatorial combat: you ought not throw sand in your opponent's eyes, for instance. Celadus is a gladiator, subject to the rules, and so he ought not throw sand in his opponent's eyes. But these rules are not *his* rules – what are they to him? Imagine that things are looking bleak – his opponent is a sadistic professional fighter, and Celadus finds himself pinned down and swordless. His only hope is to throw some sand in his rival's eyes. (Let's stipulate, with utter implausibility, that he can get away with nobody seeing him do this, just as a way of being sure that there will be no negative repercussions in the form of punishment for breaking the rules.) The rules still say that Celadus shouldn't do it, but he doesn't care about the rules – he has no particular reason to follow them, and every reason to reject them. Given that he has never entered into any form of contract to follow the rules, and that following the rules will lead to his quick and unjust demise, I

---

[5] I am indebted to Gideon Rosen (personal communication) for the example of gladiatorial rules.

think we will all agree that Celadus ought to throw sand in his opponent's eyes. He ought to do what he ought not to do.

This last statement is not in the least paradoxical, so long as we keep track of our "ought"s. The first "ought" is something like an all-things-considered "ought" – it presents *the thing to be done*. The second "ought" is an according-to-the-rules "ought." Saying that Celadus ought to do what he ought not to do is just a way of saying that he ought to break the rules. The fact that he should break them doesn't make them evaporate – they continue to *be* rules – and so there continues to be a sense in which he ought not throw sand in his opponent's eyes. If we denied this we could make no sense of the fact that Celadus was *breaking a rule* at all.

These kind of "non-evaporating" rules are discussed by Philippa Foot in her paper "Morality as a System of Hypothetical Imperatives."[6] She begins with Kant's well-known distinction between hypothetical imperatives and categorical imperatives.[7] A hypothetical imperative depends for its legitimacy on the addressee having some end or desire: "Go to the café" is good advice if I want a coffee, but if I do not have that desire, the imperative is retracted (it "evaporates"). A categorical imperative, by contrast, declares "an action as objectively necessary in itself apart from its relation to a further end."[8] I argued above that we express our moral condemnation of wrong-doers using *categorical* imperatives: someone who has committed torture may not evade our opprobrium by citing unusual desires or interests, and nor does our censure depend on an assumption concerning what his or her desires are. A sincerely unrepentant criminal may strike us as an oddity, but the lack of repentance is irrelevant to our moral censure.

Foot pointed out that systems of rules – such as etiquette, a club's rules, or gladiatorial combat, for that matter – have certain characteristics that we associate with categorical imperatives; a somewhat surprising result, since we do not think that etiquette's restriction on speaking with your mouth full has anything like the force of morality's condemnation of torture. The quality that etiquette has in common with morality is precisely what I above called "non-evaporatibility": when I discover that Mike has no interest in table manners, and cares nothing for my feelings, I don't

[6] P. Foot, "Morality as a System of Hypothetical Imperatives," *Philosophical Review* 81 (1972), pp. 305–16.

[7] See I. Kant, *Groundwork to the Metaphysics of Morals* [1783], trans. H. J. Paton (London: Hutchinson, 1985).

[8] *Ibid.*, p. 78.

retract my imperative of etiquette that he ought not to spray me with bagel while he eats. But Foot is certainly *not* saying that etiquette must be obeyed, regardless of consequences. Suppose Mike has an excellent reason for having appalling table manners – he stands to win a large bet if he annoys me over lunch. Then we might well say not only that he has a reason to speak with his mouth full, but that he has no reason *not* to. I take Foot's point to be that despite Mike's possibly having no reason to respect etiquette, an imperative of etiquette – "Mike ought not speak with his mouth full" – applies. It continues to be a rule – something he *ought not do* – even when he has a good reason to break the rule. Unlike Foot, I shall call this a kind of categorical imperative: a *weak* one.

When we say that Celadus ought not throw sand in his opponent's eyes, this is a weak categorical imperative. A Roman spectator – someone who heartily endorses gladiatorial combat and all its rules – will not retract her judgment "Celadus ought not throw sand" just because it is pointed out to her that Celadus *wants* to throw sand, and throwing sand is the best means of Celadus satisfying his own desires. Celadus' desires are irrelevant to the weak categorical imperatives of gladiatorial combat. None of this is to undermine our initial judgment that *of course* he ought to throw the sand. This all-things-considered "ought" appears to be a proper hypothetical imperative, and in this context common sense tells us that it trumps the competing gladiatorial norm (in fact, the gladiatorial norm need not carry *any* weight with Celadus).

When I said earlier that morality is not merely a set of *Dos* and *Don'ts* that we are willing to back up with force, I meant that morality is something more than a set of weak categorical imperatives. Reflect on how differently we treat "Celadus ought not throw sand" and "Gyges ought not kill people." We're content to admit that the former case is just a matter of there being a set of rules which someone from the outside is imposing on the gladiator, and these rules can be overridden by the gladiator's personal desires and interests. They need not *bind* him; they need not be *his* rules; they do not present *the thing to do*; he may legitimately ignore them. But imagine saying something analogous of Plato's shepherd: "Of course by killing an innocent person the shepherd is breaking a rule of morality, and so *according-to-the-rules-of-morality* he ought not do it; nevertheless, if he stands to gain something important by killing, then that's what he ought (all things considered) to do." That's *not* how we think of morality. Someone who reasoned in such a way might be accused of fundamentally misunderstanding what we mean by "morally ought."

The pressing question, then, is what "extra ingredient" a *strong* categorical imperative has. If the prohibitions against killing innocents are intended to have much more force than the prohibitions against sand-throwing, or speaking with one's mouth full, what is the source and nature of the force? This extra ingredient is what Foot calls "the fugitive thought," and most of her paper is devoted to showing that there is no fugitive to be found. She hypothesizes that the difference between a strong, Kantian categorical imperative and a weak, institutional categorical imperative, is that the former purports to bring with it a *reason* for action, while the latter does not. Etiquette may demand, categorically, that I do not speak with my mouth full, whether I wish to or not, but I only have a *reason* to refrain from speaking with my mouth full if I have some independent reason to be following the dictates of etiquette. Similarly with Celadus. It may be that according to the rules he ought not throw sand, but since he has no particular *reason* to follow the rules, he has no reason to refrain from sand-throwing; on the contrary, he has a very good reason to *reject* the rules, since following them will lead to an unpleasant demise.

2.2 STRONG CATEGORICAL IMPERATIVES AS REASON-BRINGING

Foot interprets Kant as holding that moral imperatives do not merely "apply" to persons regardless of their desires or interests, but imply that persons have *reasons* to act regardless of their desires or interests – and in this way they (putatively) *bind* persons, in a way that etiquette does not bind us. But she doesn't think that such reason-bringing imperatives are philosophically defensible, and so she accuses Kant of attempting to imbue morality with "a magic force." The failure of strong categorical imperatives, however, does not lead Foot in the direction of a moral error theory, since she thinks that belief in their validity is a mistake that only Kant and like thinkers have made – ordinary users of moral concepts do not generally make this blunder. My contention is that Foot is correct about the "magical force" of strong categorical imperatives, but wrong in thinking that they are expendable to morality, and this pattern of agreeing with one part of Foot's project, and disagreeing with another, is something I share with Mackie. Just to be clear, we can sum up three philosophers' attitudes towards two vital questions as follows:

	Does moral discourse centrally employ strong categorical imperatives?	Can the notion of strong categorical imperatives be defended?
Kant:	yes	yes
Foot:	no	no
Mackie:	yes	no

It is interesting to note that even Kant distinguished the two questions. After giving an account of what a categorical imperative is, he writes that "although we leave it unsettled whether what we call duty may not be an empty concept, we shall still be able to show at least what we understand by it and what the concept means."[9]

In accepting the existence of weak categorical imperatives, and distinguishing them from the strong form on the grounds that they are not "reason-bringing," Foot is denying a thesis which I shall call, for want of a better name, "Mackie's Platitude":

MP: It is necessary and *a priori* that, for any agent x, if x ought to ϕ, then x has a reason to ϕ.[10]

Mackie thinks that part of what we *mean* by "ought" is "has a reason." A potential counter-example might be uses of the predictive "ought," as in "Jenny ought to be here at any minute," which does not imply that Jenny has any reason to be here at any minute. Predictive "ought"s do not have reason-giving qualities because they may be applied to inanimate objects: we say that the snow ought to melt soon, but clearly we are not saying that the snow has reasons for melting.[11] However, the only "ought"s in which we are interested are ones that apply to actions and agents, and so predictive uses may be put aside.

[9] *Ibid.*, p. 84.
[10] This thesis sometimes goes by the name "internalism." See, for example, Brink, "Externalist Moral Realism." Gilbert Harman endorses MP, and he too sometimes calls it "internalism about reasons"; see *The Nature of Morality* (New York: Oxford University Press, 1977), pp. 84–90; *idem*, "Moral Relativism Defended," *Philosophical Review* 84 (1975), pp. 3–22. I resist this terminology so as not unduly to multiply "internal/external" distinctions. More recently, "internalism about reasons" has been used for a quite different thesis: that all practical reasons are instrumental, or "internal" in the sense outlined by Bernard Williams (see Chapter 5, below).
[11] Gilbert Harman connects the predictive "ought" to reasons by claiming that "The snow ought to melt soon" may be analyzed as "There is good reason for believing that the snow will melt soon." See his "Reasons," *Critica* 7 (1975), pp. 3–13. Mackie says much the same in *Ethics*, p. 74.

So restricted, Mackie's Platitude certainly has appeal. Imagine telling someone: "You really ought to have done that, but I accept that there was no reason for you to." It sounds very odd, to say the least. Whenever we tell someone that she ought to do something, the question "Why?" is perfectly legitimate. But we want to say something more than "Well, you simply must, and that's all there is to it!" We will want to provide her with a reason, and if we cannot, then she may feel justified in ignoring our imperative. (The thought that an "ought" claim may carry force alone, without the backing of a reason, is something that John McDowell, in no uncertain terms, calls an "insane thesis."[12]) But what about Foot's weak categorical imperatives? – aren't these precisely "ought" statements which do not carry a reason with them? To address this, we need to make a distinction between when we speak from "within" a normative system and when we speak from "outside" it.

2.3 INSTITUTIONAL REASONS

If there were an anthropologist investigating a tribe that employs a concept which she does not accept – such as that a certain person has magical powers – then, when speaking carefully, she would couch her utterances with qualifications. She would say "*According to them*, so-and-so has magical powers." (She might elliptically drop the prefix, but that would just be for the sake of brevity.) If, on the other hand, she were referring to a concept which didn't bother her in the least – say, the idea that so-and-so is chief – then the qualification could go: she would simply say "So-and-so is chief." This same distinction can be made for any normative system. One can speak from inside the institution, in which case one can be taken to endorse its rules, or from outside, explicitly or implicitly prefixing one's assertions with "According to . . ." Weak categorical imperatives admit of this distinction: one can express the fact that the rules of gladiatorial combat forbid Celadus' sand-throwing either by saying "According to these rules, he ought not do it," or simply "He ought not do it." The latter expression is what we'd expect an enthusiastic Roman spectator to say. The former is what Celadus himself might admit.

Bearing this distinction in mind, it seems that Mackie's Platitude holds. Someone who endorses etiquette thinks that the rules of etiquette just do

---

[12] John McDowell, "Are Moral Requirements Hypothetical Imperatives?" *Proceedings of the Aristotelian Society* 52 (1978), p. 14.

constitute reasons. If I am speaking from *within* etiquette – as a mouthpiece, as it were – then the question of whether one should follow etiquette doesn't arise (and in so far as it does arise then I am stepping outside of the institution). From this perspective, the rules of etiquette just *are* reasons for action. Similarly, the gladiatorial enthusiast who asserts "Celadus ought not throw sand" will also assent to "There is a reason for Celadus not to throw sand." The latter doesn't add anything that wasn't in the former; both are just ways by which she expresses her allegiance to the norms of gladiatorial contests.

This connection will be preserved when we speak from outside of the institution too: an indifferent onlooker might say "According to the rules of combat, Celadus ought not throw sand" and could just as easily say "According to the rules of combat, Celadus has a reason not to throw sand." It doesn't matter that the rules of combat, even were they formulated and written down, do not anywhere explicitly mention the contestants' *reasons*. Reasons are contained implicitly in the rules just in virtue of the presence of "ought" statements. The fact that someone who endorses the rules will say "Celadus ought not ϕ," and will smoothly say "Celadus has a reason not to ϕ," without the latter adding anything (that is, without any further facts requiring investigation), shows that reasons are implicitly contained in the rulebook, just in virtue of its being a *rule*book, all along.

At first glance, this defense of Mackie's Platitude, via the introduction of institutional reasons, seems to collapse Foot's distinction between strong and weak categorical imperatives. It seems to show that there are reason-bringing categorical imperatives after all. It is very important that we see that this is not so.

Let us return to the unfortunate Celadus. An enthusiastic Roman onlooker may say "Celadus ought not throw sand" or "Celadus has a reason not to throw sand." The onlooker isn't making a *mistake* – she is merely expressing endorsement of a normative system. But all of this only concerns what an onlooker may legitimately say without violating any rules of linguistic conduct. It doesn't affect *Celadus*. He is in the same position as we left him earlier: it is still the case that what he ought to do, all things considered – what he *really* has a reason to do – is *throw the sand*. We accepted earlier that the weak categorical imperative of gladiatorial combat doesn't bind him – that it was something that he could reasonably ignore – and the introduction of the permissibility of the onlooker expressing much the same prescription by reference to *reasons* does not alter that. We merely fall back on the same rhetoric as was employed earlier:

it may be legitimate for an onlooker to say "Celadus has a reason not to throw sand," but this doesn't provide *Celadus* with a real reason – it's not *his* reason, it is something he may legitimately ignore.

But what we are content to say about Celadus we are far from happy about admitting of Gyges. We want to say both that Gyges ought not kill innocent people and that he has a reason not to kill innocent people. But we want this to be a *"real"* reason – a reason that somehow engages the shepherd – one that he cannot legitimately ignore. In other words, in the moral case, we are not content to admit that our claim that there is a reason to refrain from killing is merely a permissible way of speaking from a perspective that endorses the dictates of morality. We are still left with a desire to say something more – to imbue the moral imperative with a greater authoritative force – and we are still left with the unsettling possibility that it cannot be done. So the introduction of these "institutional reasons" does not provide support for the kind of strong categorical imperatives that are central to our moral discourse – it merely forces us to invoke sturdier language (so far, only rhetoric) in an attempt to distinguish the authoritativeness of moral judgments from those of institutional norms.

Just to be completely clear on how "*non*-binding" institutional reasons and institutional "ought"s are, let me describe an extreme case. Suppose my friends and I have invented a bizarre game whereby we secretly stalk a stranger every day, and assign points to his various actions: if he catches the 9.30 bus he gets seven points; if he catches the 9.45 he only gets three, if he has a ham sandwich for lunch he gets bonus points, and so on. At the end of the day the points are tallied, and if he gets over a certain number, he "wins." We never interact with the stranger in any way, and "winning" doesn't equate with him having a successful day by any other standards. My friends and I might well say "He ought to catch the 9.30 bus." This is just a weak categorical imperative – Foot would accept it, but say that it brings with it no reason to catch the 9.30 bus. Mackie, on the other hand, would allow that my friends and I can also say "Of course he has a reason to catch the 9.30 bus – he gets more points that way and then he's more likely to win!" When we say this we're not making an error – we're just invoking "a special logic" (Mackie's phrase) peculiar to our game. But of course, none of this places a real requirement on anyone. If our stalkee were made aware of our little game, and made aware of the fact that *we* think he has a reason for catching the 9.30 bus, he might well say "But what's that to me?" The rules and reasons of the game need not influence his decision procedure, and may quite reasonably be entirely ignored. We do not, I reiterate, think of morality in this way. Morality purports to have more authority than this – it is not something that a person may escape (in David Wiggins's words) "by simply flying the skull and cross-bones and renouncing altogether the aim of belonging to the moral community."[13]

2.4 AN ARGUMENT FOR A MORAL ERROR THEORY

We now have the resources on the table to deploy a strong argument for a moral error theory. It is best if we state it succinctly, though with the understanding that it will be subject to refinement. For any x:

1. If x morally ought to ϕ, then x ought to ϕ regardless of whether he cares to, regardless of whether ϕing satisfies any of his desires or furthers his interests.
2. If x morally ought to ϕ, then x has a reason for ϕing.
3. Therefore, if x morally ought to ϕ, then x has a reason for ϕing regardless of whether ϕing serves his desires or furthers his interests.
4. But there is no sense to be made of such reasons.
5. Therefore, x is never under a moral obligation.

The structure of the argument is very simple:

> 1. If P, then Q
> 2. If P, then R
> ∴ 3. If P, then (Q & R)
> But 4. Not (Q & R)
> ∴ 5. Not P

Premises (1), (2) and (4) are the ones that require argument (premise (3), following from (1) and (2), requires no independent support). Establishing (4) is the most complex matter, and is the job of following chapters. In the present chapter I want to make sure that (1) and (2) are understood and settled.

The basic consideration in favor of premise (1) has already been pressed several times. When we morally condemn a criminal we do not first ascertain the state of his desires. Were we to discover that his desires were well-served by his crimes, perhaps even to the point of his wanting punishment, we do not respond "Oh, well I suppose you ought to have done

---

[13] David Wiggins, "Categorical Requirements: Kant and Hume on the Idea of Duty," in R. Hursthouse, G. Lawrence, and W. Quinn (eds.), *Virtues and Reasons* (Oxford: Clarendon Press, 1995), p. 298.

it after all." This simple consideration is enough to show that anyone is mistaken who dismisses categorical imperatives as a bizarre extravagance endorsed only by Kant and his followers. We use them all the time. Just consider our moral condemnation of Nazis. Any offering along the lines of "Well, we wanted to create an Aryan master race, and genocide seemed like an efficient means of accomplishing it" is no defense at all! But, barring an argument that their actions were in some subtle way desire-frustrating, this shows that it is a categorical imperative with which we denounce them. Of course, concerning Nazis we might not *say* "You ought not to have done that," for this sounds altogether too weak to capture the outrage – rather, we appeal to the language of "evil" and "bestiality." But the "ought" statement is implied by the stronger language – evil is, at the very least, something we ought not be.

The manner in which we condemn Nazis, ignoring any unusual desires or interests that they may have, is not a peripheral element of moral discourse; it represents a kind of reprehension that is central. A system of values in which there was no place for condemning Nazi actions simply would not count as a *moral* system. Further, I do not think that this kind of desire/interest-ignoring condemnation is a particularly modern or Western phenomenon. Despite the fact that it required an eighteenth-century Prussian to *label* categorical imperatives, I am confident that they have been with us for a long time. Did, say, ancient Chinese people retract condemnation of their own moral monsters upon discovering their unusual desires? I doubt it.[14] Perhaps Foot is correct that we could get along adequately without such imperatives. After all, we could, in the absence of making such judgments, still be justified in defending ourselves from outlaws and monsters. We might have chosen to hang Nazi war criminals without invoking categorical imperatives at all. But this, in my book, is equivalent to saying that we could get along adequately without morality (the truth of which is investigated in later chapters).

Premise (2) is Mackie's Platitude, specifically for moral prescriptions. I argued that whenever one is speaking from within a normative institution, a willingness to say "X ought to ϕ" will license saying "X has a reason to ϕ." So understood, (2) is true. So understood, however, (4) is certainly false, for we have seen that we *can* make sense of such reasons: they are merely reflections of weak categorical imperatives, which are expressions of systems of rules – and nobody could doubt the existence of systems of rules.

---

[14] I doubt it, but without an empirical survey, upon which I shall not embark, this must remain an educated conjecture.

I mean (2) to be taken in a stronger manner, which thus far I have been able to explicate only in a rhetorical way. Consider again our moral condemnation of a felon. We say (at the very least) "You ought not to have done that." We cannot end matters there, or we have nothing with which to counter the felon's "So what?" Indeed, if *all* we had to say on the matter was "You simply *mustn't*!" – accompanied by some table-pounding – then the felon's query seems positively reasonable. We seek something that might *engage* the criminal. Even if it is something that does not succeed in actually persuading her, we want something the ignoring of which would be in some manner illegitimate on her part. Looking to provide her with a *reason* appears the only possibility. I am mindful of the fact that it sounds a little odd to say that the Nazis "had a reason" to refrain from genocide. But what else are we to say? We certainly think that they *ought* to have refrained (a seriously weak way of putting it, to be sure, but not false for that), and to my ear it sounds no less odd for their moral jury to admit "You ought not to have done it, but we accept that you had no reason to refrain."

However, we do not want the claim "You have a reason not to do that" to be nothing more than an utterance licensed by our having taken the moral point of view, otherwise we've said little more than a reiteration of "You ought not do that," and we may still quite reasonably be ignored. (Nor do we want the reason to be something we *create* in the act of threatening punishment. We morally condemn no less those whom we know can evade our reprisals.) So when premise (2) links "having a reason" with a moral "ought," it is intended to be something other than an institutional reason; it is what I have been calling up until now (rather deplorably) a "real" reason. The most precise understanding we have thus far gained of "real" reasons is that they are reasons that cannot be legitimately ignored. We will try to do better in due course.

There would be no particular problem with morality (and its reasons talk) if we treated it as if it were an institution, something that people may choose to endorse or not endorse. But we don't treat it that way. We don't accept that the Nazis were at liberty to opt out of the moral framework when it suited them. Nor would there be a problem if we accepted that in defeating them and hanging their leaders we were just imposing *our* morality upon them, perhaps on grounds of self-defense. But we think of it differently. We think that the moral code that the Nazis violated was somehow *their own* rules, whether they recognized them or not. Consider, again, the comparison of the unwilling gladiator and the hurtful Gyges.

One rejects and violates the rules of gladiatorial combat, one rejects and violates the rules of morality. Yet we do not think them on a par. We invest the moral judgment with an extra authority, and it is this fugitive thought that we must try to nail down. The best place to seek the fugitive is in an account of non-institutional reasons. Thus understanding premise (2) to be referring to *non-institutional* reasons, premise (4) seems far more plausible. But before proceeding further, it is important to deal with a worry raised by Rudolf Carnap, which threatens to make the whole project of looking for "non-institutional reasons" incoherent.

2.5 CARNAP'S ARGUMENT AGAINST EXTERNAL QUESTIONING

We have seen that there can be an "institution" – a normative system – according to which various utterances are licensed, and utterances concerning reasons may be among them. But when we engage in moral evaluation we do not think that we are merely speaking in ways that an institution warrants – we think (in a sense that I have struggled to express) that the actions in question are *really* wrong or right, that the perpetrators *really* had a reason to act or refrain from acting. Of course, if speaking from a perspective of endorsing the institution of morality sanctions the utterance "So-and-so has a reason to ϕ" then it presumably also sanctions the more emphatic "So-and-so has a *real* reason to ϕ." But this gets us nowhere. There has to be some way of stepping "outside" the institution of morality, and asking "Does so-and-so really have a reason to ϕ?", "Is it really the case that she ought to ϕ?" We can make sense of this question asked from the external perspective, because the concept of "having a reason" has a wider employment than the one it enjoys within the institution of morality.

This distinction between what is accepted from within an institution, and "stepping out" of that institution and appraising it from an exterior perspective, is close to Carnap's distinction between internal and external questions.[15] Certain "linguistic frameworks" (as Carnap calls them) bring with them new terms and ways of talking: accepting the language of "things" licenses making assertions like "The shirt is in the cupboard"; accepting mathematics allows one to say "There is a prime number greater than one hundred"; accepting the language of propositions permits saying

[15] R. Carnap, "Empiricism, Semantics and Ontology," supplement to *Meaning and Necessity* (Chicago: University of Chicago Press, 1956).

"*Chicago is large* is a true proposition," etc. *Internal* to the framework in question, confirming or disconfirming the truth of these propositions is a trivial matter. But traditionally philosophers have interested themselves in the *external* question – the issue of the adequacy of the framework itself: "Do objects exist?", "Does the world exist?", "Are there numbers?", "Are the propositions?", etc. Carnap's argument is that the external question, as it has been typically construed, does not make sense. From a perspective that accepts mathematics, the answer to the question "Do numbers exist?" is just trivially "Yes." From a perspective which has not accepted mathematics, Carnap thinks, the only sensible way of construing the question is not as a theoretical question, but as a practical one: "Shall I accept the framework of mathematics?", and this pragmatic question is to be answered by consideration of the efficiency, the fruitfulness, the usefulness, etc., of the adoption. But the (traditional) philosopher's questions – "But is mathematics *true*?", "Are there *really* numbers?" – are pseudo-questions. By turning traditional philosophical questions into practical questions of the form "Shall I adopt...?", Carnap is offering a noncognitive analysis of metaphysics. Since I am claiming that we can critically inspect morality from an external perspective – that we can ask whether there are any non-institutional reasons accompanying moral injunctions – and that such questioning would not amount to a "Shall we adopt...?" query, Carnap's position represents a threat.

What arguments does Carnap offer to his conclusion? He starts with the example of the "thing language," which involves reference to objects that exist in time and space. To step out of the thing language and ask "But does the world exist?" is a mistake, Carnap thinks, because the very notion of "existence" is a term which belongs to the thing language, and can be understood only within that framework, "hence this concept cannot be meaningfully applied to the system itself."[16] Moving on to the external question "Do numbers exist?" Carnap cannot use the same argument – he cannot say that "existence" is internal to the number language and thus cannot be applied to the system as a whole. Instead he says that philosophers who ask the question do not mean *material* existence, but have no clear understanding of what other kind of existence might be involved, thus such questions have no cognitive content. It appears that this is the form of argument which he is willing to generalize to all further cases: persons who dispute whether propositions exist, whether properties exist, etc.,

---

[16] *Ibid.*, p. 207.

do not know what they are arguing over, thus they are not arguing over the *truth* of a proposition, but over the practical value of their respective positions. Carnap adds that this is so because there is nothing that both parties would possibly count as *evidence* that would sway the debate one way or the other.

Though naturally sympathetic to the claim that disputation is pointless without adequately understood terms of debate, I believe Carnap's conclusions are far too strong. Perhaps he's correct that "existence" cannot be sensibly applied to the world itself, but that is a unique case which needn't detain us. What concerns me here is the general argument: that external questions are *never* sensibly construed as anything other than practical questions. Carnap's argument boils down simply to the claim that the term "existence" – beyond a familiar *material* existence – is not properly defined by debating philosophers, that it lacks "cognitive content." But accepting that this is sometimes the case (say, for numbers and propositions), why must it always be the case? Might we not have a decent philosophical argument using a completely familiar notion of *existence*? What Carnap fails to discuss is the likelihood of a linguistic framework being "nested" within another framework, and the adequacy of the former system as a whole being appraised in terms provided by the broader one. For example, consider the European explorers encountering Polynesian "tapu" discourse. The question "Does *tapu* exist?" – as an external question pertaining to the adequacy of the whole framework – is perfectly well formed. This is because "ϕ is tapu" implies a variety of causal relations obtaining between types of event – say, among the following events: S's touching the chief's food, R's touching S, R's dying, S's not dying because he performed a purificatory rite. If a person decides that no such causal relations obtain, this need not be a "practical decision" – rather, she has employed the "thing language" and its ordinary criteria for the obtaining of causal relations, and found tapu discourse unacceptable. It's simply false that people die if they touch the chief's food and fail to perform the appropriate ritual. It's not that tapu discourse is practically suboptimal (though it may be that); rather, it's simply that there is no such thing as "tapu-ness."

We should consider the skeptic who asks "Are there such things as moral obligations?" in a similar light. Understood as an internal question the answer is trivially "Yes"; but this is clearly not the skeptic's question. Carnap would have us believe that the skeptic's question is either a practical question or a nonsensical one. But this is too hasty. I haven't addressed the reasonableness of the practical question, but merely argued that the non-practical question – "Are there *really* such things as moral obligations?" – is a sensible one. This is because there is no bizarre or alien notion of "existence" being appealed to – whatever kind of existence moral obligations have, it is a type which we are familiar with from other frameworks already accepted. Moral obligations exist, I have argued, only if *reasons for action* exist, and reasons for action are something which we are accustomed to quite independently of the moral framework. This wider non-moral notion of *having a reason* comes from practical rationality.

The unusual thing about this particular case is that the skeptic's external questioning of the moral framework *does* amount to a practical matter, since it pertains to the existence of reasons. This is not to say that Carnap is correct that the only sensible external question is a practical one – it's just that when the content of the framework revolves around reasons for action, then asking whether the framework is veridical amounts to a series of practical questions: "Should I really keep promises?", "Do I really have a reason to return this wallet?", etc. But this observation does not mean that the question "Are there really moral obligations?" may be sensibly construed only as "Shall I adopt the 'moral point of view'?"

It is important to see that even if this latter practical question were to be answered in favor of adopting the moral point of view – were we able to provide a reason for doing so – this would not thereby show that morality is *true*; that is, it would not show that we have reasons for acting in all the particular ways that morality prescribes. It may even be the case that once one has adopted the moral point of view, one *does* have reason to keep inconvenient promises (if not to do so would bring crushing guilt, for example) – perhaps from that point of view one wouldn't even dream of questioning whether one has a reason to keep the promise. But none of this shows that the person who has not adopted the moral point of view, even if she has reason to, thereby has a reason to keep promises. By analogy, there may be good reasons for me to have children, and if I were to have children then I'd have a good reason for buying some diapers – but that doesn't give me now reason to buy diapers. Another way of putting the point is this: in the prescription "You ought to adopt the moral point of view" it is far from clear that the "ought" is a moral one (it may not even make sense to think that it could be) – it does not present itself as a *categorical* imperative. In the moral prescription "You ought not break inconvenient promises, even when you know you can get away with it" the "ought" *is* categorical. Now it may be that the former hypothetical imperative is a true one – the addressee indeed might have reason (perhaps a prudential one) for adopting the moral point of view – and it may be that once that view is adopted, the agent accepts and makes categorical imperative statements like the latter. But this would not be to vindicate the particular claim about promise-breaking.

2.6 PRACTICAL REASONS AS NON-INSTITUTIONAL

But a worry remains. The above argument held that questioning morality from an external viewpoint is possible because one may do so employing the concepts of a broader, established framework: practical rationality. But isn't practical rationality just another normative institution? And, if so, aren't we merely questioning morality from a perspective to which we may *or may not* maintain allegiance? It is crucial to see why the answer is "No."

An institution, let us say, is something one may or may not adopt, something which, by its very nature, may be sensibly questioned from the outside. Certain institutions may never, as a matter of fact, be questioned – my point is that questioning them must at least be *intelligible*. The rules of gladiatorial combat are a good example: we have no difficulty imagining Celadus insisting "But what is that to me? – Why should I adopt this set of rules?" Without wanting to beg the question, I think that morality has all the hallmarks of an institution too: someone who says "Yes, I can see that morality requires me to keep that promise, but so what? – Why should I adopt that set of rules?" appears to be asking a perfectly intelligible question. Could practical rationality be just another such institution?

Whatever else it consists of, practical rationality is the framework that tells us what our reasons for acting are. We haven't yet investigated what the internal nature of this framework may be, but we know this much about it. Can we imagine someone questioning practical rationality: "Yes, I recognize that there is a practical reason for me to ϕ, but what is that to me? – Why should I adopt that set of rules?"? This, it seems to me, is incoherent (perhaps uniquely among these sorts of questions[17]). Even to ask the question "Why should I be interested in practical rationality?" is to ask for a *reason*. Thus even to question practical rationality is to evince allegiance to it. After all, what kind of answer could be provided? If the questioner is

---

[17] I say "perhaps" because I think that the same argument may work for theoretical reason, where "ϕ" denotes believing something. But it is not important here to develop this possibility. We might say that wherever "ϕ" denotes *action*, then the argument applies to practical reason alone.

already expressing doubts about whether things he acknowledges as "his reasons" should move him, then there would be no point in providing further reasons. Therefore to question practical rationality *is* unintelligible – it is to ask for a reason while implying that no reason will be adequate.

Let's be clear how this argument works. Let "M" denote *morality* and "P" denote *practical rationality*; "should$_m$" is *should according to morality* and "should$_p$" is *should according to practical rationality*. There are four questions to consider an agent asking:

(i) I know that M requires that I ϕ, but why should$_p$ I care about M?
(ii) I know that M requires that I ϕ, but why should$_m$ I care about M?
(iii) I know that P requires that I ϕ, but why should$_p$ I care about P?
(iv) I know that P requires that I ϕ, but why should$_m$ I care about P?

(ii) is self-undermining, since to ask for a moral reason is to imply acceptance of moral reasons, in which case to acknowledge that M requires ϕing is to accept that one has a reason to ϕ. However, it does not follow that M cannot be questioned at all, since one may ask (i) instead – indeed, presumably moral skeptics typically *do* ask (i) rather than (ii). Things are not symmetrical, however, when it comes to P: (iii) is self-undermining in a different way. (iii) is self-undermining not merely because to ask why one should$_p$ do something is to imply the acceptance of practical rationality, but that to ask for a reason *period* is to imply the acceptance of practical rationality. This is brought out by reflecting on (iv). To ask why one should$_m$ do something implies an acceptance of moral reasons *and* an acceptance of practical reasons; therefore (iv) is self-undermining too. All four questions, in fact, imply an acceptance of practical rationality; asking *any* practical question implies an acceptance of practical rationality. Therefore practical rationality cannot be intelligibly questioned.

This result may seem odd if one thinks of practical rationality as just another normative system on all fours with others, competing for one's action (a thought that the artificial example above admittedly encourages); but that would be a mistaken conception. Practical reasons are, by definition, those which guide our actions when everything has been taken into account: if the rules of chess are telling me to move my rook straight, the rules of etiquette telling me that I ought to let my opponent win, the rules of prudence telling me that I ought to move the rook diagonally (thereby annoying my opponent, thereby winning a bet), then practical rationality is not a *further* consideration. Rather, when I have weighed all these claims and come up with an answer of *what is to be done*, then that is the judgment of practical rationality. It couldn't be the case that practical rationality tells me that I ought to ϕ but this is overridden by another consideration – of morality, say – telling me otherwise. If the final word goes to morality, in favor of not ϕing, then that is the judgment of practical rationality too.[18] (Of course, practical rationality may still "compete" with another normative system in the sense that that system may prescribe ϕing while practical rationality tells me to refrain from ϕing. What this means, though, is that practical rationality has sided with ignoring that normative system altogether, or allowing other considerations to win out.)

The observation that practical rationality is not available for legitimate questioning is of central importance to our project. Not only does it deal with Carnap, but it suggests a lead in the search for what earlier were called "*real* reasons" – reasons that cannot be legitimately ignored. Real reasons are those that one has independently of an institution that ascribes them. Practical rationality delivers reasons claims, but practical rationality is not an institution which we may intelligibly question. If in practical rationality we have located the "real reasons" that I have been gesturing at in this chapter, then the vital question is whether one might have such a reason to ϕ regardless of whether ϕing serves one's desires or interests. If one might, then premise (4) of the argument of §2.4 is defeated. This, I believe, is the only hope for the opponent of a moral error theory: to defend the thesis that practical rationality delivers categorical imperatives, and then to forge a connection between the imperatives of practical rationality and those of morality. The objective of the next three chapters is to argue that this cannot be done. Practical rationality, I will argue, yields only hypothetical imperatives, and therefore cannot be appealed to as a way of vindicating "moral inescapability."

---

[18] Lawrence Becker, in "The Finality of Moral Judgments: A Reply to Mrs Foot," *Philosophical Review* 82 (1973), pp. 364–70, attempts a similar sort of argument regarding the "all-things-considered" nature of *moral* considerations: since moral imperatives are (he claims) all-things-considered, then to acknowledge one is to accept that there is nothing more to consider, and therefore to consider anything else would be irrational; therefore if one accepts a moral imperative one is irrational if one does not obey it. One problem with this is that if I weigh up all considerations and decide that catching the 2.30 train is preferable to catching the 3.30, and know that there is nothing else to consider, this would hardly make "Catch the 2.30 train" a *moral* prescription (so moral imperatives are not *identical* to all-things-considered ones). Further, Becker's reasoning does not obviously exclude one's giving enormous weight to prudential considerations in weighing up competing demands, and hence deciding, all-things-considered, that, say, stealing is what one shall do. It would appear that this is all it would take (for Becker) for "Steal" to be a moral imperative, the breaking of which is irrational.

A dominant theory with this consequence is what might be called "Humean instrumentalism": the view that a person has a reason for performing an action if and only if doing so promises to satisfy that person's desires. (This sketch will be expanded in the following chapter.) Thus understood, we might well rewrite premise (4) as a statement of Humean instrumentalism. This theory is in the background of both Foot's and Mackie's rejection of Kantian imperatives. Foot writes: "Irrational actions are those in which a man in some way defeats his own purposes, doing what is calculated to be disadvantageous or to frustrate his ends."[19] Outside *Ethics: Inventing Right and Wrong*, Mackie says of objective prescriptions that "[t]o say that they are intrinsically action-guiding is to say that the reasons that they give for doing or for not doing something are independent of that agent's desires or purposes" (which Mackie thinks provides sufficient grounds for rejecting them).[20] Neither philosopher, however, mounts a serious defense of the theory – content, perhaps, that they inhabit the comfortable domain of "orthodoxy" – but instrumentalism is a theory under serious pressure, and cannot simply be assumed without a contest. The following chapter investigates instrumentalism carefully. The reader may be expecting that the strategy will be to defend Humean instrumentalism, and thereby the argument above. As a matter of fact, things will turn out to be more complicated than that. A version of *non*-Humean instrumentalism will be defended, and doing so will necessitate revising the simple argument. However, these revisions leave us with a sound argument to the same conclusion.

[19] Foot, "Morality as a System of Hypothetical Imperatives," p. 310. It must be emphasized that Foot has since rejected this instrumentalism, and all my references apparently to *her* are really to a certain time slice of her from the 1970s.
[20] J. L. Mackie, *The Miracle of Theism* (Oxford: Clarendon Press, 1982), p. 115.

3

Practical instrumentalism

3.0 OBJECTIVE REASONS, SUBJECTIVE REASONS, AND PRACTICAL RATIONALITY

I have argued that the truth of a moral judgment like "It was wrong for S to do that" depends on whether we can make sense of there being a reason for S not to do that. We are asking this question from a perspective external to morality, but in doing so we are not falling into Carnap's trap of employing the concepts of a discourse in the very act of questioning the adequacy of that discourse. Outside morality we know very well what *reasons* are: most conspicuously, we have a normative framework of giving and accepting reasons for acting known as "practical rationality."

Common sense demands a distinction between reasons that an agent is aware of and those he is ignorant of. If Mary is thirsty, then it seems she has a reason to drink the liquid in the cup before her, which she believes (with justification) to be water. But if, in fact, the cup contains poison, then we also allow that there is a reason for her *not* to drink from the cup. Bernard Williams argues that there is only one reason here – for Mary to refrain from drinking – but that seems unnecessarily restrictive.[1] Mackie prefers to say that "there is no need to choose" – in one sense Mary has a reason to drink, in another she has a reason not to drink – and this seems the more natural answer.[2] The instrumentalist can accommodate this distinction smoothly:

OBJECTIVE REASONS:

S has an objective reason to ϕ if and only if ϕing will further S's ends.

SUBJECTIVE REASONS:

S has a subjective reason to ϕ if and only if S is justified in believing that she has an objective reason to ϕ.

---

[1] B. Williams, "Internal and External Reasons," in his *Moral Luck* (Cambridge: Cambridge University Press, 1981), pp. 101–13.
[2] Mackie, *Ethics*, p. 77.

Mary, then, has an objective reason to refrain from drinking, and a subjective reason to drink.[3] It is worthwhile to compare this with another distinction that has been made between types of reason: Williams's internal and external reasons. An internal reason is one which suitably connects with a person's "subjective motivational set," in such a way that it is a potential motivator of the agent. The motivational set "can contain such things as dispositions of evaluation, patterns of emotional reaction, personal loyalties, and various projects, as they may be abstractly called, embodying commitments of the agent."[4] For an action, ϕ, to be "suitably connected" to a motivational set means that the agent could, through imaginative reflection and rational deliberation, and armed with true beliefs, come to be motivated to ϕ. Although Mary is ignorant of the poison, she has a reason to refrain from drinking since her motivational set contains something amounting to "that I do not drink poison," and if she had only true beliefs on the matter (and reflected clearly), that element would ensure that she would be motivated to refrain from drinking.

If the "ends" mentioned in the account of objective reasons are identified with elements of a "subjective motivational set" (in Williams's sense), then we could speak of both objective internal reasons and subjective internal reasons: the ones that will really satisfy elements of the agent's motivational set, and the ones that the agent is justified in believing will satisfy such elements. I point this out partly as an introduction to Williams, to whom we will be returning, and partly to head-off any misunderstanding that the subjective/objective distinction maps on to the well-known internal/external distinction.

Instrumentalism brings with it an account of *rationality*:

INSTRUMENTAL RATIONALITY:

S is practically rational to the extent that she is guided by her subjective reasons.

Mary has a reason to refrain from drinking from the cup. But, given that she is thirsty and that she justifiably believes that the cup contains water, she would be *irrational* if she refrained from drinking. So we cannot simply identify practical rationality (justification) with acting in accordance with one's reasons, nor practical irrationality (lack of justification) with acting contrary to one's reasons.

---

[3] This terminology should not be confused with "subjective and objective reasons" as employed by Thomas Nagel in *The Possibility of Altruism* (Princeton: Princeton University Press, 1978).

[4] Williams, "Internal and External Reasons," p. 105.

Must the instrumentalist understand "rationality" in this way? Richard Brandt, for example, introduced a notion of practical rationality which privileges what the agent would seek to do in extremely idealized circumstances: having "every item of relevant available information," after undergoing complete and careful "cognitive psychotherapy."[5] Brandt claims that an agent is rational to the extent that his actions match those of his idealized self, which comes close to connecting rationality with an agent's *objective* reasons. One response to this would be to allow a distinction between "objective rationality" and "subjective rationality," mirroring the two sorts of reason. But this is unwarranted, for whereas the distinction between subjective and objective reasons succeeds, I believe, in capturing a useful common-sense distinction, there is no matching distinction in ordinary thought between two forms of practical rationality.

Stating that an agent is irrational is not merely to *describe* the agent's actions – it is a means of criticizing him, of saying that he is unjustified. If Mary refrains from drinking from the cup, despite the fact that she is incredibly thirsty and reasonably believes the cup to contain water (and there is no other complicating factor involved), we could hardly say that her action – or in this case, inaction – is justified. We should say that it is irrational but most fortunate. In the case of theoretical rationality, what is appraised when we call a belief "rational" or "justified" is not the *content* of the belief, but the manner at which it is arrived. We don't call any old false belief "irrational" – sometimes error is understandable, and when it is, we refrain from criticizing the erring agent. An irrational belief is one (possibly even a true one) that is arrived at in a faulty manner for which the believer is responsible, and for which he may be reasonably censured. The same thing goes for practical rationality, and for this reason it attaches far more comfortably to an agent's subjective reasons than his objective. Kurt Baier, in this vein, correctly rejects Brandt's account of rationality on the grounds that it criticizes "the merit of the content of the decision rather than the merit of the agent's performance in arriving at it."[6] This echoes a complaint that Dr. Johnson leveled at his old headmaster: that "he did not distinguish between ignorance and negligence; for he would beat a boy equally for not knowing a thing, as for neglecting to know it."[7] In what follows it will be important to remember that irrationality

---

[5] R. Brandt, *A Theory of the Right and the Good* (Oxford: Clarendon Press, 1979).

[6] Kurt Baier, "Rationality, Reason, and the Good," in D. Copp and D. Zimmerman (eds.), *Morality, Reason and Truth* (Totowa, NJ: Rowman & Allanheld, 1984), p. 195.

[7] *Boswell's Life of Samuel Johnson* [1791] (London: J. M. Dent & Co., 1909), p. 18.

is a form of negligence, not ignorance. (Whether it warrants beating is another matter.)

3.1 ENDS: DESIRES OR INTERESTS?

It is natural at this point to inquire further into what is meant by "ends" in the account of objective reasons. In particular, do we just mean something more or less covered by "desires," or might we introduce other kinds of ends as well – perhaps better called "interests"? Suppose, for example, that Wanda smokes cigarettes, and is well aware of the raised probabilities of cancer, but doesn't much care – she has a nihilistic, self-destructive streak that is more than just for show. It is tempting to describe the situation as one in which Wanda's *interests* lie in not smoking, though her *desires* go with smoking. If this is the correct description, does Wanda (according to instrumentalism) have a reason to quit smoking, or a reason to carry on smoking, or reasons to do both?

The first thing to note is that in the context of this project, the question doesn't need to be answered. Recall that what is under investigation is whether any sense can be made of the central moral notion of a categorical imperative. In the last chapter, the reader may have noticed, the description of a categorical imperative fudged this point – claiming an agent ought to ϕ regardless of his *desires or interests* – (sometimes the distinction was blurred with the phrase ". . . regardless of whether it suits him"). And I am content to leave the concept vague, since I am confident that when we morally condemn a person we often ignore *both* whether the action promised to satisfy his desires *and* whether the action was in his interests. Therefore, if I am in addition correct about Mackie's Platitude, moral language involves a commitment to agents having reasons for ϕing regardless of whether ϕing furthers their *ends* – where "ends" can be read as covering both desires and interests, and we can leave the question of whether there is a real distinction between them unadjudicated. Therefore, if we cannot plausibly defend there being such reasons – by defending instrumentalism, for instance – then moral judgments look dubious. The argument will go through with the notion of "ends" left tolerably vague throughout.

That said, however, if one were successfully to defend a more restricted type of instrumentalism, where "ends" are understood only as *the satisfaction of present desires*, then this would cast doubt on moral discourse *a fortiori*. Such an instrumentalism was defended by Hume. That Hume did not think that an agent's interests alone ground reasons is revealed by his insistence that we could not rationally fault a person for preferring and seeking his acknowledged lesser good over his greater.[8] Generally, of course, people's desires will include their own "greater good," and so desires and interests will be in accordance – and Hume thinks that this agreement is a matter of "original instinct" – but he is adamant that when they come apart, the interests *per se* do not provide the agent with reasons.

Hume does not make the distinction between objective and subjective reasons, though it appears to be open for him to do so. However, even if he were to do so he would resist the account of rationality given above, for he holds that subjective reasons *never* fail to motivate, that one is *always* guided by what one takes to be one's objective reasons. Suppose I believe, falsely, that wearing flared trousers is fashionable – an end I very much desire. Hume thinks that, absent a stronger desire to the contrary, I will be motivated to wear flares. It is true that Hume allows that this desire, because it is based on a false belief, may be called "unreasonable," but, as Christine Korsgaard rightly notes, it is only "in an extended sense" that this could be called genuine "irrationality" – relative to my beliefs, the desire is the correct one to have.[9] If I come to see that flares are horribly unfashionable, my desire to wear them will immediately vanish (Hume thinks). The moment we realize that our beliefs about how best to satisfy a desire are false, "our passions yield to our reason without any opposition."[10] One might be tempted to conclude that what this shows is that Hume thinks that we are unfailingly practically rational. However, rationality must be something that we can fall short of; a person's being rational must exclude possibilities. If we are bound to follow a principle as a matter of psychological fact, then we cannot be considered *rational* to do so – indeed, one would not truly be "following" the principle at all, but merely acting in accordance with it. The natural conclusion to draw is that Hume denies that there is such a thing as practical rationality.[11]

Yet in this Hume is surely wrong. A number of familiar phenomena may interrupt the motive force transmitting from a desire for X, via the

[8] *Treatise*, book 2, part 3 section 3 (1978), p. 416.
[9] Korsgaard, "Skepticism About Practical Reason," p. 11.
[10] *Treatise*, book 2, part 3, section 3 (1978), p. 416.
[11] A more thorough argument to the same conclusion is given by Korsgaard in "The Normativity of Instrumental Reason," in G. Cullity and B. Gaut (eds.), *Ethics and Practical Reason* (Oxford: Clarendon Press, 1997), p. 222.

The myth of morality

perception that ϕing will bring about X, to a motive to ϕ: rage, passion, depression, distraction, grief, physical or mental illness.[12] Just as such phenomena might, with respect to theoretical reason, prevent one from believing that q – upon believing that p, and that if p then q – so too might they prevent one from desiring the means that one believes optimal for satisfying one's desires. In so far as an agent's beliefs or desires are disturbed by such phenomena we call her "irrational."

There is another source of practical irrationality that Hume disallows, and that is when one desires the means to the satisfaction of an "inappropriate" desire. Hume thinks that any desire, regardless of its content, regardless of how it was arrived at, will provide the agent with a reason to satisfy it. The domain of reason in the practical sphere is restricted to determining the optimal means of satisfying our ends, but reason cannot appraise the ends themselves. As Hume memorably made the point: "'Tis not contrary to reason to prefer the destruction of the whole world to the scratching of my finger."[13] It is often thought that this rejection of the rational appraisability of ends leads directly to moral skepticism. What is seen less often is that even conceding to the anti-Humean that ends are available for rational appraisal does not in any obvious way block the path to skepticism. It all depends on the kind of rational appraisal that is admitted. In what follows I will concede to the anti-Humean that desires (ends) may be subject to rational appraisal, but continue to hold that the moral error theory still beckons. However, before continuing with that discussion it is important to deal with a certain kind of theorist who accepts Hume's limits on the scope of rationality, but hopes to build a moral theory upon that foundation.

3.2 MORALITY AS A SYSTEM OF HYPOTHETICAL IMPERATIVES

The problem, as I have argued it, is that to participate properly in moral discourse will involve a willingness to assert statements such as "S morally ought not to ϕ" when there is no reason to doubt that ϕing perfectly well serves S's desires. "So much the worse for moral discourse," says the Humean error theorist. But a Humean who does not welcome this result may try to block the presupposition of the problem: as a matter of

[12] The list, and the point it is employed to make, are from Korsgaard, "Skepticism About Practical Reason," p. 378.
[13] *Treatise*, book 2, part 3, section 3 (1978), p. 416.

58

fact every agent to whom we apply moral prescriptions has desires which are served by acting in accordance with those prescriptions.[14] Humean instrumentalism may thus be seen as a potential *savior* of moral discourse. The task that such a Humean moralist sets herself is to locate some desire which all humans have – including apparently conflict-free transgressors – towards which promise-keeping, honesty, etc., are conducive. Of course, strictly speaking it is not necessary to find a desire that is had by all; it will suffice if everyone has some desire or other which is so served. But this qualification will not help. Let us start by looking for a universal desire.

The likely candidate is self-interest: surely we are all self-interested? (This admission would be compatible with our also frequently having non-self-interested desires.) The program of founding morality upon an appeal to self-interest has a long history, with a thread running through Hume himself, Spinoza, Hobbes, Plato, back to pre-classical thinkers like Hesiod. If self-interest is inescapable, and following morality is sound advice to that end, then morality is inescapable. On this view moral imperatives would still be, in Kant's terms, *hypothetical*, in so far as they remain dependent on our having a further end – it's just that we all have that end. (Kant calls such imperatives "assertorial practical principles."[15]) Up to a point this program is likely to meet with every success; it very probably can be shown that most people in ordinary situations have good egoistic reasons for acting in accordance with morality. We might even construct our society with the purpose in mind of providing every citizen with a prudential reason to be moral, as did Hobbes with his sovereign state. However, as was argued in the previous chapter, prudence and morality will go hand-in-hand for only so far, and then must part company. As is well known, Hobbes makes no headway against Gyges, who stole, killed, and set himself up as king precisely *because of his selfishness*. We can allow that, given facts about the kind of creature he is, it is in the shepherd's interest to have friends, lovers, family, and even to feel part of a cooperative community. But he may

---

[14] See, for example, E. J. Bond, "Moral Requirement and the Need for Deontic Language," *Philosophy* 41 (1966), pp. 233–49.

[15] Occasionally one sees the hypothetical imperative characterized as prescribing action as a means of satisfying a *contingent* desire. But it is the dependence on a desire, *period* – never mind whether we all have the desire or not – that makes for a hypothetical imperative, according to Kant. Recall that Kant agrees that there are universally held desires: he accepts that we all desire the furtherance of self-interest (i.e., our own happiness), and he describes this desire as one we have of "natural necessity," as belonging to a person's "essence." Nevertheless, imperatives prescribing actions to this end are clearly taken to be hypothetical. See Kant, *Groundwork* (1985), pp. 78–80.

satisfy such desiderata in the local sphere, and do so in a sincere, non-coercive manner, while still using his ring to inflict great harm upon more distant others. To think that the shepherd, when a self-made king, *must* live a cold, unsatisfying existence, friendless and unloved – with troubled conscience and damaged soul – is at worst simply foolish, and at best requires a leap of optimistic faith that facts about human psychology are a very particular way. Alternatively, to think that the shepherd, when his circumstances are carefully stipulated in this way, lies beyond the compass of moral injunctions is to ignore the way moral discourse is employed.

Short of introducing a magical metaphysical framework wherein "just deserts" are reliably distributed, I discern no grounds for confidence concerning the thesis that self-interest and morality always coincide, let alone that the coincidence is counterfactually robust. There is, in addition, a "conceptual" worry: that moral imperatives are exactly (necessarily) those which *oppose* self-interested imperatives (if not always, then at least sometimes). Frankena, for example, insists that "prudentialism or living by the principle of enlightened self-love just is not a kind of *morality*" – in the Judaic-Christian tradition, morality is often exactly that with which we attempt to counter selfishness.[16] Frankena is appealing to the natural thought that being "morally correct" requires more than simply acting in a certain way, but encompasses the agent's motivations too, and acting from the motive of self-interest is antithetical to being a morally upstanding agent. Here I will not evaluate this further worry, for the contingent failure of prudence and morality always to coincide is quite clear enough.

Is there any other kind of desire upon which a universal morality could be based? Those optimists who hope to make out even Gyges as self-frustrating might look hopefully to a universal sense of sympathy, or fellowship, which the shepherd's actions necessarily thwart. There is solid empirical evidence (to be discussed in Chapter 6) that humans do indeed have a natural sense of sympathy, bestowed by the pressures of natural selection. And to overcome Frankena's worry, we need not understand the frustration of this sympathetic disposition in terms of a violation of *egoistic* desires – it will suffice to say that humans naturally have a desire for the good of others (a genuine altruistic desire), and immoral behavior frustrates this desire. But to form the thesis in the terms required to underwrite morality as a set of universally applicable hypothetical imperatives is to strip it of any plausibility. Whatever plausibility there is in a thesis of "natural sympathy"

[16] Frankena, *Ethics*, p. 19.

depends upon its being construed as a *disposition* or *propensity*. To present the-good-of-fellows as the object of a *desire* which all humans have (reliably, on all occasions), a desire from which no human could escape, is to divest the thesis of credibility. We're all too familiar with counter-examples. Besides, we may credit Gyges with all sorts of non-selfish desires – perhaps his caring for the interests of his friends, family and community is not motivated by self-interest at all, but he values them for their own sakes – but none of this will be sufficient for grounding imperatives proscribing his inflicting harm upon the inhabitants of the neighboring valley. So long as Plato's shepherd has a clear sense of "*my community*" versus "*foreigners*," there's no reason to think that treating foreigners in a certain way will, as a matter of psychological fact, cause him to "slide" into treating his loved ones in the same way, thus frustrating his altruistic desires.

It was noted above that it is not really necessary to find a universally held desire, so long as we can say of everybody to whom we apply moral imperatives that he has some desire(s) or other the satisfaction of which morality serves. This is ultimately how Hume argued: he appeals to a natural sense of sympathy which in many humans will manifest itself as a desire for the good of one's fellows, but for those persons in whom sympathy is altogether insensate he makes a direct appeal to self-interest.[17] But now we have canvassed two obvious candidates and found the prospects of basing morality upon either to be bleak, and we can note the unlikelihood of another contestant coming forward, the enterprise of finding a *range* of suitable desires, one or other of which is had by everyone to whom we apply moral injunctions, has all the appearance of a lost program. At this point, then, I will put aside the possibility of Humean instrumentalism being the savior of a universal morality.

The other conspicuous course for the Humean defender of morality is to deny that moral discourse does have universal scope, to deny that we would apply moral imperatives to Lydian shepherds and the like. The consequence of this view is that morality is "escapable," that someone who simply does not care, or ceases to care, legitimately evades its prescriptions. This is a consequence that Philippa Foot tolerates in "Morality as a System of Hypothetical Imperatives" (a view she later rejects), but enough has already

---

[17] The appeal to the knave's self-interest comes in the Conclusion to *Enquiry Concerning the Principles of Morals*. However, since Hume thinks that a person may even be uninterested in her own self-interest ("'Tis not contrary to reason for me to chuse my total ruin, to prevent the least uneasiness of an *Indian* or person wholly unknown to me" [*Treatise* (1978), p. 416]), an appeal to both sympathy and self-interest will still leave certain unusual agents unimpressed.

been said, I think, to show how unconvincing this is. Bear in mind that the crucial question is not the substantive one – of whether there *are* any categorical imperatives, of whether morality *does* bind everyone regardless of their ends – but the *conceptual* one – of whether it is part of our moral conceptual framework that everyone is so bound. And I am confident that the answer to the latter is "Yes." If you are told that somebody named "Jack" broke into a stranger's house, attacked the inhabitants, and all with the intention of taking their money for idle purposes, then from a moral point of view you have all the information needed to condemn Jack's action. There is no need to investigate further his desires (or ends); the judgment is not made under the assumption that his desires were a certain way. To agree with this is to agree that morality employs categorical imperatives.

3.3 SMITH'S ARGUMENT FOR MORALITY AS A SYSTEM OF CATEGORICAL IMPERATIVES

Michael Smith presents another argument against Foot's view, in favor of what he calls "the rationalist's conceptual claim."[18] I agree with Smith's conclusion that morality is a system of categorical imperatives (where this is a conceptual claim), but Smith wants to go a further step, and identify the categorical imperatives of morality with the categorical imperatives of rationality. I don't think that the argument is convincing, and seeing why it is not will lead, in an instructive way, back to the important question that was left hanging a few pages ago, concerning how we may allow for the rational appraisal of ends (desires) without this in any obvious way checking the error theorist.

Here is how Smith presents the argument:

Moral requirements apply to rational agents as such. But it is a conceptual truth that if agents are morally required to act in a certain way then we expect them to act in that way. Being rational, as such, must therefore suffice to ground our expectation that rational agents will do what they are morally required to do. But how could this be so? It could be so only if we think of the moral requirements that apply to agents as themselves categorical imperatives of rationality or reason. For the only thing we can legitimately expect of rational agents as such is that they will do what they are rationally required to do. (p. 85)

It seems to me highly doubtful that it is a *conceptual* truth that if a person is morally obliged to ϕ then we expect him to ϕ. If you simply say to me

---

[18] Michael Smith, *The Moral Problem* (Oxford: Blackwell, 1994), pp. 85–91. All textual page references to Smith are to this work unless otherwise stated.

"Jack is obliged to refrain from stealing – do you expect him to refrain?" I don't think I should hazard an answer. I'd need to know more about Jack. Even if I were cautiously inclined to think Jack would probably refrain, that wouldn't ground a conceptual claim. In the same way, if you tell me that Jane saw a hungry-looking tiger coming towards her, then I'd expect her to run away – but that doesn't make it a conceptual claim that agents run away from tigers. Most do, given typical desires about not being eaten – but some don't. Perhaps Jane, like one of Hume's radical agents, prefers her "total ruin" to a tiger's going hungry. An odd desire, to be sure, but why an *irrational* one? It is only by making a substantive assumption about the nature of practical rationality that the conclusion would go through.

In fact, the analogy of Jane and the tiger is a poor one. We're wondering whether Jack's being under a moral obligation to ϕ would ground an expectation that he will ϕ. There's no assumption that Jack is *aware* that he is under this moral obligation – perhaps he has quite forgotten about that promise he made all those weeks ago. So the better analogy would be that Jane is being approached by a tiger but is possibly ignorant of the fact. It becomes even clearer now that we should have no expectation that she would run. It matters not a whit if we stipulate that Jane is rational. Being rational may help her draw valid consequences from her beliefs, it may ensure a disposition to will the means to her ends, etc. – but it doesn't provide her with *knowledge* that a tiger is sneaking up on her.

The same goes for Jack's moral obligations. Do we really expect rational agents *as such* to act in accordance with their moral obligations? Or even in accordance with what they perceive to be their moral obligations? Note for a start that these are distinct questions, though Smith wants them to collapse into one: "we can and do expect rational agents to judge *truly*" (p. 87). But being rational won't ensure that one has true beliefs about one's moral obligations, any more than it ensures true beliefs about the location of tigers. Ignorance – unlike self-deception, or weakness of will, or illogical thinking, etc. – is not a failure of rationality. But perhaps Smith can still mount his argument without the extravagant claim that rationality involves judging truly. Perhaps instead we can start with the more modest premise that we expect agents to act in accordance with what they judge to be morally obligatory (even if they judge falsely). Add the premise that we expect rational agents *as such* to do what they themselves judge to be morally obligatory, and we may derive the conclusion that moral requirements are "requirements of rationality or reason."

Smith thinks that he can push through these premises on the grounds of having established the thesis of internalism about motivation ("MI*" from Chapter 1). With MI* in place, it can be held that any rational agent who makes the sincere moral judgment that ϕing is correct has some motivation in favor of ϕing, which may ground the expectation that he will, *ceteris paribus*, ϕ. Further, if an agent has some motivation to ϕ, then it may seem that only a rational failure would prevent him from following through with ϕing action, and so, in so far as he is rational, he will ϕ. I have already, to my satisfaction, cast doubt on MI* by drawing attention to the evil agent. Smith would describe such an agent as trying but failing to make a moral judgment, and therefore not representing a genuine counter-example to MI*. However, this will not do without further argument; it prompts the query "In virtue of what does the evil agent fail to make a genuine moral judgment?" – to which the answer had better not be "Because he lacks the appropriate motivation." Smith presents such an argument, which should be dealt with before proceeding.

3.4 SMITH'S ARGUMENT FOR MOTIVATION INTERNALISM

Smith's argument in favor of MI* turns on what we say of the "good and strong-willed" agent who changes her mind over a moral matter: we naturally expect that her motivations will change accordingly. On Monday she thought that giving to a certain charity was good and she was motivated to do so, by Friday she had learnt how that agency is squandering its money, so she now judges that giving to that charity is not morally good, and she is no longer motivated to do so. According to Smith, the externalist (in the sense of the person who denies MI*), in order to explain the shift in motivation that accompanies the shift in judgment, must credit the agent with a desire – a *de dicto* desire – to do what is good. But, Smith complains, having a *de dicto* desire to do what is good is not a characteristic we normally attribute to the "good and strong-willed person" – on the contrary, it is a vice and a moral fetish!

Why so? Smith appeals to an example from Bernard Williams, of a man calculating whether to save his wife from drowning.[19] The man thinks "Saving my wife is permissible, I want to do what's permissible, so I shall save her," and Williams, quite rightly, indicates that this would

---

[19] Williams, "Persons, Character and Morality," in his *Moral Luck*, pp. 17–18.

be a manifestation of a kind of moral vice – the man has "one thought too many"; he is calculating too much. My complaint is that Williams's example is not an appropriate one for Smith to draw attention to. Williams's point is one concerning *deliberation* – its object is to criticize a certain mental procedure that a person might go through. It's almost as if we are invited to think of the man *hesitating* for a moment on the river bank while his thought processes resolve into an answer. But it is evident that the externalist need not see the good and strong-willed person in anything like these terms. The externalist is generally a Humean concerning action being explained in terms of beliefs and desires. Let it be conceded that the externalist credits good agents with *de dicto* desires to do what is good. This is not to concede that the good person *hesitates*, and nor is it to concede that the *de dicto* desire figures in the good agent's *deliberations*. By comparison, think of how a Humean explains the following: Jane sees a tiger coming towards her and runs away. We credit Jane with a desire not to be eaten, a belief that the tiger will likely eat her, the belief that to run away will lessen the likelihood of being eaten, a desire to run away. But this appeal to a relatively complex set of explanatory posits does not entail that Jane hesitates for a moment and deliberates over these matters in a conscious way. What goes through her mind, as it were, is simply "Tiger!!" The externalist says the same of the good agent's change of heart. When the good agent sees somebody suffering and is motivated to help, to credit her with a belief that helping the suffering is good and a desire to do what is good, says nothing about her *deliberating* (in the sense of consciously calculating) at all – what goes through her mind, as it were, may simply be emotions of sympathy for the suffering before her.[20]

Smith complains that the externalist is committed to good people caring only "derivatively" for those around them, but once we have dispelled the illusion that having a *de dicto* desire for the good need concern one's deliberations, or make one "cold and calculating," then it is far from obvious in what sense this "derivativeness" is a vice. A possible source of confusion (though not one being attributed to Smith) is the thought that *de dicto* desires have something to do with conscious desires – desires with some sort of "phenomenological presence" – but this is not the case. Jane has the desire not to be eaten by a tiger. She had the desire even before she saw the tiger – indeed, we can assume that she's had it since childhood,

---

[20] This line of argument is not far removed from that used by David Brink himself – who is the "externalist" being targeted by Smith – in Brink's "Moral Motivation," *Ethics* 108 (1997), pp. 26–8.

though, like most of us, she has rarely given it much attention. Despite the fact that the desire rarely, or never, figures in her thoughts, it is a *de dicto* desire. If the animal in the third cage in London zoo is a tiger, then Jane also has the desire not to be eaten by the animal in the third cage at London zoo. *That* desire is the *de re* desire.

I have supplemented the arguments against motivation internalism given in Chapter 1 with one that directly counters Smith's main argument in favor of his version of the thesis. With motivation internalism continuing to look doubtful, Smith's argument that we expect rational agents to act in accordance with their moral judgments does not go through. If you tell me that Jack judges ϕing to be morally right, shall I expect that Jack is likely to ϕ? Only if I'm allowed to import an empirical statistical claim: that evil agents are rare and so Jack is unlikely to be one. In the absence of such a background assumption, then I would not draw any conclusions about the relation between Jack's moral judgments and his motivations. Suppose you add to the picture the stipulation that Jack is *rational* — does that weaken my reluctance to assume that Jack will ϕ? The problem now is that it depends what you mean by "rational." Smith's insistence that it is a "truism" that we expect rational agents to act morally makes it sound as if there is a clear, common-sense concept of *rationality* at hand, but this is simply not the case. If one were to endorse the Humean view of reason's limited practical role, then one would have no particular grounds for expecting that an entirely rational agent is (a) particularly likely to act in accordance with morality, or (b) likely even to act in accordance with what he judges to be morally required. Again, it is only if one is allowed to pay attention to a substantive empirical belief — that most people will not choose their "total ruin" over trivial preferences — that one can conclude that a rational person will act in accordance with what he takes to be morally required. But then, of course, the conclusion reveals nothing about what a rational agent *as such* prefers.

Thus it seems that the thesis that we may expect rational agents to act in particular ways can be put on the table only *after* a certain non-Humean view of practical rationality has been established. This being the case, it cannot be appealed to as a *truism*, as if it were simply obvious to any clear-headed thinker. Furthermore, it appears that even if one were to concede that any person who makes a moral judgment that ϕing is correct thereby has some motivation to ϕ (or is practically irrational) — there is still a gap that needs bridging to Smith's next premise. Just because an agent has a motivation in favor of ϕing it doesn't mean that she is *irrational* if she does not ϕ, and so it doesn't mean that we may expect her to ϕ as a rational agent. Perhaps she also has a motivation in favor of ψing (where ϕing and ψing are incompatible). It is certainly not irrational to have competing desires, though she might be considered irrational if she cannot settle their competition, or if she promotes both desires to the status of *intention*, or if she lets the desire with a lesser claim rule her actions. But there is nothing irrational about the agent who has a desire for the doughnut on the table across the room, and then on the way across the room spots an equally luscious looking eclair on a different table, and for a moment feels the force of both desires tugging. The second premise of Smith's argument, then, does not follow in an obvious way from MI*, and so must have independent attractions. But short of an insistence that it is a "conceptual truth" and a "truism" – both of which seem highly dubious – I am unsure whence its plausibility derives.

3.5 TAKING STOCK OF THE STRATEGY

So far in this chapter we have been dealing with a variety of issues – all important prerequisites to get straight on, but distracting us from our primary goal. Let me quickly clarify the general strategy, and then return to the heart of the matter.

In the context of arguing for a moral error theory, having resisted the conceptual identification of moral imperatives with those of practical rationality, the question arises of why we should be discussing practical rationality at all. The more predictable strategy would be to argue *for* the conceptual identification, and then attack the substantive thesis that there *are* any imperatives of practical rationality. My intentions need explaining on this point.

The conceptual commitment of moral discourse, upon which the error theory turns, is one concerning actions that we "have to" perform, regardless of what our desires and interests are. We can place next to this another commitment concerning the *content* of such imperatives: that the things we "have to" refrain from need to include breaking promises for trivial reasons, doing violence for self-gain, and the like. There may be no need to be more specific than this, if we can show that understood even in these most general terms there is no halfway plausible defense of these commitments available. In other words, a theory of imperatives that managed to supply strong categorical imperatives – that located Foot's "fugitive thought" – but for things like "Kill anyone who annoys you," "Steal when you can," etc., simply would not be a *morality*.

In the previous chapter I argued that the only hope of making sense of these commitments is to locate a kind of *reason*. The defender of morality therefore needs to produce a theory of reasons which will underwrite the commitments, and an appeal to practical rationality is the obvious choice. Moreover, I argued at the close of the last chapter (§2.6) that *only* an appeal to practical rationality will suffice, since practical rationality uniquely is inescapable, whereas any other framework of reason-giving will be just another institution which may be legitimately questioned.

I do not see an easy way of settling the question head-on of whether there is a conceptual connection between moral reasons and practical reasons. A better course, it seems to me, is to begin by investigating the nature of practical rationality. Suppose we discover either (A) that practical rationality does not produce reasons for agents to act regardless of their desires or interests, or (B) perhaps practical rationality *does* provide such reasons, but they do not condemn killing, stealing, etc. Either discovery would show that there is *not* a conceptual connection between the imperatives of morality and rationality. So the question of the connection is something we argue towards, not something we argue from. This conceptual connection being severed, one may, of course, wonder if there may not be some other way of making sense of moral reasons (Foot's elusive "fugitive thought"). But §2.6 argued that no other would suffice. Failing that, the moral error theorist has at least pushed the burden of proof firmly on to her opponents to come up with something good.

With a firmer grip on the strategy, we can return to the chase. In what follows I will continue to use Smith's discussion to frame my own views. The reason for this is not simply to define myself in opposition to Smith – on the contrary, it is because I agree with so much of what he says about practical rationality that presenting his view is profitable. However, disagreement over one point leads us to adopt conclusions that could hardly be more opposed. In short, Smith sees his non-Humean theory pointing towards moral realism; I see more or less the same theory paving the way to a moral error theory.

3.6 THE NON-HUMEAN THEORY OF NORMATIVE REASONS

Hume's notion of practical rationality – that there is really no sphere of distinctive rationality that is *practical*, but only a subset of theoretical rationality concerning means and ends – though tidy, fails to capture too much of our pre-theoretical talk of "rationality" to merit acceptance. We have already seen that it denies the existence of weakness of will: when I have another glass of wine, apparently against my better judgment, Hume will say that the very fact that I acted to have another glass of wine shows that my stronger desire was for more wine, and relative to that desire (which in itself is beyond rational censure) my action cannot be rationally faulted. We may still call such episodes "weakness of will" if we wish, but we cannot define them in terms of an agent's ϕing while sincerely judging that refraining from ϕing is preferable. The Humean agent may, of course, judge that refraining from ϕing preferable in the sense of recognizing that it is "what morality requires," but at the time of acting the agent will not be fully endorsing morality; his desire for something contrary to morality's requirements – a piece of self-gain, for example – is stronger. This no more counts as weakness of will than my acting contrary to what I judge the norms of Sufism to be. The only difference is that the Humean agent described may, on other occasions, be inclined to endorse morality, whereas I am never inclined to endorse the norms of Sufism.

But weakness of will is so familiar a phenomenon that a denial of its existence counts as a cost. We think that a person who is generally inclined to follow the dictates of morality, but on a particular occasion goes in for a piece of wicked self-gain, has not necessarily just "changed his mind" for a while – rather, it is possible that he continues throughout to endorse morality (in some sense), but a competing temptation, one that he would like to subjugate but cannot quite, has gotten the better of him. We can allow that he desires the self-gain and also desires to act as morality requires. But these desires are not on a par. The important difference is not merely (as Hume would say) that the selfish desire is stronger and thus wins the day. The important difference is that acting as morality requires is *valued* by our agent more than self-gain. (I'm not saying that agents *always* value morality more than self-gain, nor that defying morality is always a matter of weakness of will – it merely describes this one familiar illustration.) The appearance of things is that agents may have competing desires, some of which are privileged in the sense of being the agent's *values* – where this is not a matter of the strength of the desire – and that acting contrary to one's values counts as a form of practical irrationality. This appearance can be saved, I believe, though doing so requires going beyond Humean instrumentalism.

In his book *The Moral Problem*, Smith sees the proper understanding of *values* as the key to rescuing morality from an error theory. In doing so he presents a non-Humean theory of normative reasons, wherein desires are not beyond the scope of rational appraisal. Normative reasons are to be contrasted with motivational reasons, the latter being those which one appeals to in order to *explain* an agent's actions, and regarding which Smith is satisfied with, and argues forcefully in favor of, a Humean account. Normative reasons, on the other hand, pertain to how we might *justify* an agent's action – what it is *rational* for an agent to do. An episode of putative weakness of will, when described in terms of Humean motivating reasons, seems to lose all its distinctive features, becoming merely an episode of the agent acting on her strongest present desire. If we are to account for the apparent *irrationality* of the action, we must examine the *normative* reasons.[21] But Hume will not help here, for, as we have seen, he is best read as denying that there are any such things: whatever the agent does, she will be acting on her strongest desire (itself beyond rational censure), therefore never acting irrationally. I follow Smith in thinking that a non-Humean theory of normative reasons is preferable, but disagree strongly with him concerning what the consequences are for moral discourse.

Smith sees a great deal turning on the question of whether valuing is a species of desiring or of believing. The natural thought that to value X is to have a second-order desire in favor of desiring X (i.e., to desire to desire X) – something maintained by Harry Frankfurt and David Lewis, and once toyed with by Bertrand Russell[22] – Smith rejects in favor of the view that to value X is to believe that X is desirable, where this is understood as believing that one has a normative reason to bring about X, and where this in turn is understood as believing that one would endorse the bringing about of X if one were fully rational. For our present purposes it is not important to take a side on this debate.[23] What matters is that both

---

[21] Terminological point: there are many different normative systems, and therefore many different kinds of normative reasons. A person may have a normative reason to ϕ and a normative reason not to ϕ – these reasons deriving from competing justificatory frameworks. However, with Smith I will use "normative reason" in a restricted sense, to mean something that is justified according to *practical rationality*.

[22] H. Frankfurt, "Freedom of the Will and the Concept of a Person," in G. Watson (ed.), *Free Will* (Oxford: Oxford University Press, 1982), pp. 81–95; Lewis, "Dispositional Theories of Value." For Russell's thoughts, see "Is Ethics a Branch of Empirical Psychology?" [1897], "Note on Ethical Theory" [1896], and "Are all Desires Equally Moral?" [1896]: all in *Collected Papers*, vol. 1 (London: George Allen & Unwin, 1983), pp. 99–104, 204–41 and 242–4, respectively.

[23] It is important for Smith to take sides, since he has forged a link between moral judgments and rational valuing. If to value something turns out to be a species of desiring, then Smith is left in the noncognitivist camp, something he (correctly) sees as unacceptable.

kinds of theory suggest a basis for identifying certain desires as irrational. If S desires to desire X, but desires not-X, then we may consider the latter desire irrational. If S believes that X is desirable – that is, believes that she would desire X if she were fully rational – but desires not-X, then we may consider the latter desire irrational. Work would need to be done to turn either proposal into a defensible theory, but that is not our labor. What's important is that in either case S has a normative reason to φ even though she may not have a desire for that which φing brings about: an important non-Humean result.

What both theories appear to have in common is the idea that an irrational desire has not been, in some manner, properly *examined* by the agent. Even to take a second-order attitude towards a first-order desire is to be minimally *aware* of the first-order desire. And why would one fail to endorse one's own first-order desires? It is unlikely to be merely a matter of a "passion" or "appetite" which comes out of the blue. First-order desires can be like that – I might suddenly feel a desire for food, or for company, or for sleep – but second-order desires will typically be a matter of deliberation. If I am in the situation of desiring X but wishing I didn't, that second-order desire is something that I will arrive at as a result of considering my desire for X destructive, or unworthy, or fitting uncomfortably with other desires, etc. At a minimum, I will have thought about the first-order desire and evaluated it.

The same is true of Smith's account. To believe that I have a normative reason to φ is, Smith thinks, to believe that I would endorse φing if I were fully rational, and an important part of being fully rational is to deliberate correctly. The first part of "deliberating correctly" Smith draws from Williams, who describes it in rather open terms as follows:

A clear example of practical reasoning is that leading to the conclusion that one has reason to φ because φ-ing would be the most convenient, economical, pleasant, etc. way of satisfying some element in S [the agent's subjective motivational set], if not necessarily in a very clear or determinate way. But there are much wider possibilities for deliberation, such as: by time-ordering; where there is some irresoluble conflict among the elements of S, considering which one attaches most weight to . . .

The deliberative process can also subtract elements from S. Reflection may lead the agent to see that some belief is false, and hence to realize that he has in fact no reason to do something he thought he had reason to do. More subtly, he may think he has reason to promote some development because he has not exercised his imagination enough about what it would be like if it came about.[24]

[24] Williams, "Internal and External Reasons," pp. 104–5

Smith supplements this account, privileging the role of our attempting to *justify systematically* our desires. By this he means:

trying to integrate the object of [some particular desire] into a more coherent and unified desiderative profile and evaluative outlook. . . .

Suppose we take a whole host of desires we have for specific and general things; desires which are not in fact derived from any desire that we have for something more general. We can ask ourselves whether we wouldn't get a more systematically justifiable set of desires by adding to this whole host of specific and general desires another general desire, or a more general desire still, a desire that, in turn, justifies and explains the more specific desires that we have . . . [I]n so far as the new set of desires . . . exhibits more in the way of, say, unity, we may properly think that the new imaginary set of desires is rationally preferable to the old.[25]

We can tie these thoughts back roughly to the earlier consideration of weakness of will. Let "V" denote the object of an agent's value, and "T" denote the object of the desire that "tempts" the agent. V is either the object of a present desire that would survive more deliberative consideration than the desire for T, or is the object of a desire that would be created in the process of deliberation, a process that would not endorse the desire for T. The desire for V fits more coherently into the agent's wider desiderative set. If the agent were to examine that desire, consider its place in the wider set (employing adequate imaginative powers), she would be disposed to affirm its presence. (If these statements seem general, it is because I don't wish to commit myself to any particular view of deliberation to the exclusion of others.)

These observations allow us to distinguish between "rational" and "irrational" reasons. Suppose Molly has a rational desire to refrain from eating a piece of cake, but an irrational desire tugging her to eat it. I see no grounds for insisting that only one desire provides her with a reason. It seems preferable (or at least permissible) to say that she has reasons both to eat the cake and not eat the cake, but the latter is privileged – it "trumps," if you will – in virtue of deriving from a rational desire. (Alternatively, she may not have a desire to refrain at all, but still have a trumping reason to refrain if such a desire would be created in the process of deliberation.) This distinction between rational and irrational reasons is consistent with the earlier one between subjective and objective reasons. There are those actions Molly might perform which really would satisfy her rational desires, and those that she is justified in believing would. So, for example, she may well be

---

[25] Smith, *Moral Problem,* p. 159. Such a procedure, Smith adds, may also lead to the elimination of desires.

justified in believing that refraining from eating the cake is the action that will satisfy her rational desires (where her desiderative set includes a desire to avoid getting chubby – one which would survive deliberation – and she notes, reasonably, that her cake-eating habits have been pushing her in that undesirable direction). In that case she has a subjective rational reason to refrain from eating the cake. However, suppose that she is oblivious of the fact that tomorrow she will be marooned on a desert island, and the extra calories from the cake would put her in good stead for an extra day or two, perhaps even contributing importantly to the highly desirable end of saving her life. In such a case she has an objective rational reason to eat the cake. In sum: she has (i) an objective rational reason to eat, (ii) a subjective rational reason to refrain from eating, and (iii) a quite irrational desire (providing her with an "irrational reason," we might say) to eat.

3.7 RATIONALITY AND EPISTEMIC SUCCESS

Despite the complexity, I have to admit to finding the above distinctions quite commonsensical. The point of drawing them is to provide a backdrop to asking the question: "What would it be rational for Molly to do?" and the answer is, as it was before, that *she is rational to the extent that she is guided by her subjective reasons.*

This is an important fact that Smith misses. When it comes to normative reasons he would collapse the subjective/objective distinction, via making *epistemic success* (i.e., having true beliefs) a trait of the fully rational agent. This, in turn, is something he attributes to Williams, though I doubt the latter endorses it. Williams argues that an agent has a reason to ϕ (where "ϕ" denotes an action) if and only if the agent would be motivated to ϕ if:

(a) she has no false beliefs
(b) she has all relevant true beliefs
(c) she has deliberated correctly on the matter

However, it is unclear whether Williams would make the satisfaction of (a)–(c) a necessary condition for being "fully rational." Perhaps he means to identify "being rational" with (c) only, and holds that an agent has a reason to ϕ if and only if she would be motivated to ϕ were she fully rational *and* satisfied (a) and (b). But if Williams leaves the matter unclear, Smith is explicit: "[An agent] would not have the desire if he were fully rational: that is, *if he had no false beliefs* ... [An agent] would desire to do so if she were fully rational: that is, *if she had all relevant true beliefs*" (pp. 156–7, original emphasis).

When considering Brandt's account of rationality in §3.0 it was argued that appropriating "rationality" for application only to an agent with epistemic ideality is a highly questionable move. Consider the example just given of Molly deciding not to eat the cake for the worthy cause of her waistline, not knowing that tomorrow's unforeseen disaster will prove those extra calories valuable. If she were to deliberate correctly on the matter *armed only with true beliefs* then of course she would decide to eat the cake. Would eating the cake be therefore *rational*? Surely not. Consider an earlier example of Jane being approached by a hungry tiger. Let us stipulate that she is quite justified in believing there to be no tigers around (she's walking down a suburban street in San Diego); nevertheless, one has just escaped from the zoo and is stalking her. If she *knew* this, she'd run away; but given that she *doesn't* know this, that she has seen no evidence to suggest it, for her suddenly to run frantically down the street would hardly be rational. Now there *is* a reason for her to run down the street – an objective reason – but since she has no epistemic access to it, if she were to run down the street she couldn't be doing so *for* that reason; in fact, from how we've described the scenario, if she were to run down the street she'd be doing so for no reason at all. Hardly an instance of rational action. To reiterate: practical reasoning pertains to what we do with the desires and beliefs that we have; it doesn't guarantee or require that the agent is armed with *truth*. The idea that Jane – let's say now in her armchair on the evening before her being chased by a tiger – might, *through practical reasoning*, through being "fully rational," come to have the true (though utterly surprising) belief that tomorrow she will be chased by a tiger in San Diego, is an extravagant distortion of anything we ordinarily mean by "rational" and "reasoning."[26]

3.8 NORMATIVE REASONS AND MORAL REASONS

Let me purloin Smith's and Williams's sketch of practical deliberation quoted above, and say that an agent's rational desires are those that do

---

[26] In Smith's defense of his book ("In Defense of *The Moral Problem*," *Ethics* 108 [1997], p. 91) he admits, when pressured on this point by David Copp, that "the term 'rationality' is almost entirely a philosopher's term of art . . . in any case, I am not sure that anything hangs on my use of the word." But I am doubtful that this casualness over what we call it is innocuous, given that several of Smith's arguments trade on (putative) *truisms* that surround our concept of *rationality*.

or would survive such examination, and an agent is rational to the extent that he acts upon his subjective rational reasons. What I am carefully resisting is the further thought that the rational agent has only true beliefs. And now we can ask the all-important question: do an agent's subjective rational reasons, those that determine his rationality, satisfy the criteria that have been laid down for *moral* reasons? Two such criteria have been set down. First, that moral imperatives are categorical. Second, in §3.5 I noted a contentful constraint: that whatever ends up counting as a moral imperative had better bear some resemblance to what we would uncontroversially recognize as such – proscribing stealing, enjoining promise-keeping, and so forth. This second criterion is not requiring anything approaching a one-to-one mapping; it is merely saying that a theory of moral imperatives had better get them "in the ballpark" of the kind of things we uncontroversially consider such.

I will address the "all-important question" using the resources that Smith provides. He argues that an agent, S, has a normative reason to ϕ if and only if S would desire to ϕ if she were fully rational. This counterfactual is understood (in a way similar to how Peter Railton understands it[27]) in the following terms. For any actual agent, S, we may speak of an idealized counterpart of S, S+, who deliberates in a flawless manner (is fully reflective and imaginative) and who has all and only relevant true beliefs. There will be certain actions that S+ would advise S to perform. Those actions are the ones that S has normative reasons to perform. Smith would describe S+ as "fully rational," but I have already given my reasons for resisting this description. S+ *is* fully rational, of course, but she is much more than that, since she has all and only relevant true beliefs. But whatever we call S+, the important point is that she is in the ideal position to provide S with advice. Let us consider it each way in turn. First let S+ be fully rational by my lights and see whether S's normative reasons match her (putative) moral reasons, then let S+ be fully rational by Smith's lights, and see whether it makes a difference.

Imagine somebody who breaks an inconvenient promise simply because it is inconvenient, knowing that doing so will seriously upset others, but knowing that he can get away without suffering penalty. Moral discourse doesn't hesitate in saying "He ought not do that." Given the non-Humean theory of normative reasons that has been supported, we now see that it

[27] P. Railton, "Moral Realism," *The Philosophical Review* 95 (1986), pp. 163–207. See also M. Smith, "Internal Reasons," *Philosophy and Phenomenological Research* 55 (1995), pp. 109–31.

is simplistic merely to look at this character's desires and note that none is served by keeping the promise. We have to ask whether the desires he has that are served by promise-breaking would survive rational deliberation of the kind described. We have to ask whether a desire in favor of promise-keeping would be created in the process of rational deliberation. One way of understanding this is to ask whether a flawlessly deliberating counterpart of the agent (a "fully rational" counterpart, by my lights) would want the actual agent to refrain from promise-breaking.

The idealized agent certainly has desires that the actual agent does not, and vice versa. Still, the idealized agent is derived from the actual agent, and so the desires of the former will be influenced by the desires of the latter. The relation is rather like that of parent to child: what the parent desires for the child may differ from what the child desires, but the child's desires have an important effect on what the parent desires for the child. Were the child deeply to desire a motorcycle for Christmas it does not follow that the parent will want the child to get one, but it may mean the parent wants the child to get something else (a bicycle? a part-time job to pay for the motorcycle? a lesson in the ultimate insignificance of material possessions?) which the parent would not have wanted had the child desired differently. I see no ground for doubting that this may be entirely generalizable: that the things that the ideal version of myself wants for me *always* depend on what I actually desire. It is doubtful that there is any counterfactual truth concerning what he would desire for me that I cannot change by altering one or other of my desires, or, at least, that would not be false had I different actual desires. I am not assuming this is true, but merely, at this stage, pointing out that there is no reason to assume that it is not. We will turn to the argument in detail in the next two chapters.

This is why I am skeptical that there is likely to be much in the way of convergence among the desires of idealized counterparts of different actual agents. Why should there be? Actual agents have very different interests, desires, projects, ideologies, beliefs, etc., and there is every reason to think that this variation will transfer to their idealized versions. And if there is no convergence, *a fortiori* there is no convergence towards a condemnation of stealing, a praise of promise-keeping, etc. (And even if there *were* convergence in general, an extra argument would be needed to show that these kinds of things appear in the target of the convergence.)

Let us now understand "fully rational" in Smith's terms, to include epistemic success. As far as I can see, the same arguments hold. The differences that hold among actual agents that are based on *doxastic* disagreement will, of course, evaporate in their idealized counterparts, but there are no grounds for holding that all the other differences – those derived from different desires, projects, interests, etc. – will likewise be lost in the idealization. So there will be no convergence, and *a fortiori* no convergence regarding stealing, promise-keeping, etc. To put the argument another way, if there was no convergence when we understood idealization in my terms, but there is convergence when we add epistemic success to the idealized counterpart, then the question for the defender of morality is: "Which, exactly, false beliefs does the promise-breaker have?"

3.9 SUMMARY AND PREVIEW

The object of the arguments of this chapter has been to defend premise (4) of the argument presented in §2.4. It may be thought that the concessions made to the non-Humean have undermined this. Strictly speaking, this is true, but the spirit of the argument still stands, and we are now in a position to recast it more carefully. Since premise (4) contained a demonstrative referring to premise (3), we do not actually need to change the wording of (4) at all, but make alterations to the other premises. These alterations, however, are unobjectionable, and whatever considerations supported the premises as they stood in Chapter 2 will support them still. Premise (1) previously read "For any *x*, if *x* morally ought to ϕ, then *x* ought to ϕ regardless of whether he cares to, whether ϕing satisfies any of his desires or furthers his interests." This is changed as follows, and the rest of the argument reformed accordingly. For any *x*:

1. If *x* morally ought to ϕ, then *x* ought to ϕ regardless of what his desires and interests are.
2. If *x* morally ought to ϕ, then *x* has a reason for ϕing.
3. Therefore, if *x* morally ought to ϕ, then *x* can have a reason for ϕing regardless of what his desires and interests are.
4. But there is no sense to be made of such reasons.
5. Therefore, *x* is never under a moral obligation.

What the present chapter has attempted to show is that even making important and reasonable concessions to the non-Humean will leave the argument intact. The theory of reasons that has been defended is still, in my opinion, a version of *instrumentalism*, because it understands reasons only as means to an agent's ends. An agent's desires may be available for rational appraisal in a way with which Hume would have disagreed, and an agent may have X for an end (and thus a reason to pursue X) even though she does not desire X, but none of this detracts from the *instrumentality* of those reasons. I call it "non-Humean instrumentalism."[28] And because the only reasons that this theory recognizes concern performing actions that are means to one's ends, it does not support *categorical imperatives*.[29]

Apart from a disagreement concerning full rationality and epistemic success (a dispute that could largely be settled by distinguishing objective from subjective reasons), I have agreed with most of what Smith says about the nature of practical rationality. However, I am highly skeptical that this account of practical rationality promises to support a version of moral realism. On the contrary, if this is the correct account of practical rationality, then a moral error theory looks more likely than ever.

The point upon which so much turns is whether the account of practical rationality defended leads to convergence of reasons (and convergence in a particular direction), as Smith thinks, or, as I think, whether it permits

[28] Smith, it appears, would continue to call it a kind of "Humeanism" if it implies a lack of convergence among agents' normative reasons. For example, he says that Williams "is quite right to insist that he is defending a 'Humean' conception of normative reasons" (p. 165) because Williams insists on non-convergence. Smith's own view is described as "Kantian" in that we would all desire the same things if we were fully rational. Not wanting to get hung up on labels, I prefer to call my view "non-Humean" because it allows for the rational appraisal of ends. Whether it implies convergence has yet to be seen – Smith thinks it does, I think it doesn't. If it doesn't, then even though it remains "non-Humean" in an important sense, it agrees with something that Hume says. If it does imply convergence, then it is doubly non-Humean. Since Hume asserted many theses, not all of which one need agree with if one agrees with any, these confusions over what counts as "Humean" invariably arise, and it would be pointless to attempt to appropriate one of Hume's theses as definitive of "Humeanism"; one must simply clearly stipulate how one is intending to use the term.

[29] Smith would object to this (see pp. 174–5). Because he has supported the thesis that our concept of a normative reason is a non-relative one, he thinks that if S has a normative reason to ϕ in circumstances C, then *anyone* would have a reason to ϕ in C – and this he takes to be sufficient to make the imperative "Do ϕ!" a categorical imperative. I will cast doubt on the conceptual claim in the next chapter. If "C" may include the agent's desires (which Smith allows [p. 171]), then the same reasoning can turn *any* hypothetical imperative into a categorical: "Catch the bus if you want to get to town on time" becomes "Anyone has a reason to catch the bus in C" – where "C" includes "wanting to get to town on time." The important point is that if Ernie has a desire for X and Bert does not have that desire, then a fully rational version of Ernie may want Ernie to perform ϕ, while the fully rational version of Bert does not want Bert to perform ϕ. Thus Ernie has a normative reason to ϕ and Bert does not, and that difference is accounted for by their different desires. That, in my book, is enough to make the imperative "Do ϕ!" a hypothetical imperative. It is, of course, unsightly to quibble over labels, and ultimately it doesn't much matter what we call these things.

different agents to have quite different reasons. This is no small matter. For if things go the latter way, then there will be agents who, let's say, steal and break promises, but for whom there are no grounds for believing with justification that they have a reason not to. Therefore, if we have a discourse that centrally employs judgments implying that such agents *do* have a reason not to, those judgments must be untrue and that discourse must be faulty. Smith addresses this issue under the heading of whether the analysis delivers a relative or non-relative conception of normative reasons. I have declared my hand in favor of the former, but have yet to argue in a careful way for the view. This issue of relativism shall be the topic of the next two chapters.

4

The relativity of reasons

4.0 THE RATIONALIST'S DILEMMA

Any moral rationalist faces a metaethical dilemma. One horn is the alienation of an agent from her normative reasons, the other horn is moral relativism.

"Moral rationalism" I understand to center on the thesis that moral reasons are a subset of normative reasons, such that moral failing is, necessarily, rational failing. This thesis will not count as sufficient for being a rationalist, for consider if normative reasons turn out – as I think they do – to be in some substantive manner agent-relative. We might still link these practical reasons to moral reasons, to the conclusion that moral reasons are relative to agents (which is close to the conclusion that moral imperatives are hypothetical). This is the basic structure of Gilbert Harman's version of moral relativism (to be discussed later in this chapter), but it would be very misleading if Harman turned out to be a moral *rationalist*. In response to this, let us add to the above criterion for rationalism two further theses: that the imperatives of practical rationality are categorical imperatives; and that there are some true imperatives of practical rationality. The last condition is needed just to cover the unlikely case of an argument linking normative reasons to moral reasons, asserted in conjunction with a denial that there are any true normative reasons claims. (The latter denial is something I attributed to Hume in §3.1.) "Moral rationalism" had better not permissibly denote a moral error theory!

Let us consider the first horn of the rationalist's dilemma. Normative reasons claims – claims concerning what it is rational for an agent to do – must be something that potentially engage the agent to whom they are applied. This doesn't mean that the presentation of a true normative reason claim immediately results in the agent being motivated; rather, it means that the agent cannot sensibly both acknowledge that something is a normative reason for him to act and ask "But so what?" Any adequate theory of normative reasons must make out reasons to be precisely those things that forestall a "So what?" response. Some theories of reasons threaten to violate this constraint – to "alienate" an agent from his reasons. Roderick Firth, for instance, introduces the concept of *the ideal observer*, who is omniscient, omnipercipient, disinterested, dispassionate, consistent, and otherwise normal (the details need not detain us).[1] The ideal observer will approve of certain things, form desires, etc., and consequently have motivating reasons for performing certain actions. And what for the ideal observer are motivating reasons are for us normative reasons. The problem with such a theory is that it seems perfectly reasonable to say "I accept that the ideal observer would be motivated to ϕ, but what's that to me?" Why should one care about what a dispassionate person would want any more than one should care about what an enthusiastic philatelist would want? It will not do for Firth to *stipulate* that the question is unreasonable – a "So what?" question cannot be made unreasonable by *ad hoc* linguistic decree. A consequence of Firth's theory that some would count as a virtue is that it implies that every agent has exactly the same normative reasons, for the ideal observer borrows no idiosyncratic features from particular agents. Unfortunately, this is attained at the cost of alienating the agent from rationality, of making it perfectly reasonable for her to ignore these reasons claims.

Finding this unacceptable, one might prefer an account of normative reasons which avoids alienation, by tying an agent's normative reasons directly to the things that the agent is interested in. The virtue of such a theory is that it promises to answer any "So what?" demands. Hume would find the grounding ultimately in actual desires that the agent has. If one asked a person why he takes exercise he may reply that it is for the sake of his health; ask him why he desires that, and he may answer:

that *it is necessary for the sake of his calling*. If you ask, *why is he anxious on that head*, he will answer, *because he desires to get money*. If you demand *Why? It is the instrument of pleasure*, says he. And beyond this it is an absurdity to ask for a reason. It is impossible that there can be a progress *in infinitum*; and that one thing can

---

[1] R. Firth, "Ethical Absolutism and the Ideal Observer," *Philosophy and Phenomenological Research* 12 (1952), pp. 317–45. To be fair on Firth, he presents an analysis of *moral goodness* rather than *reasons for action*, but he may be interpreted as providing the basis for an analysis of the latter. See, for example, Paul Moser, *Philosophy After Objectivity* (Oxford: Oxford University Press, 1993), p. 183.

always be a reason why another is desired. Something must be desired on its own account.[2]

On this occasion Hume makes pleasure the thing that is desired "on its own account," but he does not insist that the final answer must always be an appeal to self-interest. The foundational desire may be a genuinely altruistic one – the desire may be "That my friend ceases to suffer." If asked "And why do you desire the cessation of your friend's suffering?" it is possible (Hume allows) that the correct answer is "I just do!" The only further sense that can be made of the question is that it asks for the *cause* of the desire, rather than one's reason for so desiring (e.g., a reasonable answer would be "Because we go back a long way and so I care about him" which is a different *type* of answer from those of the preceding question-and-answer sequence).

Part of the object of the previous chapter was to reject the Humean view that reasons must always be grounded in present desires. Smith's non-Humeanism allows that an agent has reason to ϕ if a fully rational version of that agent (with all and only relevant true beliefs) would desire that the actual agent ϕs. This adequately answers any "So what?" question and provides a place for the "And why should I care about *that*?" question-and-answer routine to conclude; in other words, it avoids alienating an agent from her reasons. This important result is not obvious, so let me explain.

It is quite clear that if an agent, Jill, is simply told "You should ϕ" she may quite reasonably say "Why?", or if she is told "You have a reason to ϕ" she can ask "In virtue of what?" Answering the latter question by an appeal to, say, a Firthian ideal observer invites a legitimate "So what?" response. Before considering Smith's alternative, let us examine the Humean's resources. If it were pointed out to Jill that she does want X, and she is told (and believes it) that ϕing would be the optimal means of obtaining X, then "So what?" seems blocked. For what is "So what?" if not a request for something that is relevant to the questioner, for a demonstration that the proposal ties in with her desiderative set? I realize that insisting that "So what?" must be understood in such a manner is question-begging, but we shall try to do better in due course. Assuming for the moment that "So what?" is precisely a request for evidence that the proposal fits with one's desiderative set, then to acknowledge that some action is a means to desire-satisfaction *is* to accept that the question has been answered.

[2] *Enquiry*, appendix 1 (1983), p. 87.

A further "So what?" could only be to question practical rationality itself, and we have already seen that this is incoherent (§2.6).

What now of the non-Humean instrumentalism that was argued for in the previous chapter? If told that an improved version of herself, Jill+, would want Jill to ϕ, may Jill acknowledge that this is true, yet reasonably respond "But so what?"? Much turns on the details of the "improvement" in question. We have seen that practical rationality is not something that we may legitimately question, for to question it *is* to acknowledge it. Can we use the same kind of transcendental argument to go a little further? I believe so.

To ask "Why should I ϕ?" (the politer form of "So what?") is to imply that one is in the business of accepting reasons, that one is able (at least sometimes) to recognize reasons, that one can take a potential reason claim and examine it to see if it really is a reason, that one is willing to compare this reason claim with potentially competing reason claims to see which weighs most, that one is disposed to participate in deliberative activity, that one values such things as evidence and truth. Of course, merely saying the words "so" and "what" doesn't imply these things (one can teach a parrot to speak) – but if one is *seriously* asking the question, seriously seeking an answer, then such basic general commitments are evinced. If this is correct, then we are in a position to see that Jill *does* take the desires of Jill+ as reasons, for those desires just are what Jill would desire for herself if she were fully reflective and epistemically successful. In other words, the question "I recognize that if I were to deliberate properly on the matter, armed with all and only relevant true beliefs, I would desire my actual self to ϕ, but what is that to me?" is not something we need take seriously, for just in asking the question one would be demonstrating one's valuing of deliberation and truth. This is not, to repeat, to say that whenever Jill recognizes that Jill+ would desire her to ϕ, she automatically will feel motivated to ϕ; but it is to say that the recognition is tied to her desiderative motivational set in such a way as to silence any reasonable questioning.

It is important to see what a fine line such an argument treads. For were we tempted to add a further feature to our account of "Jill+" – say, that she is *dispassionate* – then it would immediately make a "So what?" question intelligible. Asking a question in no (obvious) way implies an allegiance to dispassionateness. The fact that the non-Humean instrumentalism defended in the last chapter does not fall foul of such a problem – that it attributes to the idealized counterpart of the actual agent pretty much exactly the appropriate attributes (and no more) to forestall "So what?"

questions; that it, in other words, avoids alienating the agent from her normative reasons – is a theoretical virtue of considerable significance. That is to say, Smith's non-Humean instrumentalism (my label, not his) has the all-important virtue of avoiding the first horn of the metaethical dilemma.

In the process, however, non-Humean instrumentalism lands on the other horn: relativism. Alienation is avoided by tying normative reasons to the agent's desiderative set, but different agents have different desiderative sets (different desires, different projects, different interests) and so what is a normative reason for one person needn't be for another. Thus, claims of the form "There is a normative reason to ϕ (in circumstances C)" are not properly formed; we must understand them as shorthand for something like "There is a normative reason *for S* to ϕ in C." Therefore two people who utter the same sentence – "There is a normative reason to ϕ in C" – may well be expressing different propositions: one about S, the other about S* (thus one speaker may be uttering a truth and the other a falsehood). This is what I understand by "relativism." Someone keen to avoid relativism will need to demonstrate that agents are such that there is necessary *convergence* in their normative reasons, despite their disparate desiderative starting points, such that to claim that S has a normative reason to ϕ in C implies that S* will have the same reason to ϕ in C. In other words, the non-relativist (the absolutist) needs to show that careful reflection and full information lead to convergence of motivation. On the face of it, it's a very implausible claim, which we must subject to further scrutiny.

But another possibility beckons. If an agent is not alienated from reasons when those reasons are derived from what a fully informed and flawlessly deliberating agent would desire, but making this idealized agent a counterpart of an actual agent (with all her idiosyncrasies) introduces relativism – then can't we go between the horns? Can't we simply say that an agent has a normative reason to ϕ if and only if a fully informed and flawlessly deliberating agent would desire her to ϕ? But this, it seems to me, is a hopeless thought, and leads directly to an error theory of normative reasons. I say this because I very much doubt that a non-actual agent picked out only in such thin terms desires *anything*. It would be like analyzing a property in terms of what tall people would be inclined to choose as their favorite color. There is simply no truth about what tall persons' favorite color is. Similarly, there is no truth about the favorite color of fully informed, flawlessly deliberating agents. Although it may be true that each fully informed, flawlessly deliberating agent has a favorite color, it is a fallacy to conclude that there is a favorite color had by all such agents. Similarly, I submit that there is no truth about what a fully informed, flawlessly deliberating agent would *want*. One might be hoodwinked by the following fallacious reasoning:

> If S were fully informed and deliberated correctly, S would desire to ϕ
> ∴ If S were a fully informed, correct deliberator, S would desire to ϕ
> ∴ A fully informed, correct deliberator would desire to ϕ

But full information and flawless deliberation alone simply do not produce *desires*. They do not even produce a desire that, say, the preconditions for being a fully informed, correct deliberator be satisfied. A rational agent *as such* need not desire to be or to remain a rational agent, any more than a garbage collector *as such* desires being and remaining a garbage collector.

The idealized agent needs something to "work with" – he needs some desires, which may then be coupled with true beliefs, reflected upon properly, etc., thus resulting in "corrected" desires. But whose desires shall he start with? We can't just stipulate which desires. Suppose Jill were told that a fully informed and flawlessly deliberating version of *Bill* (someone she has never heard of) wants her to ϕ. Saying "So what?" is perfectly reasonable! Alienation is avoided only by making the counterfactual agent who provides Jill's normative reasons an idealized counterpart of *Jill*. And doing so threatens to impale one on the horn of relativism.

I have not argued that a theory of normative reasons that avoids alienation *must* stumble into relativism, and vice versa – only that it is a notable danger. If one's interest is in providing only a theory of normative reasons, then there is no real problem. Alienation, to be sure, is something to be avoided: a theory of practical reasons that allows a person legitimately to say "I acknowledge that I have a normative reason to ϕ, but what is that to me?" has gone terribly wrong. However, relativism is not in any obvious way a theoretical cost, and so to be "impaled on the horn of relativism" is in fact no disaster – one should simply embrace normative relativism. But if one is interested not only in presenting a theory of normative reasons, but is out to defend *moral rationalism* – tying moral reasons to normative reasons – then normative relativism will bring moral relativism, and that, I will argue, *is* a problem. Before that discussion, however, we must return to Smith, who thinks he can steer his theory of normative reasons between Scylla and Charybdis.

4.1 THE RELATIVITY OF NORMATIVE REASONS: THE CONCEPTUAL QUESTION

Smith embarks on the project of demonstrating that normative reasons are non-relative by breaking the question into two. First, there's the conceptual question of whether our concept of a normative reason is a relativistic or absolute concept. But even if, with Smith, we think that it's the latter kind of concept, there remains a substantive question of whether there *are* any such reasons. If the substantive question cannot also be answered in a non-relativistic way, then all Smith's labors will be for the error theorist in the end.

I hesitate to offer an opinion on the conceptual question. So long as the substantive question goes in the relativistic direction, then we do not need to call the conceptual one. Suppose rationality is substantively relativistic. Now assume, first, that our concept of a normative reason is a relativistic one. Then, so long as (i) our moral imperatives are firmly *non*-relativistic (as I have already argued, and will do so further below), and (ii) rationalism is the only plausible avenue for underwriting moral reasons – then a moral error theory will be the conclusion. If, on the other hand, our concept of a normative reason is an absolute one, then the substantive question going to the relativist will amount to an error theory of normative reasons. That being so, this time assuming only (ii), we will still be in a position to conclude a moral error theory.

I waver on the conceptual question not merely because its discussion is unnecessary, but because it is a difficult question to know how to approach. Smith himself admits that "rationality" is "almost entirely a philosopher's term of art"[3] – an admission that sits uncomfortably with his own argument, seemingly based on observation of how "the folk" typically use the term. Given that the account already given of normative reasons (that S has a normative reason to ϕ iff S+ would want S to ϕ) is supposedly derived from a "platitude," if that account suggests a relativistic reading – as it *prima facie* does – then what are we to make of further platitudes (should there be any) suggesting normative reasons to be *non*-relativistic? There are four possible courses. The first, of course, is that we should carefully scrutinize our evidence that the theses being accorded the status of "platitudes" are really anything of the sort. But let us say that this is done, and they are. Second, we might decide that our concept of *a normative reason* is incoherent, thereby offering an error theory. Third, we might try to show that the

---

[3] "In Defense of *The Moral Problem*," *Ethics* 108 (1997), p. 91.

platitude suggesting non-relativism, when properly understood, does not. Or fourth, we might try to show that the platitude suggesting relativism, when properly understood, does not. Clearly, the second option should only be adopted as a last resort. Smith plumps for the third option. It is not my intention to explore the possibilities of the fourth option, merely to point out that it is an option which, on the face of it, has symmetrical appeal to Smith's preferred route.[4]

One way of casting doubt on the concept of *having a normative reason* being non-relativistic is via another thought experiment involving translation. Suppose we were translating an alien race's language, and had done so to our satisfaction with their entire language but for a small cluster of inter-related terms that they appear to use much as we use "normative reason," "rational," etc. Let us focus on the former, and say that their term is "schmeason" (inelegant though it is). Schmeasons seem at least a lot like normative reasons. It is thought that deliberating in a clear-headed way will often lead one to see that one has a schmeason to act when one previously did not know it. If one acknowledges that one has a schmeason, but doesn't act accordingly, then one may be censured. Depression may get in the way of acting upon what one acknowledges to be one's schmeasons. It is thought that one's having a desire to ϕ doesn't necessarily provide one with a schmeason to ϕ, but if one were to deliberate in a flawless manner on the matter, with all and only true relevant beliefs, then if one still desired to ϕ then one would have a schmeason to. And so on. However, the aliens are adamant that "schmeason" is a relative term – that one person may have a schmeason for ϕing in circumstances C while another person would not have a schmeason to ϕ in C – and, moreover, observation of their practices reveals that they do indeed use it in exactly this manner. Would we translate "schmeason" to "reason"?

I'm strongly inclined to think "Yes" though I don't profess certainty; but if my being unsure is typical then that is enough to make my point. The point is that *being a normative reason* is such an imprecise and contested notion that we should be wary of speaking too confidently of "truisms." Of course there are *some* truisms concerning it. If the aliens thought that schmeasons live in the forest, and that in order to "have" one you must first go out and catch it, then the translation would be off. But on other matters there are no grounds for confidence one way or the other. It is not

---

[4] Smith's arguments in favor of the non-relativity of the concept of *having a normative reason* are effectively criticized by Christian Piller, "Critical Notice," *Australasian Journal of Philosophy* 74 (1996), p. 366.

being claimed that our concept of *normative reason* is a relativistic one, but that it is not a *non*-relativistic one either. It is not well-formed enough in this respect for us to be leaning any important argument on its being one way or the other.

4.2 THE RELATIVITY OF NORMATIVE REASONS: THE SUBSTANTIVE QUESTION

Thankfully, we do not need to, for ultimately everything turns on the substantive question. (Nevertheless, we will have further cause to discuss the conceptual question below.) To this crucial matter Smith devotes just over a page of his book (roughly, p. 188). The argument depends on mustering support for "the empirical fact that moral argument tends to elicit the agreement of our fellows." To the obvious rejoinder that there simply is no such fact, that moral disagreement is characterized more by its intractable irresolubility than any convergence, Smith makes three points.

1. First, we must remember that alongside such entrenched disagreements as we in fact find we also find areas of entrenched agreement . . .
2. Second, when we look at current areas of entrenched disagreement, we must remember that in the past similarly entrenched disagreements were removed *inter alia* via a process of moral argument . . .
3. [Third], we must remember that where entrenched disagreements currently seem utterly intractable we can often explain why this is the case in ways that make them seem less threatening to the idea of a convergence in the opinions of fully rational creatures.

These are all reasonable observations; the question is whether they jointly get us anywhere near the conclusion required to support the substantive non-relativity of rationality. (2) tells us that where there has been disagreement in the past, it has been solved by, *inter alia*, rational debate. The "inter alia" must be noted, for it tells us that things other than rational debate may also account for convergence. But this, in turn, tells us that observation of convergence of moral opinions does not, in and of itself, provide evidence that rational debate leads to convergence, for an observed convergence of moral opinions might be explained in other ways. And this point, I believe, effectively dismantles Smith's argument. Consider the convergence that the world is undergoing towards driving the same cars, wearing similar clothes, eating the same hamburgers. It would be silly to think that the convergence is driven by *rational* considerations – that rational argumentation has as its output that we should drive *these* cars, wear *these* clothes, and eat *these* hamburgers. Rather, the convergence is explained by (no doubt complex) considerations concerning cultural hegemony. I see no reason to doubt that as with cars, so with tastes, and so with evaluative outlooks. Convergence in moral opinion may be quite well explained by reference to a theory of how cultures interact and influence each other in *arational* ways. The point is that even if there were to be complete and universal convergence of moral opinion, this would not show that normative reasons are non-relative. An extra argument would be needed – presumably *a posteriori* in nature – showing that the convergence was achieved *through rational debate* (in this case, the equivalent of everybody reflecting on and discussing what each of them would desire if fully reflective and armed with true beliefs, and coming to see that their answers are all the same).

It is also worth noting that convergence *per se* may be considered valuable, and so negotiating parties may aim at it while not caring (within parameters) what they converge *upon*. Analogy: it is valuable that all countries of continental Europe drive on the same side of the road; it doesn't much matter which, so long as they decide upon one or the other. Similarly, a group of people who start out with disparate moral views may see that in order to live together cooperatively they need to adopt a shared moral policy. Let's say that there are a number of policies that are potentially acceptable to all (P_1, P_2, ... P_n), and through a process of negotiation P_3 is decided upon. Rational debate, in such a case, has led to convergence of moral policy, but it would be wrong to say that rational debate leads to convergence *on P_3* – for it might have easily converged on P_1 or P_2, etc. instead.[5] Now suppose that there were another group which is also seeking a common policy starting from the same balance of disparate opinions among its members as did the first group. Again, rational debate and negotiation leads to convergence – but this time on P_4. If these two groups interact with each other they may decide, for the same reasons as before, that a joint policy will be advantageous, and so another round of negotiations may be entered into. But suppose the two groups *don't* interact, or their interaction does not demand a common policy, and so there is no pressure for them to have the same opinion. Would we say, in that case, that rational debate leads to convergence?

---

[5] In order to block the worry that there must have been *something* about P_3 that made it preferable to the other policies – such that another group with the same starting point, going through the same deliberative procedure, *must* also alight upon P_3 rather than the others – let it be pointed out that seemingly irreconcilable desires may be forged into a group decision if all agree to draw lots or toss a coin.

Debate is most likely to lead to convergence when convergence is itself seen to be a value to aim at. But when convergence is not of use – when there are two groups who have little to do with each other, for example – then there are no grounds for assuming that, starting from disparate desiderative points, there will be convergence. In fact, the issue of whether *debate* can lead to convergence is a red herring, for it implies that the two parties are already negotiating, and that they already see a unified settlement as a desideratum. The much clearer question is whether rational reflection, coupled with true beliefs, leads to convergence over what the best course of action is, *even when the parties in question are not interacting with each other*.

We can put this in the terms set in the previous chapter. Imagine two agents, Bill and Jill, who have quite different desires, interests, tastes, etc. Bill wants to ϕ. Jill wants to refrain from ϕing. Let's stipulate that Bill+ (the fully rational and fully informed Bill) would want Bill to ψ instead of ϕ, and so Bill has a normative reason to ψ. I find the claim that we now have all the information needed to conclude what Jill+ would want of Jill to be utterly implausible. Now it's possible that Jill and Bill are partners, say, trying to form a joint policy. We might put it like this: Bill+ would want Bill and Jill to have a joint policy, and so would Jill+. If this were the case, then they will negotiate: Jill+ will take into account what Bill wants; Bill+ will take into account what Jill wants. Perhaps if their starting points are not too far apart, they will come to an agreement. And perhaps if we observe a lot of such partnerships we will observe that agreement is often reached. My complaint is that this is quite beside the point. We need to question whether Bill+ and Jill+ are likely to want the same thing for Bill and Jill respectively, *when Bill and Jill are not in a partnership*. Their being in a partnership just muddies the water, by making convergence something that they are actively seeking. The claim that the non-relativist about normative reasons makes concerning convergence is not restricted to persons or groups who are antecedently committed to a settlement.

As a final comment on Smith's evidence for non-relativism, let us turn to his third point: that some entrenched disagreements are explained because one or more of the parties is not properly participating in rational deliberation.

For example, one or the other parties to the disagreement all too often forms their moral beliefs in response to the directives of a religious authority rather than as the result of the exercise of their own free thought in concert with their fellows. But beliefs formed exclusively in this way have dubious rational credentials. They require that we privilege one group's opinions about what is to be done – those of a religious authority – over another's – those of the followers – for no good reason. (pp. 188–9)

The item to emphasize is that Smith allows that only *some* entrenched disagreements are explained in this way. But what he is committed to, in order to make his point, is that *all* moral disputes that cannot be resolved must be due either to doxastic disagreement or to rational failing such as the kind he describes (though, as we have seen, Smith thinks rational failing includes epistemic failing). In other words, if Smith's three points are to convince us, then they must work, in their pithiest form, as follows:

1. There are moral agreements and disagreements
2. The agreements are sometimes due to rational deliberation
3. The disagreements are due to the failure of rational deliberation or differing beliefs

(1) can be granted. (2) has yet to be shown. No doubt agreements are sometimes due to rational deliberation, but that may occur only when the parties' respective desiderative starting points are already quite close, or when they antecedently value coming to an agreement. Other agreements may simply be due to cultural forces, political pressures, globalization of tastes, etc. Therefore, merely adverting to widespread moral agreement tells us little about the substantive non-relativity of normative reasons. (3) is the crucial thesis, and little has been provided to make it seem compelling. The moral rationalist's position boils down to a simple and surprising claim: that moral failure is rational failure. Given this, the very first thing that can be demanded of such a theorist is a careful description of *how* a moral villain necessarily rationally miscarries (or what false beliefs he has). *Some* disagreements are doubtlessly due to rational failure – after all, if we grant, as we should, that rational failure occurs, then we should expect that its existence will lead to irresoluble disputes. But it takes little imagination to envisage a dispute that cannot be explained away in such a manner, especially given the account of normative reasons that I have adopted from Smith. It would be well to discuss a concrete case.

4.3 HARMAN'S *MURDER, INCORPORATED*

Gilbert Harman presents the following case:

[S]uppose that a contented employee of Murder, incorporated was raised as a child to honor and respect members of the "family" but to have nothing but contempt for the rest of society. His current assignment, let us suppose, is to kill a certain bank manager, Bernard J. Ortcutt. Since Ortcutt is not a member of the "family," the employee in question has no compunction about carrying out his assignment. In particular, if we were to try to convince him that he should not kill Ortcutt, our argument would merely amuse him. We would not provide him with the slightest reason to desist unless we were to point to practical difficulties, such as the likelihood of his getting caught.[6]

The criminal is attentive, appreciates arguments that are presented to him, is strong of will, consistent, etc. The criminal's rational failure, according to Smith, is that the desire that he begins with – that he will gain wealth no matter what the costs to others (when he can get away with it) – cannot be a rational desire. In other words, were the criminal to deliberate flawlessly on the matter, in conditions of full information, then he would not endorse his actual desire to gain wealth at others' expense. But why not? Smith's answer relies on something dubious that he takes as established: that the *conceptual* question of normative reasons goes the way of the non-relativist. With that established, he can make the Kantian leap: that when the criminal deliberates about what he should do, he is, in effect, legislating for everyone – that if the criminal is rational then he is committed to thinking that *anyone* who is in his position would, if they deliberated flawlessly and with epistemic success on the matter, wish themselves to gain wealth at others' expense. And if the criminal thought this, Smith holds, he would be simply mistaken: "Fully rational creatures would want no such thing" (p. 195).

It is tempting to turn the tables on the argument. Consider a law-abiding citizen, who thinks she has a normative reason to refrain from stealing. When she deliberates on the matter, she is (the reasoning goes) legislating for all: *anyone* who deliberated flawlessly with true beliefs on the matter would want themselves to refrain from stealing. But what about the mobster from Murder Inc.? – *he* doesn't think, even after deliberating, that he should refraining from stealing. So who has the true belief concerning what *all* people would want if they deliberated correctly – the mobster or the good citizen? My opinion is that the impasse here just serves to reveal the utter implausibility of the Kantian leap: that bizarre idea that when I deliberate about what I might want if I were better situated, I am thereby deliberating about what *anyone* would want for themselves if they were better situated than they are.

[6] Harman, "Moral Relativism Defended," p. 5.

Imagine us trying to reason with the mobster. "Is it rational for you to want to steal?" we ask. "Sure," he replies (in a James Cagney accent, of course); and when pressed he admits that he believes that if he were to deliberate flawlessly on the matter, and had true beliefs, his opinion wouldn't change. We go on, on Smith's (Kant's) behalf: "But do you think that *anyone* who deliberated flawlessly on the matter, and had true beliefs, would want themselves to steal?" At this point the mobster might say "No." If that is an intelligible answer (and he has not revised any previous claim), then this serves as evidence *against* the non-relativist's conceptual claim. That being so, it would be question-begging to appeal to that conceptual claim in order to discount his response. Perhaps a more predictable answer, however, would be something along the lines of: "If they'd had the upbringing I've had, and if they had the same desires as me, then sure, anyone would want to steal, even after deliberation."

The mobster's last comment is not at all obviously false – in fact, I'm inclined to think it platitudinously true. The odd thing is, however, that Smith is unfazed by this. When discussing conceptual relativism, he allowed that there is a kind of relativity that reasons claims exhibit, but that it is a benign variety " . . . that derives from the fact that what we have reason to do is relative to our circumstances, where our circumstances may include aspects of our own psychology" (p. 170). An example is your preference for wine, which gives you a reason to buy wine, and my preference for beer, which gives me a reason to buy beer. But this does not amount to the kind of agent-relativity of reasons that Smith disavows, because "I can quite happily agree with you that if I were in your circumstance – if I preferred wine to beer – then the fact that the local wine bar sells very good wine would constitute a reason for me to go there as well, just as it constitutes a reason for you" (p. 171).

Smith is resisting a kind of relativity about reasons that he attributes to Williams, but Williams is not our present concern; the question is why the above concession does not amount to all the conceptual relativity that one could hope for (or fear, as the case may be).[7] The mobster claims that he desires to steal in circumstances C, that he has a reason to steal in C, in that were he to deliberate correctly on the matter with true beliefs, he would want himself to steal in C. C includes his desires, for he certainly is not claiming that were he to have completely different desires he would

---

[7] See Piller, "Critical Notice," for much the same concern.

still have reason to steal. When he "universalizes" this claim – as Smith insists he must – then he claims that anyone with the same desires as him, in the same circumstances, would also want themselves to steal. But now, far from being false, this seems quite harmlessly true. Similarly, when the criminal considers the good citizen's honesty, he thinks, "If I were in the same circumstances as her – with the same desires – then I too would have a reason not to steal." It is not that he is preferring, without reason, his own opinion about what fully rational beings would do over other persons' opinions on the matter. All parties may agree about what rational agents will choose to do *given certain desires*. And so the criminal carries on stealing, the law-abiding citizen carries on not stealing, they both are willing to universalize their deliberations after a manner, and so one has a normative reason to steal and the other has a normative reason not to steal. If that doesn't undermine the rationalist's position in a substantial way, I don't know what does.

It would be preferable if it could be shown that the mobster suffers from a rational failing *without* relying on the unsteady thesis that our concept of a normative reason is a non-relative concept. Consider Harman's insistence that the criminal doesn't "fail to consider or appreciate certain arguments."[8] This, Smith argues, is wrong, for the mobster "sticks with this opinion [that stealing is rationally acceptable] despite the fact that virtually everyone disagrees with him" (p. 195). But appreciating an argument is one thing, *agreeing* with an argument is something else. The criminal that we are imagining certainly *listens* to arguments, he just rejects them, presumably on the grounds that a premise is implausible or a conclusion does not follow. And why should he not – for can a sound argument be offered to the criminal, showing his stealing to be irrational? Smith's whole enterprise is to provide such an argument, and his consideration of Harman's criminal is a crucial step in the argument. It is only *after* we have been shown that the criminal is irrational that we can accept Smith's rationalist claim that moral failing is rational failing. But notice the way that things are being reversed: for we are wondering what the criminal's rational failing is, and the answer is that he is failing to accept arguments. But are they *good* arguments? Failing to accept *questionable* arguments is certainly no rational failing – on the contrary! But the rationalist is not in a position – not without begging the question – to assume that the criminal is rejecting *good* arguments.

[8] G. Harman, "Is There a Single True Morality?" in Copp and Zimmerman (eds.), *Morality, Reason and Truth*, p. 39.

Smith seems to suggest that the criminal should accept arguments simply because *most* people accept the conclusions of those arguments, but that is surely no virtue of rationality to which we should aspire. By analogy, imagine an eighteenth-century Polynesian of unusual skeptical temperament: she is inclined to doubt that the things she is told are tapu really are so – she grows to doubt that there is *anything* that is tapu. She prefers this opinion in the face of universal disagreement, and "rejects the very idea that the folk possess between them a stock of wisdom about such matters" (Smith, p. 195). No doubt she is considered intellectually arrogant, but unless we can assume that the defenders of tapu-discourse are able to articulate reasonable arguments in favor of their commitments, we cannot rationally fault her.

4.4 MORAL RELATIVISM

The non-Humean instrumentalist theory of normative reasons that has been defended in this chapter and the last appears to be a relativistic theory. If it is correct, then moral rationalism is sunk, for moral reasons are conceptually non-relative. All the arguments of Chapter 2, to the conclusion that morality consists of categorical imperatives, point to morality's being non-relative. It might clarify matters further, however, if I present a sophisticated version of a theory that denies my premise – that is, that defends moral relativism – and say what I take to be mistaken about that theory.

The theory I have in mind is Gilbert Harman's.[9] Harman argues that moral imperatives are agent-relative. If this were so, then one could link moral reasons to normative reasons (which are also agent-relative), thereby rescuing morality. By the definition that began this chapter, the resulting theory would not properly be called "moral rationalism," but whatever we call it, it would be an avoidance of a moral error theory. Therefore, if my project is to succeed, something needs to be said against Harman's moral relativism.

Harman likens his view about moral judgments to a relativistic view of motion. At one time people thought of motion as absolute; it turns out there is no such thing, and we now have a relativistic view of motion. "But it would be mean-spirited to invoke an 'error theory' and conclude that these pre-Einsteinian judgments were all false!"[10] Harman urges that this does not imply that Newtonian thinkers *intended* or *meant* relative motion

---

[9] See Harman, "Moral Relativism Defended," and (with J. Jarvis Thomson) *Moral Relativism and Moral Objectivity* (Oxford: Blackwell, 1996).

[10] Harman, *Moral Relativism*, p. 4.

all along – of course they did not – but for the purposes of "assigning truth conditions" their judgments about motion should be understood as elliptical for *motion relative to spatio-temporal framework F*. Despite the fact that pre-Einsteinian thinkers would have said false things about motion, we read their utterances like "The ship is in motion" as true, by charitably interpreting their predicate " . . . is in motion" as involving one more place than they thought it involved.

One wonders why we choose to be "mean-spirited" with phlogiston and witches, and interpret seventeenth-century speakers' utterances of "She's a witch" and "This wood contains phlogiston" as false. This throws us right back to a distinction made in Chapter 1, between cases where the discovery of a fault in our understanding of the world leads us to abolish a whole discourse (e.g., with witches and phlogiston), and cases where the discovery of a fault in our understanding leads us to revise our concepts (e.g., by reading a predicate that we have heretofore assumed to be n place as $n + 1$ place – retrospectively implemented) and carry on speaking as before. The distinction must revolve around how important is the "fault" that we discover to the discourse in question. In the case of witches, for example, the whole point (one might say) of having a witch discourse was to refer to women with *supernatural* powers. To discover that no human has supernatural powers is to render the discourse pointless. Even if we were to learn that all and only the women who had been branded "witches" actually have some other distinctive property (say, playing a certain disruptive role in the patriarchal society), this would hardly show that they were all witches after all. By comparison, the point of having a "motion discourse" was to refer to the change in position of objects in space over time. There was never a particular need to refer specifically to *absolute* motion. The fact that people thought of the motion as absolute was not a vital aspect of the discourse; indeed, one doubts that they really thought much about that aspect of motion at all. So the question we must ask is: "Is moral discourse more like talk of witches or more like talk of motion?" – and the answer is that it is more like talk of witches.

Harman downplays the role of the community's *intentions* when wielding a term, but it must be recognized that an important role is being played. We could not simply decide that " . . . is good" means " . . . is pink with yellow trimmings," and rest satisfied that moral realism is established.[11]

---

[11] The example is Stevenson's ("Emotive Meaning," p. 14): If we decided that the question "Is X good?" meant the same as "Is X pink with yellow trimmings?", then ethical theory would be easy. In particular, we could have a success theory for "goodness."

Similarly, though there are empirical disclosures to be made about water, it could not be discovered that "water" is a mass term for the time between lunch and dinner. It is our intentions (considered collectively) to use the term in a certain way that preclude this possibility. It was possible to discover that water is H_2O because our intentions were open on this point – we intended to refer to a stuff we believed to be united by a common microphysical constitution – we just didn't know what that constitution was. Suppose we spent some time erroneously thinking that water is constituted by XYZ rather than H_2O – perhaps we even explicitly denied that it is H_2O. Even in that situation our intentions were to refer to whatever water is *really* made up of, and upon adequate confirmation that we had made a mistake we would have been open to revise our views. By comparison, regarding motion the best thing to say is that we were uncommitted on the issue of absolutism versus relativism: in so far as we endorsed absolute motion, it was because we had never thought very closely about relative motion.

Moral relativity is different. We have always been familiar with the notion of value relativity,[12] and there has been an overwhelming tendency to deny the thesis for the realm of moral value. To think that the shift from moral absolutism (for which we face an error theory) to Harman's relativistic "moral" replacement (which promises a success theory) is a small change in view is to misunderstand the central role that absolutism has played, and does play, in our moral concepts. Moral values are exactly those values which are *not* relative: they are the ones that apply to an agent regardless of that agent's desires or cultural placement. Our ordinary use of the concept of *motion* is not much affected when we let go of absolutism; our ordinary use of the concept of *moral rightness*, by contrast, is completely undermined without absolutism. We need not credit Newtonian speakers' assertions about motion with falsity because we recognize that they did not have all the facts before them, and had not thought in a clear-headed way about all the options. Pretend, though, that Newtonian thinkers *had* been familiar with the notion of relative motion, and nevertheless continued explicitly to deny that this was what they spoke of when they said "motion." In that case it would be appropriate for us, who know better, to deem their utterances false. This imaginary scenario – where speakers have historically been aware of both options and explicitly favored one – is, I think, the correct analog of the moral case. It is not that speakers just

---

[12] Start with Herodotus' *Histories*, book 3, chapter 38 (Harmondsworth: Penguin, 1954) and take it from there.

haven't thought much about the difference between absolute and relative value, or have remained uncommitted on the matter – rather, speakers generally *are* familiar with the notion of relative value, and they by and large insist that that is *not* what they speak of when they say "moral value."

It sounds like the argument turns on what people will actually *say* if asked, but that is somewhat misleading. Rather, what really matters is which conception of morality – absolute or relativistic – best explains and makes sense of the dominant majority of moral practices. It is possible that reading moral judgments as absolute or relativist makes no difference: observable moral practices might be equally well explained by either. This, I suggest, is the case with absolute versus relativist *motion*. However, it is not the case with moral practices. To take a dramatic example, consider the judgment and treatment of the Nazi war criminals in 1946. Moral discourse unhesitatingly demands their censure in the strongest terms. There is no possibility of their evading this denunciation by claiming that from the point of view of *their* moral framework genocide is okay. The fact that we do not pause even to *consider* what "moral framework" the Nazis may have been employing shows pretty clearly that it is not a relativistic judgment with which we condemn them. A charitable relativistic reinterpretation of the concepts involved in our moral censure of the Nazis simply fails to make sense of the judgment: it fails to make sense of what we take into account in coming to the judgment, of the fact that we will not be moved if the defendant were to claim "But from *my* moral framework these actions are acceptable."

Harman argues that "it sounds odd to say that Hitler should not have ordered the extermination of the Jews, . . . [that it] sounds somehow 'too weak' a thing to say."[13] It does sound odd, but that is not to say that it is false.[14] Ask someone whether Hitler ought not to have ordered genocide and they will certainly be perplexed, but probably answer "Of course!" The puzzlement may be similar to that which would greet the question "Is Beethoven's Fifth Symphony a piece of music?" Yet if, in the moral case, we were truly dealing with a relative notion, the question of whether Hitler was wrong might well be answered "No"! – for from *his* moral framework genocide could not be faulted. (Usually it will be understood by speaker and audience that it is *their* framework that is pertinent, but with explicit qualification a different perspective can be privileged, just as it can when talking of motion: as I stand on the cliff watching a ship go

---

[13] Harman, "Moral Relativism Defended," p. 7.
[14] See S. Darwall, "Harman and Moral Relativism," *The Personalist* 58 (1977), pp. 199–207.

by, I can intelligibly speak of myself as moving from the point of view of the passengers on deck.)

Now there are, unfortunately, some people who do not morally condemn the Nazis' actions, but this is no evidence of relativism, for a neo-Nazi does not think that Hitler's actions were right *from Hitler's perspective*, while agreeing that they were wrong from the perspective of middle-class Anglo-American values. Rather, the neo-Nazi's moral praise of Hitler is as absolutist as is our condemnation of him. And this disagreement is not merely because neither we nor the neo-Nazi have properly considered the relativity of moral evaluations. We are quite familiar with the possibility, but nevertheless take ourselves to be engaged in genuine disagreement. Compare the case of two people in passing ships with a third watching from land. Each might (if dull-witted) seriously think of himself as stationary and the others as in motion, and thus a disagreement might brew over which one of them is really stationary. However, once the possibility of the relativity of motion is revealed, all parties readily assent that there really is no disagreement. This hardly describes moral disputation. The Nazi leaders were *hanged*, and the justification was not merely because they were a threat, but because they had, grossly, acted as they morally ought not have done.

Harman claims that just as it is wrong to speak of absolute motion, or of something's being big, period (without reference to a comparison class), so too "it makes no sense to ask whether an action is wrong, period, apart from any relation to an agreement."[15] Quite so; it makes no sense. Where I disagree is that I am certain that we most emphatically *do* speak of actions as wrong, period. Indeed, I have gone so far as to claim that it is "the whole point" of moral discourse that it allows us to speak of actions in such a manner. The evidence mustered is simply observation of the ways in which we do use this language – of what information we treat as relevant and what we treat as irrelevant when making a moral appraisal.

4.5 SUMMARY AND PREVIEW

It will probably do no harm to summarize the general structure of the relatively complex argumentative thread that I have been pursuing. Let us cast our minds back to the point of departure: the argument that was presented in §2.4 (and revised in §3.9).

[15] Harman, "Moral Relativism Defended," p. 4.

I argued that moral discourse commits us to reasons-talk. Now, there are all sorts of kinds of reasons, and it has not been my intention to provide a monolithic theory. In particular, I pointed out the existence of institutional reasons: reasons-talk that is legitimated by adherence to an institution. Moral reasons, however, are not presented as institutional in nature. Morality is not presented as something than may be legitimately ignored or begged off. So the question is: What sense can be made of reasons that cannot be evaded, of non-institutional reasons, of "real" reasons? The answer I gave is that *practical rationality* yields non-institutional reasons, for to question practical rationality is self-undermining. "I acknowledge that practical rationality says I should ϕ, but why should I have any interest in that fact?" fails to express a well-formed skeptical position, and this cannot be upheld if we replace "practical rationality" with the name of any other normative system.

We then investigated, in Chapter 3, what practical rationality may consist in. I adopted a view close to Smith's: that S is practically rational to the extent that she is guided by her subjective reasons, which in turn are understood as follows: S has a subjective reason to ϕ if and only if she is justified in believing that S+ (S granted full information and idealized powers of reflection) would advise S to ϕ. The outstanding virtue of this theory is that it accounts for the non-institutionality of practical rationality; it avoids alienating an agent from her normative reasons.[16]

A key point is the realization that the non-institutional reasons that have been located (let us just call them "normative reasons") are not going to "rescue" moral reasons. The explanation is that normative reasons are agent-relative, altering depending on the desiderative profile of the agent in question. We have seen no argument that there must be convergence in agents' normative reasons, and *a fortiori* no argument that there must be convergence towards a view that approves of promise-keeping and

---

[16] Another virtue that warrants exploration is the theory's capacity to do better than Humean instrumentalism regarding the accommodation of prudence. According to the Humean, if S knows that he will have a desire for X next Tuesday, then this only gives him a present reason to act so as to bring about X if he now has a desire that his future self will have his desires satisfied. This is shown to be unconvincing by Thomas Nagel in *The Possibility of Altruism*. By contrast, the non-Humean instrumentalist, in accounting for prudential reasons, does not require that the present S has the desire that his future selves will have their desires satisfied – only that if S were to be fully informed, and were to reflect carefully, then he would want his actual self to act in a way that conduces to the satisfaction of the desires of his future selves. This seems quite defensible, though I have not space to pursue it here.

condemns inflicting harm on innocents, etc. This is what Smith attempts, but I have argued in the present chapter that his attempts fail.

One might complain: "Well, so much the worse for moral rationalism, but there are plenty of alternative programs that purport to vindicate moral discourse." However, if the arguments that I have pressed are correct, then this complaint is mistaken. Of course, there *are* alternative programs, but they are doomed to disappoint, for they will never vindicate that all-important moral *authority* that putatively binds us regardless of our desires. The rationalist at least sees the special sense of "requirement" that requires defense; it is just that his defense fails.

Another complaint along similar lines is: "Well, so much the worse for your particular version of normative reasons, but there are alternative versions available." This I take more seriously. The virtues that I have claimed for non-Humean instrumentalism don't add up to the exclusion of a theory that has all these virtues *as well as* satisfying our moral desiderata. And, of course, if such a hypothetical rationalism did rescue morality, then *ceteris paribus* it would be preferable to the theory that has been defended, for the very fact that my favored theory radically undermines moral discourse (I shan't say that *Smith's* theory does, since he would most emphatically deny that consequence) surely counts against it.

One response would be to embark on an examination of every alternative theory of practical rationality on the market, pointing out the flaws of each. This I eschew, not merely because it would fill a book in which there are more interesting things to discuss, but because it would not ultimately solve the problem – there would still be the possibility of a superior version of practical rationality appearing in the future. I prefer to tackle the issue head-on, and there appear to be two strategic avenues, the exploration of which occupy the next two chapters. Let me preview them first.

The first strategy is to attempt a straight defense of practical instrumentalism by showing that the non-instrumentalist necessarily commits an error. The only argument I know of to this conclusion is that put forward by Bernard Williams in his well-known paper "Internal and External Reasons." The following chapter therefore defends Williams's argument – or, at least, defends the spirit of the argument, for I do not agree with everything that he claims. Williams takes himself to be presenting an account of what all reasons must be like: he presents a distinction between internal and external reasons, only to exclude claims involving the latter as false. I have already presented considerations against any theory of "reasons *simpliciter*." One might instead take his argument as being restricted to normative reasons: as an account of those reasons that are justified by practical rationality. However, I do not believe that that is quite right either. I take Williams's argument to present a necessary condition for normative reasons, thus excluding non-instrumentalist possibilities.

Let me describe the backdrop against which we must consider any "theory of reasons" such as that offered by Williams. On the one hand, we must recognize that if a philosopher sets out to analyze or explicate a concept in ordinary parlance – like *having a reason* – then she must start with how the word is generally used. If enough people use the term in the "external" sense (as defined by Williams), then that usage cannot be easily dismissed as false. The linguistic population has the power to "outvote" the philosopher; if it is *their* concept that she purports to be discussing, then it is incumbent on her to provide an analysis that captures as much as possible of that concept's ordinary usage.[17] Put bluntly, if enough people use "reason" in a non-instrumental manner, then *reason* is a non-instrumental concept, whether the philosopher likes it or not. On the other hand, however, we must also recognize limits to the philosopher's subservience to linguistic democracy. The linguistic community can be unanimous but mistaken, as it was about phlogiston, tapu, and absolute motion. As we have already noted, it is the (non-negotiable) claims which the community is disposed to assert *about* such things (as reflected in their practices) that dooms these concepts to emptiness.

The same thing goes for the notion of an external reason. If a claim like "He has a reason to ϕ, even though ϕing will not further any of his ends" were just a way of talking (just a "permissible move in a language game," as it were), then the philosopher can have no quarrel. But if the speakers are also willing to make further claims – for example: "Reasons are things that it is irrational to ignore," "Reasons are things that would motivate you if you were thinking clearly on the matter and were fully informed" – then the philosopher might have something to get his teeth into. Now I am not claiming that the two examples just given *are* generally commitments that people have about reasons – they sound like something only a philosopher would say. However, I do claim that when external reasons claims are made concerning *moral* matters, then they come with concomitant commitments to "inescapability," and the impermissibility of the wrong-doer "begging off" the prescription. The philosopher then comes along (so to speak) and asks "What sense can be made of this 'inescapability'?" and the

---

[17] I thank David Lewis for helping me to see this point clearly (in correspondence).

answer he gives may be along the lines of "Someone who ignored the moral reason might be accused of irrationality." This doesn't purport to be what an ordinary person would think of saying – it is the philosopher's attempt to provide warrant for an ordinary linguistic practice. And now the philosopher really does have something to go to work on. For if the answer given truly is the most charitable explication available, but it just doesn't stand up to philosophical scrutiny, then ordinary language can be accused of error.

It might be asserted, I suppose, that such associated commitments are just further "moves in a language game," and that regarding these as well the philosopher should bow to popular linguistic practice. Against this view I would direct the reader back to §2.5, where I rejected Carnap's attempt to demonstrate that there can be no sensible criticism of a linguistic practice "from the outside." (Considerations put forward later in §6.6 are also relevant to this point.) It should also be pointed out that an error theory for morality is not *clearly and obviously* false: it seems to me that we have always had – often lurking in the back of our minds, occasionally clearly stated – a cluster of thoughts about the genealogy and function of moral language according to which the whole discourse is, to put it most bluntly, bluff (to use Williams's word). Even the most fervent moral realist, I hazard to suggest, gains her fervor largely from glimpsing a *real* opponent. If we agree that a moral error theory is at least an intelligible position (even if we think it mistaken), then we must allow its proponent the possibility of articulating a defense of his theory. But if, whenever he points out the faults of moral discourse, his opponent can simply say "Ah, but that's just another permissible move within the moral language game," then we are making an admittedly possible theory unconfirmable (and, conversely, a theory that is possibly false unfalsifiable). Any rulebook of disputation that allows this must be rejected.

It is in the context of such considerations that I regard Williams's argument. Let us all admit – as Williams does himself – that people systematically employ external reasons claims. We are in a position to find fault with the practice only if there are further things that people are willing to say (or, at least, further commitments that they evince) concerning these reasons. For example, if people were to say that all reasons are potentially motivating, then that would indeed look problematic. But do people have any such extra commitments about reasons? I am not confident that they do generally, and I don't think Williams shows that they do. However, when it comes to *moral* external reasons claims, then reasons claims are made with some pretty substantive baggage. This is what I meant earlier when I said that there would be no problem with morality and its reasons if only it presented itself as an institution. But it doesn't. It presents itself as something with ubiquitous and inescapable authority. The philosopher turns to *practical rationality* as a way of understanding this authority, for where else is there to turn? Practical rationality alone seems to have the kind of immunity from legitimate questioning that is attributed to morality.

The philosopher can then investigate the nature of practical rationality and the reasons it yields. Something he might note is that if one has a *normative* reason to ϕ then ϕing must be something that could potentially motivate one. This is not a general pronouncement about reasons *simpliciter* (as Williams takes it to be), but a claim about a sub-class of reasons: normative reasons. Because practical rationality is hardly a familiar notion concerning which ordinary speakers have many firm convictions, in giving an account of it the philosopher is less at the mercy of the whims of the linguistic community. Williams's argument against external reasons – which, as we shall see in the next chapter, revolves around their inability to motivate those to whom they are ascribed – tells us something important about practical rationality, not about reasons claims in general. That, in any case, is how I read matters.

I said that there are two strategic approaches against the practical non-instrumentalist. The second is what might be called the "genetic" strategy, which is the subject of Chapter 6. Here we ask "Why and how has morality developed?" Suppose that the most plausible answer does not require that any of our moral discourse be *true*; rather, all that the hypothesis requires is that people have by and large *believed* morality to be true. Suppose that we discover that it would be of evolutionary advantage for humans to develop a sense of "to-be-doneness" regardless of whether there really is anything answering to that concept in the world. Perhaps we find that this evolved sense lies behind our judgments of moral obligatoriness, as much as behind earlier notions about the demands of the gods, the demands of tapu, the demands of the ancestral spirits, etc. None of this would be to demonstrate that these concepts are flawed, but it would put into perspective any attempt to vindicate them. We could predict that people *would* try to vindicate them, for these concepts are the expression of something deeply rooted in us.

Suppose that we start seeing the practical non-instrumentalist – or, more specifically, the moral rationalist – in this way: as someone whose project is to vindicate a concept with which evolution has endowed us; and suppose we note, further, that this project has been going on for a very long time without being able to articulate a convincing case. Again, this would not be to show that a convincing case cannot be made, but it casts the project into a suspect light. At the very least it breaks a looming impasse by placing the burden of proof on the rationalist, and until that burden is discharged a moral error theory is to be preferred. In other words, there is a position available that explains all there is that cries out for explanation – a position that combines an instrumentalist theory of normative reasons (which accounts attractively for all our intuitions concerning normative reasons but fails to cover moral reasons), a moral error theory, and an evolutionary hypothesis about why we have a tendency to commit this error. Nothing mysterious remains; the work is done. The rationalist is someone who is unsatisfied – who insists that there is more work to be done. But the evolutionary hypothesis predicts exactly that: that we *will* feel dissatisfied with the answer. Put in unflattering terms, the rationalist is someone who invents an unnecessary riddle and then tries to solve it. Perhaps he will find a solution, but until he does, the former package of theses is preferable in that it recognizes no unsolved mysteries.

5

Internal and external reasons

5.0 INTERNAL AND EXTERNAL REASONS

Bernard Williams presents a theory of reasons in many respects like that of Smith's theory of normative reasons. The theory is designed to show that the opposition – one that supports non-instrumental reasons – necessarily makes a mistake. The purpose of this chapter is to describe and develop Williams's position, and then to criticize some of the opposition it has faced. I do not pretend that this list of opponents will be exhaustive, but it is hoped that they represent some basic types of anti-instrumentalist argument.

Williams claims that one has a reason to ϕ if and only if one would be motivated to ϕ after a process of fully informed correct deliberation. As before, I should prefer to drop the "... and only if ...," allowing elbow room for other kinds of reason. Suppose Molly has been exposed to ample evidence that ϕing reliably attains X – so much so that she is quite justified in believing it – but it is actually false (she is not fully informed). Let us say that she deliberates carefully and flawlessly on the matter, and her desire for X survives the process. I see no grounds for resisting the admission that it would be rational for her to ϕ, that she has a (subjective) reason to ϕ; and I find the insistence that she does not have a reason to ϕ (because if she had *true* beliefs she would desire otherwise) clashes with commonsensical attribution.

It may appear that Williams's account at least comes close to capturing what I have called "objective reasons," since granting Molly all relevant true beliefs, relieving her of any false ones, and asking what she would want *then*, accomplishes much the same job as assessing what would *really* satisfy her carefully considered desires. The accounts are not equivalent, however, since Williams's includes that new desires may be created (and old ones destroyed) not just in the process of deliberation, but also through

106

having been granted epistemic success.[1] Consider the following situation. After full deliberation Molly desires X – call this a "rational desire." She's justified in believing that ϕing will satisfy the desire for X, though in fact ψing will. According to my view, she has a subjective rational reason to ϕ and objective rational reason to ψ. It may appear that this is equivalent to saying that if she had all true beliefs on the matter, she would want to ψ rather than ϕ. However, having true beliefs may alter her desires: if she comes to see that ψing is the only way to attain X – and ψing, let's say, is incompatible with some other desire that she has – then her desire for X may be destroyed. So according to Williams, she may have reason neither for ϕing nor ψing.

I'm inclined to construe this not as a choice that is forced between two competing theories, but rather just further evidence of how varied is the array of reason-attributions. There is nothing to prevent constructing an even more elaborate theory of reasons that accommodates both the reasons that Williams admits and the ones to which I have drawn attention. Furthermore, it strikes me that even though we would have to introduce more unlovely terminology in order to distinguish the types of reason, doing so would not fail to track reasonably commonsensical distinctions. For the present purposes this task is not strictly necessary, but just to show the compatibility, let me add layers to a case like that described at the end of §3.6.

Molly is watching her weight, yet is tempted by the cake in front of her. She has an irrational desire to eat the cake, and were she to do so we could explain her action by reference to that desire. Thus (perhaps) she has an irrational reason to eat the cake. Yet the desire is *irrational*, in that her better judgment – the desire she endorses after deliberation, the one that is associated with her *values* – tells her not to eat the cake. Thus Molly has a (rational subjective) reason to refrain from eating. Unbeknownst to her, tonight she will be forced to skip dinner, and will wish she had eaten a big lunch. At present (lunch-time) she has a rational desire that she should not go hungry this evening, and therefore, since eating the cake will help satisfy that desire, she has a (rational objective) reason that she is unaware

---

[1] And in this Williams is surely correct. Cf. Hume: "Reason . . . can have an influence on our conduct only after two ways: Either when it excites a passion by informing us of the existence of something which is a proper object of it; or when it discovers the connexion of causes and effects, so as to afford us means of exerting any passion" (*Treatise*, book 3, part 1, section 1 [1978], p. 459). The process of rational deliberation, in other words, can create desires.

of: to eat the cake. However, were she at present to believe that tonight she will be forced to skip dinner, she would realize that today is the perfect opportunity to fast for the whole day – something she has been meaning to do for a long time – and she would form a desire to do so. If this desire would survive all further fully informed correct deliberation, then Molly has a (Williams-style) reason to refrain from eating the cake.

My point is not that all of these types of reason are on a par; merely that none of them, with the possible exception of the first, seems objectionable. There is no obvious reason for resisting the admission of all of them. However (as I have said before), it seems best to say that Molly's *normative* reasons – what it is rational for her to do – go along with her "rational subjective" reasons, not her "rational objective" reasons, nor her "Williams-style" reasons. But if Williams's account of reasons provides neither the necessary and sufficient conditions for *having a reason* in general, nor even the conditions for *having a normative reason*, then why are we discussing it?

Our interest in Williams lies in the argument he employs to exclude external reasons. All types of reason admitted in the above example are potential motivators of Molly, and therefore none count, in Williams's terms, as external reasons. An external reason claim is one that is applied to the subject of the ascription regardless of what are his desires; and Williams argues that although we make such claims, they are all false. His argument turns on the claim that reasons have to be able to explain action:

> If there are reasons for action, it must be that people sometimes act for those reasons, and if they do, their reasons must figure in some correct explanation of their action . . .

In other words, something is a reason only if its consideration could potentially motivate the agent. I do not support this strong conclusion, for I do not think that the philosopher has the right to "outvote" a widespread practice in the way that Williams appears to. However, if we consider ourselves to be discussing only *normative reasons*, then the above constraint seems far more reasonable. This point dovetails with my earlier claim that an adequate account of practical rationality must not leave an agent alienated from her reasons. If a normative reason could not potentially motivate an agent, then, if presented with such a reason, an agent could say "Yes, I accept that is a normative reason for me, but so what?" – and this, I have urged, is unacceptable. Having noted this important difference of opinion between myself and Williams, however, I propose for the rest of this chapter more or less to ignore it, in the interests of discussing Williams and his critics on their own terms, without inelegantly twisting things to my own project. In other words, I will speak as if I were supporting the conclusion that all reasons are internal, though in fact my position is more focused: that all normative reasons are internal.

5.1 EXTERNAL REASONS AND MOTIVATION

How could an external reason fulfill the condition quoted above? Let us first see how an internal reason does. Suppose I am thirsty, but unbeknownst to me the cup of coffee I am (reasonably) reaching for contains poison. I have an internal reason not to drink, in that I have a desire not to poisoned, and refraining from drinking helps satisfy that desire. Because of my ignorance, of course, the reason explains nothing about my actions – but it *could*. If I were to be granted true beliefs on the matter, then I would refrain from drinking, and the reason would explain that inaction. This explanation would presumably be a matter of psychological causation: the belief that the coffee was poisoned coupled with the desire not to be poisoned *causes* my act of refraining.[2] (This is not to say that these two states *automatically* result in that action – I may be irrational and drink the poison anyway.)

Back to the external reason. Suppose it were claimed, instead, that I have a reason to refrain from drinking the coffee because it is tapu and must not be touched. This reason claim will be urged regardless of what I may say about my indifference to tapu, or my citing of nihilistic desires to tempt the hand of fate. *Regardless* of my desires (it is claimed) I ought not drink – I have a reason not to drink. But how could that reason ever explain any action of mine? Could the external reason even explain my refraining from drinking? Clearly, in order to explain it the external reason must have some causally efficacious role among the antecedents of the action (in this case, an omission) – I must have, in some manner, "internalized" it. The only possibility, it would seem, consistent with its being an external reason, is that I *believe* the external reason claim: I believe that the coffee is tapu. There's no doubting that such a belief can play a

---

[2] See Donald Davidson, "Actions, Reasons, and Causes," in his *Essays on Actions and Events* (Oxford: Oxford University Press, 1980), pp. 3–19. Although I have boldly stated that the relevant explanatory relation is causal, I must admit to some hesitancy on the matter, but it need not distract us now.

role in explaining actions – including my refraining from drinking the coffee. The question is whether the belief *alone* can produce action, to which the correct answer is "No." A very familiar and eminently sensible view says that in order to explain an action the belief must couple with desires (such that those same desires had in the absence of the belief would not have resulted in the action). And this seems correct: if I believe that the coffee is tapu *but really just don't care about that*, then I will not refrain from drinking it. So in order for the belief to explain action it must couple with desiderative elements – but in that case the putative external reason collapses into an internal one.[3]

We started out discussing normative reasons, but, if we follow Williams, the argument quickly becomes one about motivating reasons, and about the Humean conception of action in general. In short, if Hume is correct that action requires belief and desire operating together, then an external reason could never explain an action, for even if the subject *believes* the reason claim, action will ensue only if certain desires are present.

It would be strategically tidy at this point to present a swift and watertight defense of the Humean theory of action, but – though I am cognizant of the sophisticated opposition that the theory has faced – in the present study I am content to accept it as a reasonably stable premise. The great virtue of the Humean framework is its simplicity, its explanatory breadth, and its apparent intuitiveness. These virtues, in my opinion, are not manifest in the opposition. The anti-Humean (bear in mind we're talking about the anti-Humean concerning the explanation of action, rather than the anti-Humean concerning normative reasons) is committed to there being mental states that are neither beliefs nor desires, but another kind of unitary state (playing the role that the Humean assigns to beliefs and desires), which, with J. Altham, we might call "besires."[4] If there were such a thing, it might fit the bill for the defender of external reasons: if I *besire* that the coffee is tapu then that besire may count both as my representing to myself the coffee's being tapu *and* as the explanation of my refraining from drinking it.

---

[3] This is so even if we see the content of the belief as something like this: that a fully informed and correctly deliberating counterpart of myself would want me not to drink the coffee. I have presented arguments that one cannot legitimately remain indifferent to this consideration, but this does not mean that such a belief automatically motivates. The emphasis is on the "legitimately." Even if one has such a belief, one may remain indifferent to the action in question, but then one's indifference would be irrational. To be motivated to perform the action in question will still require an appropriate desire.

[4] J. Altham, "The Legacy of Emotivism," in G. Macdonald and C. Wright (eds.), *Fact, Science and Morality* (Oxford: Basil Blackwell, 1986), pp. 275–88.

The first thing to note is that the whole background against which we have framed our questions from the start – distinguishing in Chapter 2 between categorical and hypothetical imperatives, etc. – was built upon the assumption of the commonsensical Humean division between beliefs and desires. To bring it into question now would require the reframing of the previous chapters in very different terms. "So much the worse for the previous chapters," one might respond. But I think that they are safe, because there is in reality no well-formed challenge. Several philosophers have been tempted by "besire-psychology," even if not under that name, but their enterprise has been quite effectively quashed by considerations raised by, among others, Michael Smith.[5]

Smith understands beliefs and desires in terms of directions of fit, which he in turn understands in counterfactual terms. If I have a mental state that p, and I observe that not-p, then (i) if I am thereby disposed to change my mental state to not-p, then it is a belief, and (ii) if I am thereby disposed to change the world to p, then the mental state is a desire. In either case the end-result is that the world and mind are brought into harmony. This may not stand as an analysis of beliefs and desires, but any adequate analysis, it seems correct to say, must underwrite it. So how could there be a mental state with *both* directions of fit?

Suppose I besire that p, and I observe that not-p. Qua belief, I am disposed to alter my mental state to not-p, but qua desire, I am disposed to change the world to p. If I succeed on both counts, and then observe the fruits of my labor, I will see that the world contains p. But now my mind contains not-p. The new mental state, let's say, is either a belief, a desire, or a besire. If it's a belief, then I'll change it to p, in which case the result of the whole process was as if I had simply desired that p in the first place. If it's a desire, then I'll change the world to not-p, in which case it is as it would be if I had initially believed that p. If it's is a besire, then we just go through the whole business again, *ad infinitum*. Surely a reductio?

Smith then considers a "more subtle" besire theorist, who does not require that the "belief element" and the "desire element" of the besire have the same content. The besire may be normative in nature, such as "that ϕ is right." That, at least, is the doxastic part of it; but we need not understand the desire element as follows: that upon perceiving that it is not the case that ϕ is right, one is disposed to alter the world to make ϕ

[5] Smith, *Moral Problem*, pp. 92–125. Smith's explicit opponents – the anti-Humeans regarding motivation – are Thomas Nagel, John McDowell, Mark Platts, and David McNaughton. See also David Lewis, "Desire as Belief," *Mind* 97 (1988), pp. 323–32.

right. Rather, the desire element is simply a disposition to perform ϕ – perhaps, to put this in direction of fit terms: upon perceiving that one is not performing ϕ (or not performing "the right thing"), one is disposed to do so. But now these two elements have been granted different contents, the question that immediately arises is "Why are they not just *two* different states that are causally linked? – Why are they not, to be precise, a belief *and* a desire?" The obvious test is whether we can imagine them coming apart. And it seems no great feat of the imagination, and no great distance in modal space that need be traveled, in order to do so, for we have already discussed agents who judge that actions are right but feel no motivation to perform them: if not evil agents, then those who are weak of will. Alternatively, we can easily imagine someone disposed to perform some right action ϕ while not believing that ϕ is right.

I don't propose to pursue this defense of Humean psychology further here, though there is no doubt much more to be said. I am satisfied to note that Williams's challenge leads to a well-worn battlefield, upon which he has a decided advantage. But there remain other places to apply pressure to Williams's argument. One is to question the assumption that generates the argument – that for S to have a reason to ϕ, that reason must potentially explain S's ϕing action. Another strategy is to argue that Williams's argument undermines itself, and that even his account of internal reasons is committed to the existence of external ones. A third critic complains that Williams has left his account of "correct deliberation" so open that even if he is correct that there are no external reasons, he grants the non-instrumentalist everything she could have asked for. I will take them in turn.

5.2 MILLGRAM'S CHALLENGE TO WILLIAMS

Elijah Millgram attempts to argue by straight counter-example: providing a case of S's having a reason to ϕ though that reason could not explain any of S's actions, not even her ϕing.[6] We are invited to imagine Archie, who is rather insensitive to those around him. His insensitivity deprives him of certain satisfactions, but these are satisfactions the value of which he cannot appreciate because he is insensitive. The important thing is that this insensitivity is a *deliberative* incapacity: it blocks him from recognizing that he has reasons to be sensitive. Suppose, for example, that if Archie were more sensitive then he would have more fulfilling friendships. But there is

---

[6] Elijah Millgram, "Williams' Argument Against External Reasons," *Noûs* (1996), pp. 197–220. All textual page references to Millgram are to this article.

no element in Archie's "subjective motivational set" that would be satisfied by his having more fulfilling friendships, and no amount of deliberation will get him to desire the actions that will lead to fulfilling friendships, precisely because he is so insensitive. "But were he to experience them, he himself would acknowledge the extent to which his life had improved" (p. 204). Because of this, according to Millgram, it "is natural to say that Archie has reason to change his ways."

Millgram is concerned to counter the potential complaint that Archie does not really have a reason to be sensitive at all, but the more pressing worry is that he does have such a reason and it is an internal one. Granted that there is no element in Archie's motivational set that being more sensitive will satisfy, but that is not Williams's criterion. We need to imagine an improved Archie, who deliberates correctly and is fully informed: does *he* desire fulfilling friendships? And the answer seems a straightforward "Yes," on two counts. First, Archie *ex hypothesi* has a deliberative incapacity – if he were deliberating correctly, then he would not be insensitive, and so would not be blocked from recognizing his reasons. Second, he fails to realize that better friendships will improve his life. But a fully informed Archie would know this: he would know that his well-being is better served through fulfilling friendships, and that it is just the flawed Archie's insensitivity that is preventing him from seeing this.

Perhaps I am being unfair on Millgram by discussing the wrong reason. Let us say that the reason that Archie has concerns the performance of some action that will lead to his becoming more sensitive – let's say *going to counseling*. The actual Archie has no desires that counseling will further, since he has no desires that sensitivity will satisfy, no desires that having more fulfilling friendships will serve. But nor does the fully informed and deliberatively flawless Archie have reason to go to counseling, for he doesn't need to!

This problem is dissipated if we think carefully about the matter. We are imagining that S has a reason to ϕ, even though S+ would not have a reason to ϕ – and this is possible precisely because ϕing may be an action needed to move one from a state of being S to a state of being S+. But we have at no point defined S's reasons in terms of what S+'s reasons are, nor in terms of S+'s desires or actions. Rather, we have defined S's reasons in terms of what S+ would want *for* S. S+ is not the exemplar, but the advice-giver.[7]

---

[7] See Smith, "Internal Reasons," pp. 110–12.

Let us say, then, that Archie has a reason to go to counseling because that's what the fully informed, sensitive, etc., Archie+ would want Archie to do (even if Archie+ himself wouldn't want to).[8] Now the question is: Could that reason ever explain any action that Archie performs? Let us imagine a continuum of improving counterparts of Archie – Archie$_1$, Archie$_2$, . . . Archie$_n$, Archie+ – improving with respect to deliberative capacities and epistemic success. Archie has a reason to go to counseling but doesn't know it; Archie+ has no reason to go to counseling, but (we are assuming) is aware that Archie does. What happens in between? There are two pertinent ways that the continuum may go. On either, some counterpart – say, Archie$_7$ – comes to realize that fulfilling friendships, etc., are of value. Now he will get to that state only if he has already grown somewhat more sensitive than Archie, which is consistent with the continuum mapping, *inter alia*, improvement of deliberative capacities. On one continuum, Archie$_7$ also comes to realize that what remains of his insensitivity is standing in the way of his attaining this value, realizes that counseling would be a good way of overcoming it, and so goes to counseling. This action is explained by his awareness that this is a good means of satisfying his desires. Therefore, Archie's reason to go to counseling *does* explain a possible action that he would perform under improvement. This reason

---

[8] Millgram ("Williams' Argument Against External Reasons," fn. 14) claims that we had "better not" say this. "Even if he [your improved counterpart] is in a position to figure out what *he* ought to do, does this put him in a position to advise *you*? . . . [W]hy . . . should you listen to what he tells you?" But these challenges may be answered. My improved counterpart is in a position to advise me because, being fully informed, he knows all about me. Why should I care about full information and deliberative excellence? Because even to ask the question reveals my commitment to such values. Millgram suggests that it is quite possible that S is actually so uncaring that even her improved counterpart will not care about S (being uncaring, unlike being insensitive, is not in any obvious way a *deliberative* incapacity), and yet, for all that, S may have a reason to be more caring. How could this be? Millgram argues the case on the grounds that if S *were* to become more caring, she would acknowledge that she is better off; yet at the same time it is important that this "satisfaction" is not understood in terms of the satisfaction of any element of S's motivational set (and no element of a set improved by better deliberation and full information), or it just becomes an internal reason. But S+ is not only an improvement on S in terms of deliberative prowess, but is fully informed. Therefore, if we start with the assumption that S, were she to be more caring, would acknowledge that this is an improvement in her life, then we must accept that the fully informed counterpart of S is aware of this fact and therefore will value caring. If, on the other hand, we start with the assumption that even the fully informed counterpart of S does not value caring, then we must let go of the view that S, were she to have certain experiences, would acknowledge that she is better off caring. If we go the former route, then S's reason to be caring is an internal one; if we go the latter route, then there remain no grounds for assuming that S has any reason at all to be more caring.

is an internal reason, since it depends on Archie's subjective motivational set – or, more precisely, a subjective motivational set that is accessible through practical deliberation (and having been granted full information) from the actual flawed Archie's set.

On the other continuum, we can imagine that by the time Archie's sensitivity has improved to the stage where he can see that having fulfilling friendship is a value (by the time he becomes Archie$_7$), he no longer needs the counseling. So on this continuum Archie never actually goes to counseling, and so that action never calls for explanation. This possibility may look like it continues to make trouble for Williams, since there is a reason that Archie has, we are imagining, but it appears that the reason can never explain any action that Archie might perform.

However, there is really no problem here, since it is not being claimed that one continuum describes Archie's improvement while the other does not: there are many different routes to improvement that one may follow, and different sequences of improvement that one may undergo. And that's all that Williams needs. It's perfectly *possible* that Archie would improve in the former way, and therefore there is an action that Archie *could* perform – going to a counselor – that would be explained in terms of the Archie's having a reason to go to a counselor. These modal terms do, of course, need to be treated with caution here, but Williams has told us roughly what is being included and what excluded: the possibility extends to granting the agent full information and no deliberative flaws, and not beyond. Within those limits there are certainly actions that Archie *could* perform that would be explained by the reason in question, even though neither the utterly flawed nor the utterly ideal Archie would be interested in performing that action.

There are other arguments that Millgram puts forward, but my point here is that he has not succeeded in refuting what I am calling "the presupposition" of Williams's argument – that any reason must be a potentially motivating reason (i.e., must explain an action that the agent might perform).

5.3 HAMPTON'S CHALLENGE TO WILLIAMS

It is not clear to me whether Jean Hampton, in the course of her multi-fronted attack on Williams, denies the presupposition of his argument.[9]

[9] Jean Hampton, *The Authority of Reason* (Cambridge: Cambridge University Press, 1998). All textual page references to Hampton are to this book.

Rather, she attempts to find his argument self-undermining: that in his identification even of internal reasons he commits himself surreptitiously to true external reasons claims. Williams leaves the notion of *correct* deliberation unashamedly vague – he sees doing so as a desideratum – but he doesn't think that any old practical reflection counts as correct deliberation. "Correct deliberation" being a normative notion (i.e., involving "ought" statements), it implies reasons claims. Hampton asks:

Are these reasons regarding deliberation internal or external? If Williams answers "internal," how does that answer make sense, given that, in order to use it, he would have to invoke the concept of deliberation he is trying to define? (p. 76)

The accusation is one of circularity. Let's simplify the sequence. Williams defines "internal reason" in such a way that a notion of *correct deliberation* is ineliminably used. Hampton asks "Are the reasons involved in correct deliberation internal or external?" "Internal," replies Williams. "A-ha! – Circularity!" cries Hampton. But it is easy to see that this is quite unfair. The reasons involved in correct deliberation *are* internal, but Williams hasn't *defined* "correct deliberation" with reference to internal reasons, and there are no grounds for thinking that he needs to. Compare a parody of the argument. Mary defines "species" in a way that makes central reference to, let's say, individuals being able to interbreed and produce fertile offspring. John asks: "So these offspring you speak of – are *they* members of species?" The fact that Mary would answer "Yes" in no way shows her original definition was circular. The accusation of circularity will only take hold if Williams needs to invoke the concept of an *internal reason* in order to define what he means by "correct deliberation." Yet even if the circularity objection doesn't go through, might there still not be something implausible about the thought that our reasons to deliberate are *internal*?

We need to be more precise concerning just which reasons to deliberate we're talking about. Hampton mentions three areas: "[i] reasons directing how we are to deliberate, [ii] what counts as correct deliberation, and [iii] when we are to deliberate" (p. 76). It is important to see that the third does not pose a problem. Nobody is claiming that we must always deliberate (beyond, perhaps, a minimum). It would help to have a concrete example to discuss. Presumably included in "correct deliberation" will be something like "If you desire something, then you should consider whether the satisfaction of that desire will interfere with the satisfaction of any of your other desires." If I'm being chased by a lion, then it is simply not true that in such I should consider how my desire not to be eaten fits in with all my other desires. I have a reason *not* to deliberate, and *a fortiori* I have a reason not to deliberate correctly. If, when being chased by a lion, I have reason not to deliberate, then what kind of reason is that? The answer is that deliberating is likely to get in the way of my acting quickly, and if I don't act quickly I shall be eaten, and I don't want to be eaten (if, for some perverse reason, I *wanted* to be eaten, then it would be a different story); in other words, my reason for not deliberating in that circumstance is an internal reason, depending on my having a desire (which I would continue to endorse under improvement). When I am in calmer circumstances, then I may have reason to deliberate because doing so is conducive to the satisfaction of my desires. Not just my actual desires, but those that I would have after correctly deliberating under conditions of full information. Isn't *that* circular? No, because at this stage we're not *defining* anything. We've said that S has reason to ϕ iff S+ (who correctly deliberates) would want S to ϕ. There is no circularity if it turns out that the advice that S+ would give includes "In circumstances C, deliberate carefully" (in other words, "In C, try to be more like me").

So the reasons that pertain to *when* we ought to deliberate may be internal. Regarding Hampton's other two areas, I must admit that I cannot see a clear distinction, so I will treat it as one potentially problematic claim, concerning the *content* of correct deliberation: when one does have reason to deliberate, then one has reason to do it *this* way, as opposed to any other way. To use the example from above: if I do have a reason to deliberate, then I have a reason to consider whether the satisfaction of one desire clashes with my other desires. But this strikes me as an odd claim, because checking my desires for clashes is partially *constitutive* of deliberating. If I have a reason to deliberate (in C) – and it is an internal reason – then I have a reason to check my desires for clashes (in C) – and that too will be an internal reason. Compare an analogous case: suppose I have a reason to climb the highest mountain in France – perhaps my reason is to impress my girlfriend. Now that reason gives me a variety of other reasons: to buy some climbing gear, to locate my French phrase book, etc. But it also gives me reason to do the things that are constitutive of climbing the highest mountain in France – it gives me reason to climb the Mt. Blanc. Whatever reason I have to climb Mt. Blanc just *is* the reason I have to climb the highest mountain in France: to impress my girlfriend (unlike my reason for buying all that climbing gear, which is so that I can climb the mountain).

I just claimed that checking one's desires for clashes (for example) is partially constitutive of deliberating, but is that quite right? Isn't it only partially constitutive of deliberating *correctly*? Perhaps one could deliberate without checking desires for clashes, and in doing so one would be deliberating *poorly*. We had better get straight on this. Just as there may be circumstances in which S has no reason at all to deliberate, there may be circumstances where S has reason to deliberate *somewhat* (e.g., she has only twenty seconds to make up her mind whether to ϕ or ψ), or quite a lot, but not perfectly. There may even be circumstances where S has reason to deliberate very badly (e.g., she has some false beliefs, and deliberating well from those beliefs will lead to disaster; her fully informed and perfectly deliberating counterpart would want her to deliberate badly). As before, there is no circularity in claiming that all these reasons are internal. When S has an internal reason to deliberate *somewhat* in C, then any activity that is constitutive of deliberating somewhat (say, reflecting with moderate but not total attention, making some but not every effort to check for clashes among desires, etc.) is something that she will also have an internal reason for doing in C. Likewise, *mutatis mutandis*, if S has an internal reason to deliberate *correctly* in C.

Whatever S has reason to do – even if it's to deliberate in an mediocre manner – she has so in virtue of the fact that her counterpart, S+, who deliberates *correctly* on the matter (with full information) would want S to act in that way in the circumstances. An exact account of what counts as *correct deliberation* has not been given; Williams provides some thoughts on the matter, but intentionally leaves it open (see the quotes in §3.6). But Hampton seems to have a further complaint: that however this is cashed out, it will, just in virtue of involving a notion of *correctness*, invoke an external reason (pp. 76–8). Her reasoning seems to be this: if a particular brand of deliberation counts as *correct*, then that means it's the deliberation we *ought to* partake of, which implies that we have a *reason* to. Correct deliberation (surely) isn't just whatever we want it to be, therefore we *ought to* deliberate in this way regardless of whether we want to, therefore we have reason to deliberate in this way regardless of whether we want to – which is (roughly) an external reason.

But we have already seen that something must be wrong with this argument, for it is simply *not* the case that we always ought to deliberate correctly. Williams claims that we always have reason to act in accordance with the desires of a counterpart of ourselves – a fully informed and correctly deliberating one – but that is a far cry from claiming that we always have reason to deliberate correctly. Hampton is perfectly correct that "correct deliberation" is a normative notion, implying reasons, but

118

she misdescribes the implication. Correct deliberation is something we always have reason to act in accordance with, not something we always have reason to *do*.

With this clarification, might her challenge nevertheless be pressed? When it is claimed that one always has reason to act in accordance with how a fully informed and correctly deliberating counterpart of oneself would want one to act, might *that* be an external reason? The claim that one always has reason to act in accordance with correct deliberation may be expressed as follows:

$\forall x \forall y$, x has a reason to perform y iff a fully informed and correctly deliberating counterpart of x would want x to perform y

Hampton's challenge amounts to this: "You claim that Jim has a reason to ϕ if a fully informed, correctly deliberating counterpart of him would want him to ϕ – so is that reason internal or external?" We are not asking after Jim's reason for ϕing – for that is an internal reason – rather, we are asking after a *conditional reason*: Jim's reason for ϕing-if-a-fully-informed-and-correctly-deliberating-counterpart-of-him-would-want-him-to-ϕ. And the worry is that this is not an internal reason, for Jim cannot escape it by altering his desires.

It is important to remember that the above biconditional represents, for theorists like Williams and Smith, an attempted analysis, or explication, of the concept of *having a reason*. As such, it is an instance of the general form:

$\forall x \forall y$, x has a reason to y iff Rxy

This biconditional, presumably, is not a matter of personal choice. If it's correct, but Jim doesn't like it, that's tough luck for him: if Jim stands in relation R to some action, then he has a reason to perform that action, whether he likes it or not. But it does not imply that he has a reason to perform an action whether he likes it or not. It means that whether he likes it or not, *if* he stands in a certain relation to that action then he has a reason for performing it.

That something has gone awry with Hampton's challenge can be brought to light by mounting an analogous challenge, where "R" denotes what Hume would have it denote:

$\forall x \forall y$, x has a reason to perform y iff x has a present desire that performing y will satisfy

As before we can ask: "You claim that Jim has a reason to ϕ if he has a present desire that ϕing will satisfy – so is that reason internal or external?" Again, we are not asking after Jim's reason for ϕing, but his reason for ϕing-if-he-has-a-present-desire-that-performing-ϕ-will-satisfy. And again, this conditional reason looks like it may be external, since, if the Humean biconditional were correct, Jim will have the reason regardless of his desires or ends.

It is clear that this kind of challenge can be mounted regardless of what "R" denotes, and so it threatens to make the existence of external reasons trivial. But the fact that one might thus squeeze an external reason even from radical Humean instrumentalism should arouse suspicion. The most important thing that I would highlight about this kind of challenge is that it does not promise to work as a foot-in-the-door strategy to any other external reasons. For a start, it works only with a conditional reason: a reason to ϕ-if-one-stands-in-R-to-ϕing. Moreover, it's not just any antecedent that is being plugged in – it's not like asking "Do we have reason to save a drowning child if one exists?" or "Do we have reason to give money to someone if we have promised to do so?", etc. Rather, "R" denotes the proposed analysans, or explicans, of the very concept of *having a reason*. Thus the case will be *sui generis*: to understand how it works is to understand why it is unique.

In the context of debating a moral error theory, it is not sufficient to locate a single external reason and think that that puts an end to instrumentalism. Of course, it would, strictly speaking, represent a counter-example to premise (4) of the argument presented at the end of the Chapter 3. But that chapter also identified a *contentful* constraint on opposing an error theory (§3.5): in order to defend moral discourse one would have to defend categorical imperatives attaching to such things (roughly) as not stealing for fun, not killing innocent people, keeping promises when breaking them is a moderate inconvenience, etc. (I am being approximate here because there is no need for greater precision.) If the only external reason that can be mustered is the kind of special one discussed above, then there is no cause for optimism that this will lead to external reasons even in the ballpark of proscribing stealing for fun, etc.

Let me sum up and then develop my argument against Hampton. First, her circularity charge is ill-founded, since at no point does one need to define "correct deliberation" with reference to internal reasons. Second, her attempt to find an external reason attaching to the *correctness* of "correct deliberation" at best locates a special case, and there is no reason to think that it creates leverage against the substantive argument for a moral error theory. However, I doubt we even need concede that much. These "conditional reasons" are very shady customers. Take what seems to be a straightforward one mentioned above: one's reason to save a drowning child if one exists. There are two readings:

(i) If there exists a drowning child, then S has a reason to save him/her.
(ii) S has a reason to save a drowning child if one exists.

The absence of a comma after "child" in (ii) makes the difference. (ii) is saying that S has the reason all along: when there are no drowning children, when S is asleep, while S is watching TV, etc. And that, I think, is a counter-intuitive interpretation. It is far more natural to say that in general S has no reason to save any drowning children, but when there exists a child drowning, then (and only then) does S *get* a reason to save him/her. The consequence of disagreeing with this is to lumber all of us with all sorts of bizarre reasons: you, right now as you read this, would have a reason of the following sort: to push the purple "eject" button on the panel in front of you if there is an aggressive alien in your cockpit, if you are a thirty-first-century space pilot defending Earth from the Plutonian invasion, if there were aggressive Plutonians (which there actually aren't), if . . ., etc. But that is not a reason you have now! Surely the correct thing to say is that you have no reason of the sort, but *if* you were to find yourself in that terribly unlikely scenario, *then* you'd have a reason to push the purple eject button.

This observation is entirely generalizable, to the conclusion that there are not really any "conditional reasons." Anything true of the form "S has a reason to ϕ if C obtains" should be read as "If C obtains, then S has a reason to ϕ," *not* "S has a reason to ϕ-if-C-obtains." In the case of the "*sui generis* external reason" found above, it is perfectly possible to argue that it is nothing of the sort. The reason S has to act in accordance with what a fully informed and correctly deliberating counterpart's desires for S, amounts to this: "If S+ wants S to ϕ, then S has a reason to ϕ," but not this: "S has a reason to ϕ-if-S+-wants-S-to-ϕ." So understood, what kind of reason is it that S has to ϕ? An internal one.

If this argument is correct, we can draw an important result. I have argued that "ought" claims imply reasons claims. As well as making claims of the form "You ought to ϕ," we make conditional claims of the form "You ought to ϕ if in C." The latter can be read in two ways: "You ought to ϕ-if-in-C" or "If you are in C, then you ought to ϕ." Call these "type 1" and "type 2" readings. The argument provided above – that there are no conditional reasons claims – forces us to the second reading. The implications of this are significant, allowing us to address a worry that Hampton and others have had concerning the status of the Humean's instrumentalist principle: "If you want X, and ϕing is the best means of achieving X, then you ought to ϕ."[10] Hampton tries to squeeze from this an external reason to which the Humean is committed; one might just as easily try to find in this a categorical imperative to which he is committed. But the argument fails to notice the difference between type 1 and type 2 conditional imperatives. The Humean need not, and should not, accept the following imperative: "You ought to (ϕ if you want X and ϕing is the best means of achieving X)." Rather, the Humean endorses this: "If (you want X and ϕing is the best means of achieving X), then you ought to ϕ." On the second reading, the only thing that is being prescribed is the action of ϕing, and it is being done so hypothetically. So the Humean's allegiance to the instrumentalist principle does not commit him to the very thing he is striving to avoid. Were it otherwise, then creating categorical imperatives would be trivial. One could just say: "You ought to catch the 2.30 train if you want to get to London by 6.00, if you are in Sheffield, England." That would be an imperative that, right now as you read this, binds the people waiting in the check-out line in a small supermarket in Alaska (to say nothing of even stranger imperatives involving spaceships and Plutonians).

The person who thinks that there is a categorical imperative buried in the Humean account needs to provide something (to which the Humean is committed) of the form "You ought to ψ." I have objected that allowing "ψ" to stand for something of the form "ϕ if conditions C obtain" leads to an absurd theory. Instead one might claim that "ψ" stands for ". . . follow this principle: if you want X, and ϕing is the best means of achieving X, then you ought to ϕ." But the Humean can complain that this is just iterating "ought"'s needlessly, and is nothing he need endorse. Consider, for example, someone who asks "Why ought I get on the train?" The Humean thinks that an adequate answer might be "Because you desire to go to London, and getting on the train is the best means of achieving it." But the person continues with a second question: "Why does the mere fact that I desire something give me a reason for performing an action

---

[10] I'm putting this in terms of opposition to Humean instrumentalism, but clearly this dispute might be reframed as one concerning the non-Humean instrumentalism favored in this book.

that will lead to its satisfaction?" Now at this point what the Humean should *not* do is trot out a more general imperative: "Because you ought to follow this principle: if you desire X, and ϕing is the best means of achieving it, then you ought to ϕ." This would be futile, for the mere fact that the person needed to ask the second question shows that she is not going to accept this as an answer. Rather, the Humean thinks that the questioner does not properly understand what the word "reason" means. He needs to provide her with tuition, perhaps beginning by asking her what *she* understands a good reason to be. He might try to show that in even asking the second question the questioner is evincing an allegiance to instrumentalism. I'm not claiming that the Humean is obviously correct, and the two may need to discuss a lot of paradigm cases of people having reasons, and embark on some philosophical discussion. My point concerns what the Humean *doesn't* do: provide another imperative. The question of what kind of normative foundation instrumentalism can receive is a good question (that I have tried to address in earlier chapters), but what is being argued here is that instrumentalism need not be presented as a grand imperative, nor as something that one has a reason to follow. *A fortiori* the instrumentalist principle is not a categorical imperative, nor something that one has an external reason to follow.[11]

5.4 KORSGAARD'S CHALLENGE TO WILLIAMS

As has been noted, Williams leaves the notion of "correct deliberation" rather vague. Several commentators have thought that this imprecision undermines his theory.[12] It is not that it shows that Williams's argument is unsound, but rather shows that in excluding external reasons he has not excluded an important theoretical option. Suppose, for example, that one argued that "correct deliberation" will always involve reasoning to a particular conclusion – say, vegetarianism – regardless of what one's deliberative starting point is. Since Williams allows that "correct deliberation" can involve the elimination of desires in one's initial subjective motivational set, and the creation of new ones, then there is in principle nothing to

---

[11] Cf. James Dreier, "Humean Doubts about the Practical Justification of Morality," in Cullity and Gaut (eds.), *Ethics and Practical Reason*, pp. 81–99.
[12] See Rachel Cohon, "Are External Reasons Impossible?" *Ethics* 96 (1986), pp. 545–56; R. Jay Wallace, "How to Argue about Practical Reason," *Mind* 99 (1990), pp. 376–8; Thomas Scanlon, *What We Owe Each Other* (London: The Belknap Press of Harvard University Press, 1998), appendix.

exclude such a possibility. Williams cannot evade this contingency by re-stricting deliberative activity to an instrumental nature, on pain of begging the question. Thus, anyone you care to name might have an internal rea-son to perform any action you care to think of, so long as you are able to back it up with the appropriate account of deliberation.

An obvious procedure here would be to tighten up the notion of "correct deliberation" in a manner to which all parties will agree, and then see whether relativism or non-relativism of normative reasons fol-lows. However, that strategy would require a lengthy treatment which I am not willing to undertake. (I don't mean to imply that I can foresee how such an argument would run, for it must be admitted that I cannot.) What I will be satisfied with is the establishment of a "burden of proof" case against the non-relativist, accompanied by a criticism of one prominent attempt to discharge that burden.

Establishing the burden of proof is straightforward. There is such a thing as instrumental deliberation: we deliberate about how best to satisfy our desires, and we deliberate about how those desires fit together as a whole. Since it is incontestable that different people have different desires, some-times my deliberations will come to the conclusion that I ought to ϕ in C, whereas your deliberations will conclude that you ought not ϕ in C. This much is platitudinous. It is the person who wants to go beyond this picture (as opposed to developing its details) who has the explaining to do.[13]

The opponent that we are interested in here is the non-relativist: the person who argues that from disparate desiderative starting points, correct deliberation will lead all parties to the same conclusions, at least concerning certain matters. To defeat the moral error theorist, these "certain matters" must involve things like refraining from stealing, from initiating hostility, etc. In order to sharpen the non-relativist's thinking, we can set him a challenge: let him consider Harman's Mafia hit man (of §4.3), and tell us exactly what deliberative defect(s) this imaginary agent is suffering from. This, I think, is a perfectly reasonable task to set. If it cannot be passed, then we cannot say that the hit man has a (non-institutional) reason to refrain, in which case we cannot legitimately say that he ought not refrain, in which case – given that users of moral discourse do, unhesitatingly, condemn the killing of innocents – the moral error theory would be with us. It will not do if we show that the hit man *might* be suffering from

---

[13] For more on the burden of proof, see J. David Velleman, "The Possibility of Practical Reason," *Ethics* 106 (1996), pp. 694–726.

a defect of reasoning (as Thomas Scanlon seems to think[14]); we need to show that in calmly choosing to kill another human being he *must* be manifesting deliberative failure.

We have already seen Smith attempt and fail to pass the test (§4.3). Another contender is Christine Korsgaard, whose argument I will discuss because it appears a prime representative of a type of response.[15] Korsgaard attempts a similar move to Smith, which I previously called "the Kantian leap." The idea, roughly, is that when one makes a reasons claim about oneself, one is, in some sense, legislating for everyone – one is claiming that anyone in the same circumstances would have the same reason. When discussing Smith, my objection was that it is unclear what is being included in "same circumstances." If they include the desires of the agents, then it is trivially true. However, in that case it loses all bite: the mobster is willing to universalize his reasons to kill, the law-abiding citizen is willing to universalize her reasons to refrain from killing, and neither is contradicting the other. On the other hand, if "same circumstances" do not include agents' desires, then the thesis is, I claim, false.

First, for ease of reference, let's baptize our mobster "Al." There are various facts about Al that Korsgaard argues for, which can be granted without comment. As a reflective being, someone who is able take a second-order attitude towards his desires and impulses, Al is a reason-seeking being. He thus cannot but see himself as autonomous, as a "self-legislator." The thing that determines the domain of Al's legislations is the range of conceptions he has of his personal identity.

> The conception of one's identity in question here is not a theoretical one, a view about what as a matter of inescapable scientific fact you are. It is better understood as a description under which you value yourself, a description under which you find your life to be worth living and your actions to be worth undertaking … Practical identity is a complex matter and for the average person there will be a jumble of such conceptions. You are a human being, a woman or a man, an adherent of a certain religion, a member of an ethnic group, a member of a certain profession, someone's lover or friend, and so on. And all of these identities give rise to reasons and obligations. Your reasons express your identity, your nature; your obligations spring from what that identity forbids. (p. 101)

---

[14] Scanlon, *What We Owe Each Other*: "it *may*, in the case of cruelty and insensitivity, involve some other failing or deficiency" (p. 372, my italics), and so long as this, and a couple of other criteria, are satisfied, then "everything really important is in place" (p. 373).

[15] Christine Korsgaard, *The Sources of Normativity* (Cambridge: Cambridge University Press, 1996). All textual references to Korsgaard are to this book.

Since one of Al's central self-conceptions is as a member of "the family," it would appear that he has a reason to kill Ortcutt after all. But Korsgaard points to one self-conception that is *sui generis*, which underlies all others: one's identity as a human. Al *must* value his own humanity, since any other self-conception he has depends upon it.

> Most of the time, our reasons for action spring from our more contingent and local identities. But part of the normative force of those reasons springs from the value we place on ourselves as human beings who need such identities. In this way all value depends on the value of humanity; other forms of practical identity matter in part because humanity requires them. Moral identity and the obligations it carries with it are therefore inescapable and pervasive. Not every form of practical identity is contingent or relative after all: moral identity is necessary. (pp. 121–2)

Let us accept that Al must value his own humanity if he is to value anything at all (putting aside the subtleties of Korsgaard's arguments leading to this point). The crucial question is how we get from this premise to the conclusion that Al's decision that he has no reason to refrain from killing Ortcutt involves him in a deliberative failure. Korsgaard's strategy is to move from Al's valuing his own humanity, to Al's valuing humanity *per se*, to Al's valuing Ortcutt's humanity. Thus in valuing his own humanity but not that of Ortcutt, Al is being inconsistent.

The predictable response, which I endorse, is that even if we allow that in valuing his own humanity, Al, on pain of irrationality, must accept that others value their own humanity as he does, this falls dramatically short of his being rationally required to value their humanity. Korsgaard is perfectly aware of this concern, and develops an argument designed to show that it is based on a false view about reasons. Reasons, she argues, are agent-neutral; they essentially have a shareable, public character.

She argues for this unusual conclusion via an invocation of Wittgenstein's views on a private language. Wittgenstein, recall, invites us to imagine someone who has a kind of "inner sensation," and who gives that sensation a name.[16] His objection is that this act of imagination is incoherent, for the person could not trust his memory in order to know that one occurrence of the sensation is of the "same kind" as an earlier one, and so there is nothing that counts as a correct instance of naming an episode of the sensation, and nothing that counts as incorrect. Nor could we possibly teach such a language to others. Conclusion: we cannot have a language the denotata of which are "private" mental occurrences.

[16] L. Wittgenstein, *Philosophical Investigations*, §258–§275. (Oxford: Basil Blackwell, 1963), pp. 92–6.

It is my contention that this appeal to Wittgenstein is misplaced. Korsgaard, in sliding from talk of "agent-relative reasons" to talk of "private reasons," has blurred an important distinction. "Private," in the context of Wittgenstein's argument, is an issue of communicability: were I to label my own sensations, then I could never teach that language to another, and in this sense it would not be a "language" at all. But a reason may be *relative* to an agent – it may be a reason for her and her alone – without thereby being *incommunicable*. In this respect the shift to the language of "privacy" and "publicity" is deceptive, for it allows one to trade on an ambiguity. We speak, for example, of "private property," usually meaning land that is owned by a person and to which others have no rights of access. But we may also speak of a piece of property as "private" in the sense that it is unavailable to scrutiny – being surrounded by a tall hedge or wall. Clearly, a piece of property may be private in either sense without being private in the other. Agent-relative reasons are like private property in the first sense: they belong to a person, they bear a relation to him that they do not bear to others. But it doesn't follow that in considering such a reason, the agent (as Korsgaard puts it) "backs into the privacy of his practical consciousness, reviews his own reasons, comes up with a decision, and then re-emerges to announce the result" (p. 141). The fact that a reason is relative to an agent doesn't put it behind a tall hedge. I can say to you: "This slice of pie is mine and not yours" and you will understand perfectly well what I have said. I can say to you: "I have a reason to climb Mt. Blanc but you do not" and you will understand perfectly well what I have said. In this sense – the sense of communicability and understandability – agent-relative reasons are public and shareable.

That this is obvious suggests that Korsgaard intends something else by appealing to Wittgenstein's argument. Perhaps the point she wants to high-light does not concern the incommunicability of a private language, but the normativity of language. Part of Wittgenstein's concern is that if I try to baptize a type of sensation with the word "red" (say) by "ostension" to a token, then I would have no criterion of correctness for using the word in application to other tokens, in which case I would not be intro-ducing a piece of language at all. Korsgaard seems to sum up this point as follows: "to say that X means Y is to say that one ought to take X for Y; and this requires two, a legislator to lay it down that one must take X for Y, and a citizen to obey" (p. 137). I am doubtful that this relation between "legislator and citizen" is something Wittgenstein was aiming to express. The "normativity" of language requires public denotata because

127

only then does it make sense to speak of our being able to test whether we are applying the word correctly; it is not (in any obvious way) because only then can we demand the linguistic obedience of others.

It is, besides, unclear why, and in what sense, normativity "requires two." It turns out that one of the two need be only counterfactually present: Korsgaard allows that a person may have a *personal* language (Robinson Crusoe, say, baptizing features of his island), but claims that the strength of the argument is that this personal language must be in principle communicable to somebody else (p. 138). Parallel reasoning is supposed to show that "it takes two to make a reason" (p. 138), presumably with the same qualification: Robinson Crusoe may have reasons for going hunting in the morning, so long as those reasons are in principle communicable to others. So it seems that the argument has something to do with communicability after all, in which case my above objection holds: an agent-relative reason may be perfectly understandable by others. Perhaps instead what Korsgaard will insist on is that Crusoe's reasons must be in principle *justifiable* to others.[17] But we can now draw attention to the presence of the "in principle." Just as the mere fact that I cannot communicate with a certain person does not show that my language is "incommunicable" – for perhaps the person with whom I am trying to converse speaks only Swahili – so, too, the mere fact that I cannot get a person to understand, appreciate or endorse my reasons for acting in a certain manner (in other words, I am unable to justify myself to her) does not show that those reasons cannot be justified to others. Perhaps it just requires that I find an audience with similar eccentric tastes.

Let's get back to Al and the unfortunate Ortcutt. Imagine Ortcutt realizing that Al has arrived to carry out the contract (the gun pointed at his head gave it away), and an opportunity for discussion, for exchange of reasons, arises. It is easy to imagine that Ortcutt will appeal as follows: "How would you like it if someone did this to you?" We are invited to think that in saying this Ortcutt is drawing attention to an agent-neutral reason against killing. Al is supposed to see that if someone were pointing a gun at *his* head, he would accept that she would have a reason to refrain from killing him (that she would have an obligation not to), and

---

[17] I owe this thought to "Korsgaard on Reasons" by Mark LeBar, who was kind enough to allow me to read an early draft. My discussion on Korsgaard is also much indebted to James Skidmore, who likewise permitted me to read his paper "Skepticism about Practical Reason: Transcendental Arguments and their Limits." Both papers were presented at the 1999 APA Eastern Division Meeting.

this (Ortcutt hopes) will lead Al to see that there is a reason to refrain from killing Ortcutt. Thus, in making his appeal, Ortcutt attempts to force Al to acknowledge the value of his (Ortcutt's) humanity, and obligates him to act in a way that respects it.[18]

This is wholly unconvincing as an account of what Ortcutt's appeal amounts to. Is it even true that Al, if faced with his own would-be assassin, would think that there is a *reason* for the killer to refrain? Certainly he would desperately wish that the killer would not carry out her assignment, and he may accept that *he* has a reason to try to prevent her, but I doubt that he would represent that wish, even to himself, in terms of an obligation and a reason that *she* has. By the same token, I do not think that Ortcutt need consider Al to have a *reason* to refrain from killing him. He may understand perfectly well that Al will make money from carrying out the contract, that he will suffer reprimand from "the family" if he does not, and so there is nothing odd in the idea that Ortcutt well-understands that Al has a very good reason to kill him, and no particular reason to refrain. But that, of course, doesn't mean that Ortcutt has to *like* it, nor that he cannot reason with his killer.

Gilbert Harman tells another imaginary story of intelligent aliens landing on Earth, who commence calmly slaughtering humans.[19] Suppose their motivation is that human brains are a great gastronomic delicacy. Would we, if thus beset, have any trouble in admitting that the aliens have a *reason* to kill us? Certainly they have a reason – it's because our brains make a good *hors d'oeuvre*. Their reason is communicable and intelligible, even though it is a reason only for them, and not for us. (And even if *we* could not understand their having this reason, it would not follow that their reason is "in principle unintelligible to anybody else.") It might be claimed that even if we admit that they have a reason to kill us, we will also hold that they have an additional and overriding reason to refrain from killing us. But where would that additional reason come from? One might say that if we value our lives, then we could articulate this in terms of "there being a reason that we not be killed." But ascribing reasons to states of affairs (as opposed to the actions that may bring them about) is sensible only within limits. If I think that something is the product of design, I might say that there is a reason for the existence of some feature of it ("There must be a reason for this lever's being here"); or I may advert to causal

---

[18] Here I am almost quoting Korsgaard, *The Sources of Normality*, p. 143.
[19] Harman, "Moral Relativism Defended," p. 5.

antecedents via reason talk ("There must be a reason for all these fallen trees"). However, we would be doing neither of these things if we said, as a way of expressing our distress at the prospect of losing our lives, "There is a reason that we not be killed." That this is even something which we would say in such circumstances just doesn't ring true. We might well say "Given that we value our lives so greatly, there is a reason for us to do all in our power to resist being killed," but this is very different from thinking that the aliens have an overriding reason to refrain. When something we care about is under threat from another agent, it is simply false that we will naturally express our anxiety by claiming that the other has a reason to forbear.[20]

A capacity to extinguish empathetic sentiments is, one presumes, part of an assassin's expertise. If the first rule that novices are taught at Assassin School is "Shoot first, ask questions later" it is not merely because doing so precludes the possibility of getting shot yourself – it is because engaging in conversation threatens the suspension of natural empathy, making it harder to shoot at all. If Ortcutt can get Al talking to him about anything – football, books, Italian food – then he will be improving his own chances of survival, for in doing so he will be forcing Al to see him as a human, with projects and values. However, what is important to understand is that Ortcutt's attempt to "humanize" himself in Al's eyes is an attempt to engage his capacity for *empathy*, not to get him to acknowledge a reason. The plea "How would you like it if someone did this to you?" serves the same function as talking about football: in either case the subtext is "I am a person with a life just as you are," the intention of which is to arouse Al's natural social nature, to stir in him a desire not to execute his plan. In this respect, the plea is an attempt to *create* a reason for Al to refrain from killing, not force him to recognize one that already exists.

If Al is an effective assassin, then Ortcutt's entreaties will not work (indeed, the conversation would not be taking place). But this is not to say

---

[20] In all this discussion I am purposely leaving moral discourse out of the picture. If we are adherents of the institution of morality, and we think that the aliens are obligated to refrain from slaughtering us, then we may well express this by asserting: "They have a reason not to kill us." But, as we saw in Chapter 2, this is a kind of reasons claim that the aliens may legitimately ignore. Moreover, what is under investigation here is whether a potential wrong-doer, like Al, could, through deliberation, come to see that he has reasons for not killing people, via imaginative acquaintance with scenarios in which he would recognize that others have reasons not to kill him. To show that someone *who endorses morality* would recognize that others have reasons not to kill her – and, thereby, come to recognize that she has reasons not to kill others – is hardly a remarkable conclusion. We are interested in the agent who doesn't give a fig for morality.

that Al has no empathetic sentiments at all – it is merely that he deploys them selectively. For this reason I do not think, as Korsgaard does, that the issue here is one of *egoism*. Al need not be an egoist. For all that we have said, his motivation for killing Ortcutt may be an altruistic one: the bank manager's death is the wish of the family patriarch, the desires of whom it is Al's heartfelt ambition to serve. This is an important point to note, because in seeing the threat to be combated as simply being that of the egoist, the defender of morality may, as I believe Korsgaard does, employ an argument that misses the target. Perhaps Korsgaard is correct that reasons must be public in some sense – they must be communicable, shareable, intelligible, justifiable. The reasons of the *egoist* can be presented as internal, private, essentially individualistic things which have none of the mentioned characteristics. But as soon as we realize that the immoral agent need not be an egoist, that he may be a member of a sub-group or sub-culture which stands against moral values, then we must concede that his reasons are communicable, shareable and justifiable *to some*. Korsgaard may respond that she didn't intend communicability etc. to be limited in this way – that by "shareable" she means "shareable by *all*." But, first, this cuts both ways. Are the reasons of a morally upstanding citizen shareable by all? Perhaps Al and his "family" think that ordinary law-abiders are naive fools. Second, the move from "shareable" to "shareable by all" will require a new argument. Wittgenstein argues that words do not denote private sensations which cannot be shown to others; but it does not follow that words must denote items that can be shown to *everyone*.

We do not need to speculate in order to know what Korsgaard may say in response to the challenge of Harman's hit man, for G. A. Cohen presents her with much the same example in reply to her lectures (pp. 183–8). She responds that Al (I'll still call him that, though obviously Cohen and Korsgaard don't) has conflicting obligations – those that spring from his place in the "family," and those that arise from his being a reflective human – and the latter trump because his "obligation to be a good person is . . . *deeper* than his obligation to stick to his code" (p. 258). The metaphor of "depth" appears to be a counterfactual matter. Being a "family-member" is something that Al could shed, whereas being a human is inescapable. There are two comments I wish to make about this. First, arguments have already been provided to undermine the claim that Al's reasons which find their source in his own humanity require him to value the humanity of others. In other words, there are no grounds for assuming that the assassin's obligations *are* in conflict. Second, even if they were in conflict, it is

131

unclear why the counterfactual asymmetry between Al's "identities" requires that the more counterfactually robust one yields the overriding reasons. The answer, presumably, has something to do with the idea that if Al were to violate the humanity derived reasons, he would be more dramatically undermining himself. To violate "the conceptions of ourselves that are most important to us ... is to lose your integrity, and so your identity, ... it is to no longer be able to think of yourself under the description under which you value yourself and find your life to be worth living ... It is to be for all practical purposes dead or worse than dead" (p. 102). How much of this is rhetorical relish it is hard to say until we know what it is to "violate one's identity as a human." If it is to give up on being an animal that sets itself ends, that reflects on how to achieve those ends, then "for all practical purposes worse for dead" is a reasonable description. But this just brings us back to the first point: in what way does Al give up on himself as a human in *that* sense when he chooses to act on "family" values? There are, sadly, people like Al in the world, and there is no particular reason to assume that their lives are afflicted with such dramatic disorders as living "at random, without integrity or principle" (p. 121), much less that they are mere vegetables, unable to set themselves practical ends and act upon them. We should allow that such people may be happy, may have loving relations with friends and family, and may gain satisfaction in their projects. If they are, in the course of such lives, violating their identities as humans, then we must ask why the reasons that have their source in human identity take precedence over those that spring from other contingent identities. And if, in the course of such lives, they are *not* violating their identities as humans, then Korsgaard's whole enterprise of showing that we have reason to behave morally, that correct deliberation will lead us to see this, has failed.

Let me tie this examination of Korsgaard back into the discussion of Williams and the broader strategy. Williams thinks that what reasons a person has for acting will depend on what desires she actually has. It has been objected that whether Williams is entitled to this conclusion depends on what conception of "correct deliberation" is favored. Rather than attempt to establish a theory of deliberative correctness, I have thrown down a challenge: consider someone who is, by any moral standards, a wrongdoer, and show us where his deliberations fail. Korsgaard takes up the challenge by attempting to establish the agent-neutrality of reasons: the interests of the victim obligate the wrongdoer, they provide him with reasons for respectful behavior, regardless of the desires that he may have brought to the deliberative process; and if the criminal were to deliberate correctly on the matter, he would see himself as so obligated. I have objected that even if Korsgaard's arguments show that reasons must be shareable, communicable and justifiable, this falls well short of their being non-relative. More to the point, it falls short of showing that motivations to act in accordance with morality will be created through correct deliberation regardless of the desires that one brings to the process.

My argument has not shown that it *must* be true that one's actual desires determine the limits of where correct deliberation can take one. It merely deflects an attempt to show that they do not. So the challenge stands – and (who knows?) perhaps it may yet be met. I do not take the strength of my arguments in this book to *demonstrate* that a moral error theory is true, merely to show that the weight of evidence leans in that direction to a sufficient extent that it is reasonable to believe that it is true. In the same way, I do not consider that at this stage relativism about practical reasons has been demonstrated, but enough has been said, I believe, for confidence that the burden of proof lies with the non-relativist to show us that the natural belief in relativism is mistaken. I do not think that this burden has yet been discharged.

5.5 SUMMARY

Let me remind readers that my apparent defense of Williams in this chapter must be importantly qualified. I have argued as if supporting his contention that the only true reason claims concern internal reasons. But I would not in fact go so far as to say bluntly that any use of an external reason is false. We must recall the discussion of institutional reasons from Chapter 2: reason claims that are legitimated by the rules of an institution, and which may well be external in nature. My objection is only with external reason claims that do not know their place – that overstep themselves by claiming to transcend all institutions. Such, I have argued, are moral reasons. Williams's constraint on reason claims – that a reason must be a potential motivator – is best construed as a necessary condition of *normative* reasons. I have discussed Williams's argument because it promises to act as a "knock-out" argument against any non-instrumental account of practical rationality. And with non-instrumental practical rationality out of the picture, we can see clearly that an appeal to practical rationality is not going act as the savior of moral inescapability. Moral rationalism is sunk.

I consider the argument for a moral error theory now to be complete. In short, when we say that a person *morally* ought to act in a certain manner, we imply something about what she would have reason to do regardless of her desires and interests, regardless of whether she cares about her victim, and regardless of whether she can be sure of avoiding any penalties. And yet after careful investigation we have found no defensible grounds for thinking that such reasons exist. Few people in the actual world may be so heartless or so impregnable to recrimination, but that is beside the point. Moral judgments are untrue not just because they sometimes ascribe reasons for (say) honesty to people who have no such reasons. They are untrue even when they ascribe reasons for honesty to people who *do* have reasons for being honest, in that they imply that those reasons would remain in place across counterfactual situations when in fact they would not. The distinctive authoritativeness which characterizes our moral discourse turns out to be well-entrenched bluff.

But the question remains: why do we employ these mysterious imperatives? Perhaps the whole point of morally condemning somebody is to do so with a particular inescapable force, but what is the point of wanting to do *that*? What has led us systematically to commit this error?

6

Morality and evolution

6.0 THE EVOLUTION OF MORALITY: HELPING KIN

A proponent of an error theory – especially when the error is being attributed to a common, familiar way of talking – owes us an account of why we have been led to commit such a fundamental, systematic mistake. In the case of morality, I believe, the answer is simple: natural selection. We have evolved to categorize aspects of the world using moral concepts. Natural selection has provided us with a tendency to invest the world with values that it does not contain, demands which it does not make.

This is an empirical hypothesis and should be tested as such. In the context of the present work, however, it must be left with the status of "plausible speculation" backed up with some references to other studies. I do not pretend to argue here the case in detail, but am content to outline the content of the hypothesis.

Most parties agree that the origins of morality lie in the development of human cooperation. Few will object to the view that the human tendency to help each other in certain circumstances is a trait that has been naturally selected for.[1] In the past few decades we have gained a clear picture of how helping traits can be favored by forces of natural selection – something which, perhaps, seems initially puzzling. The first step is helping behavior among family members. Why should an individual provide aid even for his or her offspring? The answer is that offspring contain 50 per cent of an individual's genetic material, and therefore (among certain kinds of creatures) those who look out for their young will enjoy an increased probability of having offspring in subsequent generations over those who

---

[1] See, for example, M. Ruse, *Taking Darwin Seriously* (Oxford: Basil Blackwell, 1986); R. Axelrod, *The Evolution of Cooperation* (New York: Basic Books, 1984); R. Alexander, *The Biology of Moral Systems* (New York: Aldine de Gruyter, 1987); R. Wright, *The Moral Animal* (New York: Pantheon Books, 1994); J. Q. Wilson, *The Moral Sense* (New York: The Free Press, 1993); E. Sober and D. Wilson (eds.), *Unto Others: The Evolution and Psychology of Unselfish Behavior* (Cambridge, Mass.: Harvard University Press, 1998).

do not. This will go for helping tendencies towards siblings as well, and, to a lesser extent, cousins, nephews and nieces, etc. (bearing in mind that several nieces/nephews are worth more, genetically speaking, than a daughter or son). I use the word "help" rather than "cooperation," since none of this implies that the help need be paid back in any manner.[2]

All that is required for this selection to occur are certain helping *behaviors*, but we need to ask how the appropriate behaviors will most efficiently be regulated at the psychological level. The whole thing *could* have been governed by a kind of "gene selfishness" – where the individual thinks something like: "Well, I really want my genes to do well in subsequent generations, and helping out my cousin is conducive to that end" – but how would evolution provide us with knowledge of genes and our genetic relations to others? (It is worth noting in passing that anyone who thinks that from the thesis that helping is an evolved trait it follows that all human actions are, at bottom, selfish, is committed to exactly the preceding absurd view.) A more serious answer is that we would be granted by evolution a general *desire* to look after the interests of our family members. Of course, the *de dicto* content of that desire need not specify "family members"; rather, having an individual play a certain role in one's life – such as being very familiar during childhood, or having emerged dramatically from one's own body – will prompt one to form a desire to look out for *him* or *her*. Thus, it is hypothesized, not only are we naturally helpful towards family members, but we are naturally *sympathetic* towards them (where "sympathy" denotes a motivating feeling). The evidence that such a sense of sympathy is a natural human trait is compelling, yet I question whether it can be the whole of the matter.

The problem with desires is that they are unreliable things. After a hard day's hunting and gathering, one may be so weary as to have one's desire to look after the children enervated or quite dissipated. The long-term satisfactions of child-rearing may be under-appreciated due to phenomena like distraction, weakness of will, or simple exhaustion. The desire is likewise under threat if one's nephew, say, has accidentally broken one's favorite spear, thus provoking intense annoyance. Desires can be overridden by stronger, contrary desires, and desires for intense, immediate gratification can be temporarily re-evaluated to the detriment of satisfying longer-term, calmer desires. One might think, then, that natural selection

---

[2] The classic statement of the mechanism of "inclusive fitness" comes from W. D. Hamilton, "The Genetic Evolution of Social Behavior," *Journal of Theoretical Biology* 7 (1964), pp. 1–52.

should have simply rendered desires more stalwart and reliable, but it is the very flexibility and adaptability of desires in many areas of life that is their great virtue. Because of these kinds of limitations of desire, an individual does better (in the sense of being more reproductively fit) if she has her desires in favor of family members supplemented by a sense of *requirement* to favor family members. It is not merely that an individual *wants* to help out his sister's son, but he feels that he *ought* to – he feels that he *must*. An individual with a sense of requirement – attached, that is, to the appropriate actions – is more reproductively fit than one in whom such a sense is lacking, whose cooperative activities depend upon the presence of the right desires. In pressing this point I am in agreement with the position argued for by Michael Ruse.[3] Ruse and I also agree regarding the thesis that the fact that moral thinking is a naturally evolved trait has error theoretical implications (of which, more later).

Such a sense of requirement, supplementing sympathy, could only develop in a species that already has the cognitive wherewithal to think in such terms, but in the case of ancestral humans there is every reason to think that such cognitive capacities were in place a million years ago (merely to choose a conservative round number). The point was made by Darwin:

Any animal whatever, endowed with well-marked social instincts, the parental and filial affections being here included, would inevitably acquire a moral sense or conscience, as soon as its intellectual powers had become as well developed, or nearly as well developed, as in man.[4]

The emphasis on the development of a *conscience* is key here. If my helpful behavior towards my family is regulated solely by a strong sense of sympathy towards them, then failing to act accordingly would merely be an instance of my failing to act so as best to satisfy a desire, and the feeling that such a failure produces should be described perhaps as "regret," but certainly not "guilt."[5] Guilt is the negative feeling an agent has when she believes that she has acted in a way she ought not have, and it is a necessary and important element of any system of values deserving the

---

[3] See Ruse, *Taking Darwin Seriously*. See also his "Evolutionary Ethics: A Phoenix Risen," *Zygon* 21 (1986), pp. 95–112.
[4] Charles Darwin, *The Descent of Man* [1871] (Princeton: Princeton University Press, 1981), pp. 71–2.
[5] The same point goes for the opposite of guilt, which is possibly most accurately described as "self-praise": merely satisfying a desire does not prompt "self-praise," whereas doing something that I feel I *ought* to have done does.

name "moral." I find it odd, therefore, that so many recent studies that purport to explain "the origins of morality" in evolutionary terms rest content if they manage to explain the origins of sympathy. A creature with a sense of sympathy, no matter how strong it may be, does not thereby have anything recognizable as "a moral sense." We need only think of what emotions such a creature would experience if, for some reason, it let a companion down: the regret of having failed to satisfy a desire. Regret over unsatisfied desires can certainly be powerful and motivating – my complaint is that it's not the *sort* of feeling that we associate with morality. We do not think of the moral wrongness of, say, killing innocents, in terms of "I would just hate to do that"; rather, we think "I *mustn't* do that." A group that merely disliked killing, and had no desire to do so, would not thereby have a moral system. Moreover, if all there were in the picture was sympathy, then there would be no sense to be made of our applying moral injunctions to others, including those who are lacking in the appropriate sentiments of sympathy. We do not think of a human murderer in the way we think of a killer shark: we do not simply *dislike* what the former does – we judge that the murderer does something that he *ought not* to do, and we do so regardless of whether he lacks that sentiment of sympathy.

For evidence that we have naturally developed not only a sense of fellow-feeling, but the capacity to feel guilt (and therefore something that deserves the name "a moral sense"), we can turn to empirical observations of non-human primates.[6] Among such primates there is evidence of the capacity to feel guilt – or, at least, a "proto" form of that capacity – thus giving credibility to Darwin's claim that the faculty of conscience is an evolved trait. Unlike, say, canines, whose familiar tail-between-the-legs groveling after having chewed up the newspaper might be described as "guilt," but is just as likely to be punishment-avoiding appeasement, monkeys and apes manifest symptoms of guilty consciences that cannot be easily explained by other hypotheses.

Christopher Coe and Leonard Rosenblum conducted experiments on the behavior of subordinate male macaque monkeys, focusing on their submissive behaviors towards the dominant alpha male. Usually the sexual activity of subordinate males is impeded by the presence of dominant males, and they remain no less deterred when the alpha male is physically separated but able to watch through plexiglass, despite their being free to

---

[6] For the information in this and the following paragraph I am indebted to Frans de Waal's *Good Natured: The Origins of Right and Wrong in Humans and Other Animals* (London: Harvard University Press, 1996).

engage in sexual activity with the females without risk of attack. However, when the alpha male is removed from the scene entirely, then episodes of sexual contact between the lower-ranking males and females increase dramatically. What is most interesting is the behavior of the subordinate males when the alpha male is reunited with the group. Their submissive behaviors towards him are far more frequent when they have been enjoying sexual freedom than when they have not been. Coe and Rosenblum conclude that this provides evidence "that animals can incorporate behavioral rules which are associated with their social role and can respond in a manner that acknowledges a perceived violation of the social code."[7] Frans de Waal, reporting Coe and Rosenblum's study, claims that chimpanzees would not act in this manner, for such unprompted sycophantic behavior would immediately arouse an alpha male chimp's suspicions. We can turn instead to observations made by Toshisada Nishida of chimpanzees in the wild. He reports a dominant male's "sneak attack" upon a subordinate – one which overstepped the usual rules of hierarchical combat. This attack provoked an immediate and sustained violent reaction in the subordinate, from which the dominant male did not defend himself nearly as much as one would predict. Nishida describes the younger male as "confident that, because he was on the side of justice, there would be no retaliation," while the older male's reluctance to return aggression is put down to his "guilt" at having transgressed the social code.[8] These are just two instances, granted, but it is not my intention here to establish the empirical hypothesis firmly, merely to point to the kind of evidence that is available.

If it is true that we have an innate sense of "requirement," why need it have anything to do with mysterious categorical imperatives? I will return to this question later, but we already have said enough to give a rough answer. The alternative is that the individual thinks of helping actions as *hypothetically* required: required in order to bring about some

---

[7] C. Coe and L. Rosenblum, "Male Dominance in the Bonnet Macaque: A Malleable Relationship," in Patricia Barchas and Sally Mendoza (eds.), *Social Cohesion* (Westport, Conn.: Greenwood, 1984), p. 51.

[8] T. Nishida, "Review of Recent Findings on Mahale Chimpanzees," in R. W. Wrangham, W. C. McGrew, F. de Waal and P. G. Heltne (eds.), *Chimpanzee Cultures* (Cambridge, Mass.: Harvard University Press, 1994), p. 390. Nishida is Director of the Mahale Mountains Chimpanzee Research Project, in Tanzania. For a discussion of chimpanzees' cognitive and emotional abilities – covering such things as role-taking, attributing responsibility/intentions to others, deception, and their concept of self – see D. J. Povinelli and L. R. Godfrey, "The Chimpanzee Mind: How Noble in Reason? How Absent in Ethics?" in M. H. Nitecki and D. V. Nitecki, *Evolutionary Ethics* (Albany: State University of New York Press, 1993), pp. 277–324, as well as many papers in Wrangham *et al.*

end. What would that end be? Obviously not any conscious awareness of genetic survival. A desire for the good of the family member, then? But I have already objected that helping dependent on the presence of sympathetic desires may lose out in the evolutionary struggle to helping that is governed by something stronger. Feelings of "inescapable requirement" will, in certain circumstances, serve reproductive fitness more effectively than clear-headed calculations concerning desire-satisfaction, because they will enforce cooperative behavior, at the motivational level, more resolutely.

In saying this I am not claiming that a belief in a categorical requirement *alone* can provide motivation, for that would be to retract the Humean view of motivation that was argued for in §5.1. John Stuart Mill commented that there is "a disposition to believe that a person who sees in moral obligation a transcendental fact, an objective reality belonging to the province of 'Things in themselves,' is likely to be more obedient to it than one who believes it to be entirely subjective, having its seat in the human consciousness only."[9] Mill goes on to disagree with this supposition, claiming that whether we think of the sanction of morality as internal or external (these being Mill's terms), a person's obedience to the moral law depends upon her "subjective feeling." There's a sense in which Mill is quite correct: mere awareness of the authoritative basis of a moral claim will not suffice to carry motivation with it. Even if the Kantian program were entirely successful, and wrongdoers could be accused of irrationality, this will hardly stay the hand of the criminal who couldn't give a fig for practical consistency. What determines whether morality makes any difference to us is the attitude we take towards it, not its ontology. But Mill fails to recognize that the attitude we ultimately take towards morality can be influenced by how "external or internal" we conceive morality's authority to be. Whether I obey a person's orders depends on whether I want to, of course – but if I believe that person to have legitimate authority over me then it is far more likely that the desire to comply will be prompted. Similarly, if I believe that a kind of action *must* be done, then the entertainment of other courses of action may be excluded from my deliberations, affecting my motivations.[10] This is the distinctive behavior-modifying value of moral concepts: they are imbued with maximal authority. They are nature's optimal means of getting intelligent social beings to act together.

[9] J. S. Mill, *Utilitarianism* [1863], chapter 3 (Cambridge: Hackett Publishing Company, 1979), p. 28.
[10] See Williams, "Practical Necessity," in *Moral Luck*.

Some might think that it's just bizarre to credit prehistoric humans with the use of categorical imperatives, but I do not think so at all.[11] The term "categorical imperative" may have been introduced by Kant with all his characteristic philosophical intricacy, but it captures a quite simple mental (and, derivatively, linguistic) phenomenon. If a person thinks, concerning, say, the help of her child, "I just have to," and if, when pressed for a reason why she has to, is disposed not to provide an answer but simply reiterate "Well, I just *have* to" (or something amounting to that), then she is wielding a categorical imperative. (Of course, the categorical imperative may lie a little deeper: she may have answered "Because she's my child," but when pressed on why she should help her child she might have revealed "Because one just should.") Clearly, this kind of question-and-answer routine is somewhat artificial. What it's designed to capture is a kind of "feeling" which the agent may not even be able to articulate: the vague sense that there are certain rules of conduct that have intrinsic authority, that mustn't be questioned, that are there in the nature of things.

6.1 THE EVOLUTION OF MORALITY: RECIPROCAL HELPING

Once there is in place a cognitive faculty for thinking of family helping as required, it may be exploited by natural selection for other useful ends.[12] One obvious such end will be helpful behavior towards non-kin individuals on the expectation that they will reciprocate.[13] This is useful because a group of cooperating individuals can often attain desirable ends that small kin-groups cannot.

---

[11] Nor did Freud, who wrote: "It may begin to dawn on us that the taboos of the savage Polynesians are after all not so remote from us as we were inclined to think at first, that the moral and conventional prohibitions by which we ourselves are governed may have some essential relationship with these primitive taboos and that an explanation of taboo might throw a light upon the obscure origin of our own 'categorical imperative'" – *Totem and Taboo*, p. 22. (I am assuming, without argument, that Freud would be willing to countenance a connection between what he calls "savage Polynesians" and humans in a prehistoric state.)

[12] For a detailed account of how natural selection could create a moral primate through "re-wiring" the mammalian brain, using for raw material the structures already in place to regulate parent–offspring exchanges, see J. Turner, "The Evolution of Morality," *Critical Review* 11 (1997), pp. 211–32.

[13] See R. L. Trivers, "The Evolution of Reciprocal Altruism," *Quarterly Review of Biology* 46 (1971), pp. 35–57; Axelrod, *Evolution of Cooperation*; L. Cosmides and J. Tooby, "Cognitive Adaptations for Social Exchange," in J. H. Barklow, L. Cosmides and J. Tooby (eds.), *The Adapted Mind* (Oxford: Oxford University Press, 1992), pp. 163–228.

Helpful behavior towards non-kin is, on the face of it, vulnerable to exploitation from the character who accepts help but does not give it, therefore if a trait for reciprocal help is selected for at all it is likely that accompanying it will be a particular sensitivity to "exploiters": a trait which spots them, remembers them, and is hostile towards them. An exploiter among a group of unthinking helpers may do well, but an exploiter among a group of helpers *who have sensitivity and hostility towards exploiters* will do badly, and be selected against. This is another place where we can see that the tendency to feel that certain cooperative activities are *required*, as opposed to the individual merely desiring to perform them, is the better trait to have. An individual who thinks that cooperating in certain circumstances is required will see others as bound by that requirement too, and thus will see another who does not cooperate in those circumstances as being deserving of criticism and punishment.

Observations and experiments from primatology again provide numerous examples of "moralistic aggression" towards cheaters when they are caught out. De Waal tells of a female chimpanzee named "Puist" who had supported the male Luit in his struggles with another male, Nikkie. When Nikkie later acted aggressively towards Puist, she held out her hand to Luit, indicating a plea for support. "Luit, however, did nothing to protect her against Nikkie's attack. Immediately Puist turned on Luit, barking furiously, chased him across the enclosure and even hit him."[14] Often defection brings retaliatory punishment not merely from the faulted individual, but from the whole group.[15]

A single exploiter does badly in a group of helpers who are hostile to exploiters, and, conversely, a single helper in a group of exploiters will also do badly. This latter observation has led some people to worry about how cooperation could get started in the first place, requiring, as it appears to, some individual to stick his neck out, while there is no evolutionary explanation for why others should not promptly chop it off.[16] But this is not really a problem, so long as we allow that kin-help will already be firmly in place. Thus reciprocal helping can get started within groups that are already cooperating to a large extent. Suppose, for example, that within a population is the trait to help out cousins in certain circumstances,

---

[14] Frans de Waal, *Chimpanzee Politics* (Baltimore: Johns Hopkins University Press, 1982), p. 207.

[15] See, for example, de Waal, *Good Natured*, pp. 91–2, 158; and *Chimpanzee Politics*, p. 56.

[16] See, for example, A. Rosenberg, "The Biological Justification of Ethics: A Best-Case Scenario," *Social Philosophy and Policy* 8 (1991), p. 98.

though not as much as one would help out a sibling – let's say one helps a sibling "a lot" and helps a cousin "moderately." Reciprocal helping may begin by an individual helping out his cousin a little more than moderately. This is not for the individual to open himself up to wholesale exploitation, since the cousin is already disposed to refrain from doing so. Thus kin-helping can lead to more generalized cooperation within a small inter-related population through gradual steps, and once it has done so, the group does even better than before, participating in various activities that more fully exploit the environment.

When the trait of reciprocal help has developed in the small population, that group does much better than the group of mutual exploiters in the neighboring valley (by "mutual exploiter" here I mean someone who has developed a helping tendency only towards his or her kin, and who, from non-kin, might accept help but will not repay it). If there's a bad year, the neighboring exploiters may go extinct (or almost so), leaving space for the reciprocal helpers to expand. But supposing there is not a "bad year," what happens when mutual helpers encounter mutual exploiters? First, note that the mutual helpers, considered collectively, are doing better than the mutual exploiters, and it follows that a given area of land will support more cooperators than it would exploiters. Consider the tract of land bisected by the "border" between the two populations. The area of land on the helper's side of the border will contain more helpers than the equally sized, equally resourced portion of land on the exploiter's side contains exploiters. Thus if the two populations geographically merge, there will be thrown into the mix more helpers than exploiters. And so long as a certain ratio of helpers to exploiters is maintained, one is better off being a helper. The more helpers there are in the population (helpers, that is, with the trait of sensitivity towards exploiters) the more disastrous it will be to be an exploiter. In these ways reciprocal help, once it is firmly established in a small population, is likely to spread throughout a larger population.

Again we can ask "But why should categorical imperatives be involved?" – after all, with reciprocal help there is a pretty clear end that the helper may have in mind: the expected pay-back. Why can't non-kin reciprocal help be regulated by means/end reasoning with self-gain as the motivating factor? The answer is that it *could* be regulated in such a way, but it may be regulated *better* in another way. Picture a group of humans hunting. Consider an individual among them, Stig. What kind of companions will Stig want at his side? His choice is between (1) companions who care about him, (2) companions who have a feeling of requirement to help him, and (3) companions who help him because they see that he will probably repay them (or that they will at least be "repaid," even if not by Stig). Comrades of the third sort are the *least* desirable, for their cooperation is based on a calculation that things are working to their benefit, and as soon as circumstances change (a saber-toothed tiger appears on the scene, for example), they will decide that their self-interest is best served by abandoning Stig and running. Moreover, if Stig is hunting with a single partner, then an egoistic calculator is risky: at any moment the "companion" might decide that owning Stig's club and bear-skin cape is worth more than any future service Stig might do him. This allows us to make a further important point: that the trait of being sensitive and hostile towards "exploiters" is likely to extend as far as a sensitivity to others' motivations. A "calculating helper" is always a potential exploiter, and should be identified, remembered, and at the very least be treated carefully. What one wants in one's companions is not just helpful behavior, but helpful behavior that has the appropriate *motivation*. In other words, one wants *altruistic* companions.[17]

A lovely example to back this up empirically is the human tendency to blush. Blushing is a public signal that something is amiss with the external front being advertised. Someone who blushes when he says that you can trust him shouldn't be believed. By the same token, someone who has been observed to blush over a trivial matter (thus signaling a sensitivity to guilt), but who does not blush when indicating allegiance over something more important, has shown trustworthiness. De Waal writes: "The uniquely human capacity to turn red in the face suggests that at some time our ancestors began to gain more from advertising trustworthiness than from fostering opportunism. And what more effective way to do so than by telltale signs beyond their control?"[18] I am reminded of Groucho Marx's maxim: "What you need to get on in politics is sincerity; if you can fake that you've got it made." There's a serious evolutionary point there:

[17] "Altruism" is a much abused term. Here I use it in what I hope is a "non-abusive" way, to refer to actions that are motivated by non-selfish ends. Biologists can, of course, co-opt and define terms as they wish, but in my opinion it is a mistake to use the terms "altruistic" or "selfish" to refer to the danger calls of groundhogs, birds, etc. It is a mistake because when the biologists' theories are applied to humans there is much confusion caused by these labels to no compensating purpose. A groundhog is neither selfish nor altruistic (and nor are its genes). Humans, by comparison, are frequently selfish and frequently altruistic (but again: their genes are neither).
[18] De Waal, *Good Natured*, p. 116.

in a group of sympathetic cooperators, sensitive to potential defection, anyone who can *fake* sympathetic tendencies, but remain disposed to defect whenever he can get away with it, is at a decided advantage. Perhaps at some point in prehistory sympathetic cooperators faced just such a threat from within. Blushing can be seen as a remedy provided by natural selection. Darwin reported a colleague, Burgess, "who believed that blushing was designed by the Creator, in 'order that the soul might have sovereign power of displaying in the cheeks the various internal emotions of the moral feelings,' so as to serve as a check on ourselves, and as a sign to others that we were violating rules which ought to be held sacred."[19] With a tweak here and there, Burgess was correct.

For reasons that I have already sketched, Stig will prefer (2) to (1), though perhaps the optimal situation is to have both motivations operative. Having comrades who *like* you is all very well, but it's not something you want to rely on. What if last week Stig accidentally injured one of his hunting partner's children? – he could hardly hope that that partner will carry on feeling an active *desire* for his well-being. What if the hunters are so frightened by the approaching tiger that all such warm feelings are driven from consciousness? Surely what Stig would most prefer is that his companions have a sense that they *must* help him, even if they don't much like him. With this motivation, cooperative activity is entered into most reliably. Of course, nothing guarantees cooperative behavior, but the best that one can do is invest that behavior with the strongest sense of authority available: the requirement that must be obeyed regardless.

The above argument was put in terms of "what Stig would prefer," and one might well object that this is neither here nor there: Stig would no doubt prefer companions who would sacrifice their lives for him, but that trait is hardly going to be selected for. But talking of Stig's "preferences" is just shorthand for discussing what kind of motivating bonds will be optimally efficient among a group, under the assumption that cooperation enhances reproductive fitness. A pair of hunters faced with a saber-toothed tiger are in a classic Prisoner's Dilemma scenario.[20] Suppose two hunters

---

[19] C. Darwin, *The Expression of the Emotions in Man and Animals* (London: John Murray, 1873), pp. 337–8. The moral component of blushing, as well as many other detectable physical and physiological changes, is discussed by R. H. Frank, *Passion Within Reason* (London: W. W. Norton & Company, 1988), pp. 114–33.

[20] The example is from Peter Singer's *The Expanding Circle* (Oxford: Clarendon Press, 1981), p. 48, though I am bending it to make a rather different point.

standing together have a 90 per cent chance of driving off a tiger without either being killed. Suppose that if one runs but his partner stays, then he'll be safe and the partner will be the tiger's dinner. Suppose, lastly, that if both run the tiger will choose one at random, and certainly get him. Self-interested calculations will lead one to run, since if one's partner also runs, then one is facing a 50 per cent chance of death if one runs versus a 100 per cent chance if one stays, whereas if one's partner stays, then one has a 0 per cent chance of death if one runs versus a 5 per cent chance if one stays: either way, one is better off running. But hunters will be better off (reproductively fitter) if they have in place a mechanism that makes them stay and fight side by side. We can assume that the potential psychological mechanisms which enjoin cooperation are inevitably imperfect. Once in a while they break down, leading to a collapse of cooperation (and hunters getting unnecessarily eaten). If one such mechanism breaks down less frequently than another, then, *ceteris paribus*, the former will be selected for. This, I submit, is the case when a sense of sympathy is supplemented by a sense of moral duty, versus a sense of sympathy alone.

Saying that humans have a natural moral sense is not, of course, to argue that every particular moral prescription is subject to direct evolutionary explanation. The claim is, firstly, that the tendency to employ the basic general categories of moral appraisal is innate. I will understand this as meaning that we have a "hardwired" predilection to believe that moral obligations exist. A second, stronger, thesis is that we have a natural tendency to believe that certain types of action bear such moral properties – things such as caring for the young, looking out for family members, avoiding incest, not initiating hostility towards members of the community, repaying debts, playing fair, being antagonistic towards exploiters. Cultural influences may cause this sense of requirement to be transferred to any number of other types of actions – say, in Roman Catholic priests towards sexual celibacy, or in historical Polynesian cultures towards the touching of the chief's food. And cultural pressures may also cause the widespread "detachment" of requirements from those actions to which they are innately ascribed – the Pharaonic Egyptians' toleration of limited incest, for instance. Thucydides tells of the abandonment of all moral restraint amongst the Athenians under the pressures of war and plague[21] – the

---

[21] Thucydides, *History of the Peloponnesian War* (Cambridge, Mass.: Harvard University Press, 1969), book 2, 53 and book 3, 82.

kind of moral collapse, perhaps, that was observed in detail by Colin Turn-bull, in his study of the Ik people of Uganda.[22]

Talk of "hardwiring," though obviously metaphorical, remains rather misleading. It encourages neglect of the thought that natural selection has provided us with psychological *dispositions* which require environmental cues to become "manifest." So even if something very particular like "the belief that *p*" had been selected for, it would not follow that every individual believes that *p*. A child raised isolated in a windowless room will not believe in moral obligations any more than she will develop the ability to focus visually on things in the distance.

Over the years there has been much hostility expressed towards the idea that behaviors and motivations that humans have *now* might be given an explanation in terms of the forces of natural selection operating on hominids millions of years ago. My hunch (I shall have to call it that, since I can hardly argue it) is that much of that antagonism is really directed at a rather different program: that the fact that certain behaviors and attitudes can be given an evolutionary explanation might amount to some sort of *justification* of those behaviors and attitudes now. To object to the latter program is right and proper, but I know of no sound reason why one should object, in general, to the former. Of course, there may be particular proposals of evolutionary explanations that are implausible or downright silly, but that shouldn't tarnish the general framework. We have evolved the psychological structures that prompt us to care for our children as much as we have evolved the physical structures that prompt us to cough when choking. The account that has been argued here takes what is true of caring for children, claims that this mechanism will work optimally in humans if regulated by a sense of "requirement," and extends it into other fields. I may well be mistaken in the details, but there should be nothing in principle objectionable about this provision of evolutionary explanation.

But if all that has been described thus far is a genealogy and not a justi-fication, what relevance does it have to discussing our present moral dis-course? One conclusion is that, complementing the arguments for an error theory of the previous chapters, it accounts for the origin of a widespread and natural mistake, and thus discharges a burden that any error theorist owes her critics. But I will argue that we can draw a stronger conclusion:

---

[22] Colin Turnbull, *The Mountain People* (New York: Simon and Schuster, 1972); though note that Bernd Heine paints a picture of the Ik very much at odds with Turnbull's in "The Mountain People: Some Notes on the Ik of North-Eastern Uganda," *Africa* 55 (1985), pp. 3–16.

the very fact that morality is the product of natural selection provides evidence in favor of the error theory. Before embarking on that argument in §6.4, however, I wish, in the next two sections, to deal with those theorists who seek to overcome the distinction mentioned between explanation and justification: who hope to take the kind of evolutionary genealogy that I have favored and, working from that premise, to *vindicate* moral discourse.

6.2 EVOLUTIONARY ETHICAL NATURALISM

Several enthusiasts of "evolutionary ethics" have sought in natural selection a justification of morality, putting forward what we can call "an evolutionary success theory." A success theory, recall, is one that holds that our moral discourse is not fundamentally in error, that many of our utterances – such as "You mustn't ϕ" "John is a morally good man," etc. – are true. An *evolutionary* success theory holds that the kind of fact in virtue of which such judgments are true is, in some manner, a fact about human evolution. The first and probably most famous proponent of this kind of theorizing was Herbert Spencer, but – with his misguided assumptions that natural selection leads to heterogeneity and improvement, with his crass application of the model onto class struggle – he need not detain us. I shall discuss some late twentieth-century proponents, whose attempts to put forward more subtle evolutionary success theories warrant more careful rebuttal.

William Rottschaefer and David Martinsen agree that humans have evolved to have a certain kind of response to certain kinds of stimuli, and that this fact explains, in the large part, our tendency to employ moral judgments.[23] They then submit that there is a dispositional property, which we can describe as "such that humans have evolved to respond with [say] approval," and this property can be identified with (say) *moral rightness*. So moral rightness exists after all, and a similar story can be told, no doubt, about other moral properties.

This kind of move is a familiar one to philosophers of color, and it is instructive to compare the cases. A person may be tempted, upon a little reflection, to decide that colors are not really a feature of the world at all, and think that the fact that they seem to be says something about how we,

---

[23] W. A. Rottschaefer and D. Martinsen, "Really Taking Darwin Seriously: An Alternative to Michael Ruse's Darwinian Metaethics," *Biology and Philosophy* 5 (1990), pp. 149–73. The same concerns I express in the text hold for Rottschaefer's more detailed position in *The Biology and Psychology of Moral Agency* (Cambridge: Cambridge University Press, 1998).

in perceiving objects, take an inner experience of color and "project" it on to our experience of the world. This was the view held by Hume, who extended it to moral categories too: "Vice and virtue may be compared to sounds, colors, heat and cold, which, according to modern philosophy, are not qualities in objects but perceptions in the mind"[24] – moral judgments are a matter of the "gilding and staining [of] natural objects with the colors borrowed from internal sentiment."[25] Regarding the ontology of color, it has been a popular strategy in recent years to accept Hume's basic projectivist premise, yet nevertheless to place colors in the world, as a dispositional property of the surfaces of objects. Redness, for example, is said to be the dispositional property of producing the phenomenological response *redness* in normal human viewers (as they are actually constituted) under good viewing conditions (i.e., in broad daylight).[26] There is a kind of objectivity here, since had a tomato ripened fifty million years ago it would still be red, in so far as *were* a normal human to observe it in good viewing conditions (never mind that there weren't any humans in existence) that human *would* have a certain response. We might say that this analysis makes colors existentially independent of, though conceptually dependent on, human minds.

If we're accepting the premise that the attitude favoring cooperative activity is an evolved trait, then it cannot be denied that such activity does instantiate the kind of relational property gestured at, but a crucial question remains: "Is that property the referent of the term *rightness*?" Regarding color, the point is put succinctly by Michael Smith: "Someone who denies that colors are properties of objects need not deny that objects *have* these dispositions, all he has to deny is that colors *are* such dispositions."[27] The mere availability of a dispositional account of a concept does not force that analysis upon us. After all, for *any* predicate we can find a dispositional property had by all and only the items in the predicate's extension. All and only the objects satisfying ". . . is a manatee" are (trivially) such that they

---

[24] *Treatise*, book 3, part 1, section 1 (1978), p. 469.

[25] *Enquiry*, appendix I (1983), p. 88.

[26] See J. McDowell, "Values and Secondary Qualities," in T. Honderich (ed.), *Morality and Objectivity* (London: Routledge and Kegan Paul, 1985), pp. 110–29. For related discussion see M. Johnston, "How to Speak of the Colors," *Philosophical Studies* 68 (1992), pp. 221–63; J. Campbell, "A Simple View of Color," in J. Haldane and C. Wright (eds.), *Reality, Representation and Projection* (New York: Oxford University Press, 1993), pp. 257–68.

[27] M. Smith, "Objectivity and Moral Realism: On the Significance of the Phenomenology of Moral Experience," in Haldane and Wright (eds.), *Reality, Representation and Projection*, p. 239.

would prompt the response "There's a manatee!" in an infallible manatee spotter.

Is there reason to resist thinking that this "Darwinian dispositional property" identified by Rottschaefer and Martinsen is the referent of a familiar moral term of positive appraisal? Yes. For such a property cannot underwrite the notion of moral *requirement* – and what is moral rightness, if not something we are required to pursue? Consider again our unrepentant moral villain, familiar from previous chapters. We can allow that the action he performed had the following relational property: being such that humans have evolved to respond with disfavor. According to Rottschaefer and Martinsen, then, the action was *wrong* – really, objectively wrong. Unfortunately, moral naturalism does not come so easily. For at the heart of our moral discourse is the idea that the criminal *ought not* to have performed the action, that he was somehow *required* to refrain, and therefore (I have argued) that he had a *reason* to refrain (regardless of his desires, and regardless of whether he is aware of the fact). But why do the things favored by natural selection bind him in this manner, or provide him with reasons?

It would be tempting, but futile, to appeal to the fact that our criminal *is* a human, with all the natural human dispositions, and therefore has reason to act in accordance with natural selection. This is, in effect, how Robert Richards argues in presenting his version of evolutionary success theory.[28] Since, according to Richards, all humans have evolved to act for the community good, we may say to any human: "Since you are a moral being, constituted so by evolution, you ought to act for the community good." He likens this derivation of an "ought" to that occurring in "Since lightning has struck, thunder ought to follow." This is surprising, since the "ought" of the latter is an *epistemic* or *predictive* one. Such "ought"'s still, arguably, entail reasons: "That lightning has struck gives one reason for believing that thunder will follow."[29] But the *moral* "ought" that Richards hopes to derive surely is not an epistemic one: when we say that the villain ought not steal, we are not saying that we are able to predict, on the basis of some antecedent concerning evolution, that he will not steal; and, by the same token, the reason entailed by the "ought" pertains to *his* reasons for not stealing, not *our* reasons for believing that he won't steal!

[28] R. Richards, "A Defense of Evolutionary Ethics," *Biology and Philosophy* 1 (1986), pp. 265–93.
[29] See Harman, "Reasons" (1975); Mackie, *Ethics*, p. 74.

Presumably what Richards hopes to do is to make moral imperatives *hypothetical*, depending for their legitimacy on an end with which all humans, as a matter of fact, have been assigned by natural selection: the good of the community. If our moral villain has this end, then he ought (*ceteris paribus*) to do whatever will satisfy it; he has a (*prima facie*) reason to do whatever will satisfy it. The important point to hold in mind, however, is that whatever else we may say about evolutionary forces, it is utterly implausible to think that they have bestowed upon us all an active *desire* to promote community good – at most, we are endowed with a *disposition*, or *capacity*, to form that desire (as Richards recognizes). But why does a mere disposition provide an "end," or ground an "ought" statement? Allow that evolution has endowed a moral felon, Jack, with a disposition to favor the promotion of the community's good, but imagine that his upbringing was such that the disposition went quite undeveloped, and now has been effectively quashed. Why *ought* he still act for the community's good? Why does he still have a *reason* to?[30]

Richards toys with the idea of simply branding Jack a "sociopath," therefore not fully human, and therefore not a proper subject of moral injunctions. Perhaps this would stick if Jack lacked the disposition altogether, as the result of a genetic abnormality, but we are not claiming any genetic anomaly – Jack still *has* the disposition, it has just gone utterly undeveloped, and now, let's imagine, it is too late for him to develop it, in much the same way as it is now too late for him to become a concert pianist.[31] It's important to note that our "villain," despite earlier characterizations, need not be the serial killer stalking back streets, need not be the suicidal teenager heading to school with an automatic rifle in his bag. The kind of self-centered person we encounter every day – one who regulates his or her actions consciously and solely in terms of perceived self-gain – will suffice perfectly well as an example of someone whose altruistic

---

[30] I must say, in fairness to Richards, that he does *not* think that the mere fact that we have, as a product of natural selection, a disposition to favor altruism entails that we ought to be altruistic. He notes that we also have evolved aggressive tendencies, but he doesn't think it follows that we ought to act on them. See "A Defense of Evolutionary Ethics," pp. 288 and 342. However, I must admit that I do not properly understand Richards's attempt to argue for a principled distinction on this point.

[31] It is important to stress that the sense of "disposition" under discussion is specific: an inherited trait that regulates the formation of certain attitudes when the agent is exposed to certain environmental cues at a certain point in development. Thus when I claim that Jack "has the disposition," this is a claim about his genetic package; it does not follow that there are any environmental stimuli that Jack could encounter *now* that would result in his forming the attitudes in question.

dispositions have been quelled. Bearing this in mind, talk of "sociopaths" who fall short of satisfying the criteria for *being human* seems wildly overstated.

Consider such a character: pleasant enough to interact with, has a successful career, a family, etc. But if she has made a promise that will be inconvenient to keep, and she sees that she can break it without incurring penalty (perhaps she can make a decent excuse), then, despite her knowledge that doing so will seriously penalize others, and, say, harm the community in general, she will not hesitate to break the promise. Let us point out to her that the action of promise-breaking has a certain "Darwinian" dispositional property: it is such that humans have evolved to disfavor it. She accepts this, but notes it with unconcern (along with facts about the evolution of manatees). Let us inform her that she herself has this disposition, in the sense that had she received a certain kind of upbringing she would have favored the good of the community (and may pass this disposition on to her offspring). But, given that she *didn't* receive that upbringing, but one that left the disposition dormant, why does she now have a reason to refrain from promise-breaking? To say that the disposition *must* have some manifestation, such that in some sense she, in acting against the community's good, *must* be subtly undermining her own projects and interests, is just desperate.

I have reiterated the question of why facts about evolution provide persons with reasons, why they ground moral "ought" statements – and it should be clear that my answer is: "They don't." Of course, if evolution has endowed me with a disposition to favor cooperation, and my upbringing has been such that this disposition *has* developed fully, then indeed I have a (*prima facie*) reason to cooperate. But now all the work is being done by the fact that my upbringing has provided me with certain attitudes and traits that are now actively operative – and these attitudes would ground "ought" statements even if they had nothing to do with evolution. It will not do to maintain that any agent in whom such dispositions lie untapped (and now "untappable") is simply a sociopath, who lies beyond the pale of moral injunctions. Such agents are possibly quite common, and they certainly remain the subjects of the dictates of moral discourse. We think that a person – regardless of an upbringing that left her intractably selfish – morally *ought not* break promises for the sake of convenience. Pointing to a relational property pertaining to natural "fitness," indicating that natural selection provides humans with certain dispositions against promise-breaking, does not help. And if an ethical theory cannot account for so central and familiar a moral judgment – that a selfish person ought not break an inconvenient promise – it has not gotten off the ground.

6.3 EVOLUTIONARY ETHICAL NATURALISM AND THE NATURALISTIC FALLACY

Proponents of evolutionary success theory always appear sensitive to the accusation that they are committing the dreaded naturalistic fallacy. The evolutionary naturalists discussed above are no exception, and all go to some effort to show that no such transgression is taking place. But it is not the naturalistic fallacy that I accuse such theorists of, for, I hereby admit, I have little idea what that fallacy is, nor why ethicists – especially those interested in evolution – seem so fearfully mesmerized by it.[32] I should like in this section to put that fallacy to rest (though no doubt it will live on), and in the process identify what it would take for an evolutionary success theory to be acceptable.

It has become commonplace to assume that G. E. Moore's notorious fallacy does for "good" what Hume did for "ought," but no part of *Principia Ethica* that I am familiar with bears resemblance to Hume's claim that one cannot derive an "ought" from an "is."[33] It is true that nothing like the following is formally valid (if by this we mean "is an instance of a theorem of the predicate calculus"):

1. Things of type ϕ are such that humans, by the process of natural selection, are disposed to have attitude A towards them.
∴ Things of type ϕ are morally good

But no naturalist would claim such a thing. Rather, she will treat the above as an enthymeme, inserting a major premise if required:

2. If things of type ϕ are such that humans, by the process of natural selection, are disposed to have attitude A towards them, then things of type ϕ are morally good.

It is no good complaining that (2) reproduces, in conditional form, a formally invalid argument, for the naturalist does not claim that (2) is "valid," merely that it is *true*. Nor can it be simply insisted that (2) commits

---

[32] In particular, I have never understood why William Frankena's sensible 1939 article – "The Naturalistic Fallacy," *Mind* 48, pp. 464–77 – did not put an end to the whole business.
[33] G. E. Moore, *Principia Ethica* [1903] (Cambridge: Cambridge University Press, 1948).

"the naturalistic fallacy" in virtue of relating a fact to a value, and therefore must be false. That's just begging the question. It is also important to remember that the "fallacy," according to Moore, is committed no less by statements of the following kind:

(Yellow) Having the natural properties P, Q, R, *is* what it is to be yellow.

So he evidently did not think that it is the "evaluativeness" of goodness that powers the fallacy, but its *indefinability*. But again, we cannot simply *assume* that goodness is indefinable (or unanalyzable), for that is precisely a point at issue. When we look at the heart of Moore's description of the fallacy (in §12 of *Principia Ethica*), what we actually find seems to be advice that one ought not confuse the "is" of identity with the "is" of predication. Moore thinks that the hedonic naturalist, when she claims "Pleasure is good," may be saying something true so long as it's an "is" of predication; but to mistake it for an "is" of identity (a *definition*, by Moore's lights) leads to absurdity. In the same way, if I say "The book is red" and "The book is square" – but these are taken as identity claims – I'm left with the crazy conclusion that redness is squareness.

Keeping track of one's "is"'s is surely good advice – perhaps to confuse them may even be called a kind of "fallacy" – but Moore is quite mistaken if he thinks that the naturalist *must* be confused over "is." (2) can be seen as entailed by a naturalistic thesis:

(Naturalism) For any ϕ, ϕ is a type of thing towards which humans, by the process of natural selection, are disposed to have attitude A iff things of type ϕ are morally good.

There is one "is" of predication there. With rewording, the biconditional might be strengthened into an "is" of identity flanked by property names. Thus naturalism might be an *a posteriori* claim, comparable to "Water is H_2O," or an *a priori* (but covert) thesis, like "Knowledge is justified true belief." But in neither case need the naturalist fall foul of the problem that *Moore* called "the naturalistic fallacy." Moore does allow that *some* things may be defined without trouble: his stock example is a definition of horse. (That's Moore's syntax; I'd much rather speak of a definition of "horse" or a definition of *horseness*. Since he's adamant he does not intend the former, I assume he means the latter.) So what is it about *yellowness* and *goodness* that makes them different from *horseness*? Moore's answer is that they are "simple," "non-natural," and "indefinable" – but this cannot be treated as a self-evident datum, for it is exactly what the naturalist, in offering something like (Naturalism), denies. Oddly, of this all-important premise, Moore writes: "As for the reasons why good [*sic*] is not to be considered a natural object, they may be reserved for discussion in another place." It appears that this "further discussion" is the very next section of *Principia Ethica* – where the Open Question Argument is deployed. But the woes of that argument are well-documented, and won't be rehearsed here.[34] (I'll merely note that it doesn't even work for Moore's favorite example of the definition of *horseness* – for the analysis he offers is *a posteriori* in nature – making mention of a horse's *heart* and *liver*, etc. – such that a perfectly competent speaker might be certain that X is a horse, but uncertain that X has a heart, liver, etc.)

Consider something like (Naturalism) – what Rottschaefer and Martinsen would call a "robust Darwinian naturalism" (and I have called "an evolutionary success theory"). The question, I have argued, is not whether it commits a "fallacy," but whether it is *true*. If it is true, then it is either an *a priori* or an *a posteriori* truth. The relevant model for the former is a philosophical analysis like "Knowledge is true justified belief." We do not come upon such truths (pretending that it *is* a truth) simply by doing a bit of quick introspection, or by looking in a dictionary. Smith suggests that one way of proceeding is to gather all our platitudes about knowledge – a platitude being something one comes to treat *as* platitudinous in attaining basic competency with the concept – and then to systematize those platitudes.[35] "True, justified belief" may be the best systematization, or encapsulation, of our epistemic platitudes (though it probably isn't). But it is clear that no description worded centrally in *evolutionary* terms is going to be the best systematization of our moral platitudes. Moral concepts, it may be assumed, preserved their identity criteria throughout the nineteenth century: someone saying "Slavery is morally wrong" in 1890 was not expressing a different proposition to someone uttering the same sentence in 1810 (otherwise, were the 1810 speaker instead to assert "Slavery is morally permissible," she would not be in disagreement with the 1890 speaker, in which case we could not say that moral attitudes towards slavery changed over the course of the nineteenth century). If this is true, then, according to the theory under question, it was *a priori* available to pre-Darwinian speakers to systematize their moral platitudes in such a way

---

[34] For effective criticism, see, for example, Harman, *Nature of Morality*, p. 19; H. Putnam, *Reason, Truth and History* (Cambridge: Cambridge University Press, 1981), pp. 205–08.

[35] See Smith, *Moral Problem*, pp. 29–41.

that *natural selection* centrally figured in that explication. But that is absurd, so robust Darwinian naturalism as an *a priori* thesis is a non-starter.

How will it fare as an *a posteriori* thesis? The model here is "Water is H$_2$O." According to the *a posteriori* naturalist, we can "find out" that two kind terms, perhaps both in common parlance, are, and always have been, co-referential.[36] This sounds closer to what the robust Darwinian naturalist will presumably claim: when we consider a term like "moral rightness," and examine the kind of things to which we apply it (and the kind of things from which we withhold it), and then bring in evolutionary theory, perhaps boosted by detailed empirical confirmation, we might discover that (pretty much) all and only the things to which we apply ". . . is morally right" instantiate a property, or cluster of properties, which may also be described by the predicate ". . . is a type of thing towards which humans, by the process of natural selection, are disposed to have attitude A." This is potentially threatening to a moral error theory, for we have agreed that there *is* such a property had by (pretty much) all and only the things to which we apply our predicate ". . . is morally right," so is that not immediately to give the game to the (*a posteriori*) evolutionary success theorist?

I don't believe so. The worry with this kind of *a posteriori* theory is that it threatens to achieve far too much. Consider our term "witch" that was once applied to actual persons. It is possible that all and only the persons to whom we applied "witch" had a certain property, or cluster of properties – perhaps they were women who tended to be of a certain social class, playing a certain socio-political role, who threatened the patriarchal authorities in a particular way (I'm not suggesting that it's anything so simple – it may be disjunctive and vague). But to locate such a property clearly would not be an *a posteriori* vindication of "witch discourse," because when seventeenth-century speakers made assertions employing the predicate ". . . is a witch" something more was going on than merely applying it to some objects, withholding it from others. They were disposed to claim something *about* those women to whom it was applied – namely, that they possessed supernatural powers. This concomitant statement had an important status: it was a central part of the *meaning* of the term "witch"

[36] See, for example, R. Boyd, "How to Be a Moral Realist," in G. Sayre-McCord (ed.), *Essays in Moral Realism* (Ithaca: Cornell University Press, 1988), pp. 181–228; D. Brink, *Moral Realism and the Foundations of Ethics* (Cambridge: Cambridge University Press, 1989); W. Lycan, "Moral Facts and Moral Knowledge," in *The Spindel Conference: The Southern Journal of Philosophy*, supplementary volume 24 (1986), pp. 79–94.

(in the sense discussed in Chapter 1). And since these women did not have supernatural powers – since no women have supernatural powers – there are no witches. The same pattern of argument can be used regarding tapu, phlogiston, zodiacal influences on personality and, many would think, the gods. It is not being claimed that there always is some property shared by all and only the objects to which such terms are applied; merely that even if we were to locate such a property (and there is no reason why it might not be an odd and gerrymandered one), it would not shake our proper conviction that such discourses are fatally flawed.

The same thing will go for moral discourse. It is not enough to find some property had by all and only the things to which we apply our moral terms. There are also very important things which we endorse *about*, say, morally right actions – such as they are the ones which a person *ought to* perform regardless of his desires, they are the ones that we have overriding *reason* to perform, they are the ones the recognition of which will *motivate* an agent. But, as I argued previously, the kind of property adverted to by the robust Darwinian naturalist does not satisfy such a sense of "inescapable requirement." Therefore this Darwinian dispositional property, though very probably existing, does not deserve the name "moral rightness."

The naturalist might respond: "So much the worse for our sense of *categorical imperative* – why not just admit that this aspect of our moral discourse is faulty, and carry on with a revised naturalist discourse?" Well, why couldn't defenders of "witch theory" just revise their theory when it was discovered that there are no supernatural powers, insisting that all along they had been talking about, say, certain disempowered women who play a certain communal role, and regarding whom they had held some false beliefs about supernatural abilities? When Lavoisier gave us oxygen theory in the late eighteenth century, why couldn't the fans of phlogiston just revise their theory, insisting that they had been talking about *oxygen* all along, concerning which they had held some false beliefs about its being stored and released? The reason that witch theory could not be revised and vindicated in this manner is that the bit about the supernatural powers was the whole *point* of discussing witches. Similarly, the thesis about a stuff that is stored in bodies and released during combustion was too central to phlogiston theory to be negotiable – one might say that the whole point of phlogiston discourse was to refer to a *stored and released* material. By the same token, I believe, the whole point of having a moral discourse is to prescribe and condemn various actions with *categorical* force.

6.4 MORAL GENEALOGY, MORAL ERROR, AND THE GENETIC FALLACY

There is little cause for optimism that the fact that our moral sense is innate might provide justifying foundations for moral discourse; on the contrary, I think that the fact that morality is an evolved trait undermines it. This is not an original thought. Indeed, when Darwin's *The Descent of Man* was published in 1871, the *Edinburgh Review* pronounced that if exposed to these doctrines "most earnest-minded men will be compelled to give up these motives by which they have attempted to live noble and virtuous lives, as founded on a mistake; our moral sense will turn out to be a mere developed instinct . . . and the revelation of God to us, and the hope of a future life, pleasurable daydreams invented for the good of society. If these views be true, a revolution in thought is imminent, which will shake society to its very foundations by destroying the sanctity of the conscience and the religious sense."[37] The *Edinburgh Review* was, I contend, right about at least one thing: if Darwin is correct about our moral sense being the product of natural selection, then our moral pronouncements are "founded on a mistake." (Whether we should therefore "give up these motives" is another matter, to be addressed in the later chapters.)

The kind of genealogy presented in §6.0 and §6.1 is an explanation of why humans would tend to employ moral predicates regardless of whether those predicates have empty extensions, non-empty extensions, or (if we wish to countenance it) no extensions at all. One might be tempted to think, then, that an error theory is in the offing via Ockham's Razor: everything that needs explaining is explained by an evolutionary story concerning how and why we have a disposition to make moral judgments, with no need for an additional theory according to which the judgments are *true*.[38] But it can now be seen that Ockham's Razor won't suffice – not, at least, in such a brisk and decisive manner – for the kind of robust Darwinian naturalism that has been under discussion does not posit any extra *ontology* – it rather points to dispositional properties, the existence of which all parties to the debate should antecedently agree to.[39]

---

[37] Quoted in R. W. Clark, *The Survival of Charles Darwin* (London: Weidenfeld and Nicolson, 1984), p. 181.

[38] See, for example, M. Ruse and E. Wilson, "Moral Philosophy as Applied Science," *Philosophy* 61 (1986), pp. 186–7.

[39] Compare the kind of "non-natural" property that Moore thought is the referent of "good". If we had a well-confirmed theory that explained all relevant phenomena by appeal only to our *making judgments* that such non-natural properties exist, then Ockham's

The innateness of moral judgments undermines these judgments being true for the simple reason that if we have evolved to make these judgments irrespective of their being true, then one could not hold that the judgments are *justified*. And if they are unjustified, then although they *could* be true, their truth is in doubt. Consider an analogy. John makes judgments that Sally is "out to get him." After talking to John's psychiatrist, we discover that John is neurotically paranoid about Sally, and would form these judgments about her regardless of what she did. If whatever evidence John is provided with concerning Sally's intentions, he will make exactly the same paranoid judgment, then there is absolutely no reason to think that his judgments are true. It is *possible* that they are true, of course, but his having made the judgment does not make that possibility in the least *probable*. Furthermore, if we were able to make a well-grounded judgment about the likelihood of Sally's being out to get him (independent of anything to do with John's judgment about her), and decide that it is terribly unlikely (after all, how many people are really "out to get" others – say, 0.1 per cent?), then we would have grounds for concluding that John's judgment, given the circumstances of its genesis, is extremely *unlikely* to be true.

The claim that the circumstances of a judgment's origin provide direct evidence of the likelihood of its being true will provoke immediate accusations that the so-called "genetic fallacy" is being committed. But (as with its naturalistic relation) I am far from confident that I understand what is meant by the label "the genetic fallacy." The earliest identification of this fallacy was probably in 1914, but within a few decades there was much confusion as to just what "the genetic fallacy" was supposed to denote: two articles written in the 1960s between them identified *thirteen* different things that pass by that name![40] The confusion settled into a cluster of slogans: "Don't confuse the origin of something with its nature," "Nothing is objectionable simply because it has an objectionable

Razor should serve to establish an error theory – for in order for those judgments to be *true* we would be required to posit some extra kind of entity in the world (i.e., non-natural properties), but this additional ontology would not explain anything that was not explained by the theory that appealed only to (untrue) judgments.

[40] The 1914 article is M. R. Cohen's "History *Versus* Value," *Journal of Philosophy* 11 (1914), pp. 701–16. I suspect it was *An Introduction to Logic and Scientific Method*, by Cohen and E. Nagel (New York: Harcourt, Brace and Company, 1934), that popularized the fallacy. The two 1960s articles mentioned are T. A. Goudge, "The Genetic Fallacy," *Synthese* 13 (1961), pp. 41–8, and N. R. Hanson, "The Genetic Fallacy Revisited," *American Philosophical Quarterly* 4 (1967), pp. 101–13.

origin," "Always distinguish between context of discovery and context of justification." Putting slogans to one side, the claim seems to be that the circumstances under which a belief is formed have no bearing on the likelihood of that belief being true; and this, I contend, is simply false. (The following discussion is indebted to Elliott Sober's views on the matter.[41])

Perhaps there is a "fallacy" of thinking that from facts about the circumstances of origin one might *deductively infer* the truth or falsity of a judgment. The following argument is clearly invalid:

1. John's belief that Sally is out to get him is the result of his paranoid neurosis
∴ Sally is not out to get John

But who would think otherwise? If we forget about deduction, and consider the relation between premise and conclusion to be one of *probabilifying* or, more simply, *support*, then there is more to be said in favor of the argument. If a belief is formed in a thoroughly unreliable way – such as being based on a roll of the dice, based on the opposite of whatever the evidence suggests, or the product of paranoid delusion – then this should very much influence our judgment concerning the likelihood of that judgment's being true! A belief is likely to be true if it is the product of a process that in some reliable manner demonstrates sensitivity to the evidence. Sober calls this a "dependence relation" holding between the manner in which a judgment was reached and the truth of the judgment. If an independence relation obtains between the mode of judgment formation and the content of that judgment – as in the case of paranoia – then we can conclude that the judgment is dubious.

Here "dubious" is intentionally an indeterminate word. It might mean that we have no evidence one way or the other concerning the truth of the judgment, and so should withhold assent, or it might mean that the judgment is actually unlikely to be true, and so we should (tentatively?) disbelieve it. With an exception noted below, the former is the correct option. In the previous example of John's paranoid neurosis, the conclusion that his belief is *unlikely* to be true required the importation of a substantive background belief: that few people are ever really "out to get" others, and therefore that of an arbitrarily selected person – Sally – it is quite improbable that she is out to get John. In other words, if we were to

[41] See E. Sober, *The Philosophy of Biology* (San Francisco: Westview Press, 1993), pp. 205–8; and *idem*, "Prospects for an Evolutionary Ethics," in L. Pojman (ed.), *Ethical Theory: Classical and Contemporary Readings* (Belmont, Calif.: Wadsworth Publishing Company, 1995), pp. 110–20.

pay attention *only* to the fact that John's judgment was the product of an unreliable process (one that bears an independence relation to the facts) we could conclude nothing about whether it is likely or unlikely to be true. For such a conclusion we would have muster direct evidence about the probability of Sally's being out to get him. Perhaps this is what people mean by "the genetic fallacy." Suppose, however, that John's beliefs are not just produced by paranoia, but by a defective process of belief formation whereby he believes things *contrary* to what the evidence suggests (we might call this an "inverse dependence relation"). If we know this about John, and we note that he believes that *p*, then we have grounds for positively *doubting* the truth of the judgment. On the other hand, if we were to know instead that John's judgment is generated by a perfectly reliable process, one that is sensitive to the facts, then we would be able to conclude that it is likely to be true. Either way, it is simply mistaken to claim that the circumstances of judgment formation have no bearing on the likelihood of a judgment's being true. Of course, *frequently* circumstances of genesis are irrelevant − one shouldn't reject a theory on the grounds that its originator was an alcoholic, or a Nazi sympathizer, for instance. My complaint is against the sweeping generalization that the genetic fallacy usually embodies. It's a matter of whether the characteristic imputed to the originator is one that is likely to cut loose belief from evidence.

With these thoughts in mind, let us return to the matter of natural selection and moral judgments. Suppose that the pressures of natural selection have created an animal that is "hardwired" to believe that *p*. The belief that *p*, presumably, is terribly useful for the animal to have (in the sense of improving reproductive fitness), even if the belief is false. If we were to consider only these facts, we would have no grounds for thinking that *p* is likely or unlikely to be true. It is, however, implausible that natural selection would generally work in this manner regarding doxastic matters. What is surely useful about a belief system is its very plasticity, its very sensitivity to the environment, the very fact that particular beliefs are generally *not* hardwired.[42] Consider my belief that Paris is the capital of France. There's a sense in which my having that belief can be explained by evolution: evolution has granted me a complex brain that is able to form beliefs, the capacity to move around my environment (preferably towards Paris) tracking facts, and the capacity to communicate with others who

---

[42] See R. Nozick, *Philosophical Explanations* (Oxford: Clarendon Press, 1981), pp. 284–6.

can testify to geographical facts. But that is a very weak sense of "evolutionary explanation." Nor does such an explanation render my belief in the least dubious. On the contrary, what evolution has provided me with are systems for forming beliefs in accordance with the available evidence – beliefs that are, if anything, more likely to be true than false.

We have already allowed that moral beliefs have a certain plasticity – after all, the judgment that slavery is wrong is not "hardwired" – so should we not draw exactly the same conclusion concerning moral beliefs as beliefs about the capital of France: namely, that they are the product of a reliable process of judgment formation, and therefore likely to be true? There is an important difference. I have, in the course of experience, somehow acquired the concept *Paris* and the concept *France* and the relational concept ... *is the capital of*. ... I have no natural tendency, or disposition, to form beliefs containing any of these elements. In the case of moral beliefs, however, it was argued in §6.0 and §6.1 that the very concept of "requirement" is the product of natural selection. When, for example, I judge that slavery is forbidden, certainly the concept *slavery* is something that I have acquired, but the concept *forbidden* is not. It would be a mistake to conclude from this that my belief that slavery is wrong is the product of natural selection. Rather, it is my belief that there exist forbidden actions (or that forbiddenness exists) that is so-produced. This is not to say (to repeat) that given any upbringing anyone will employ the concept *forbidden*: aberrant environments can nullify natural dispositions (where "aberrant" need mean nothing more than *different from the ancestral environment*). Nor is it to deny that we have to learn the *word* "forbidden" (if we speak English) – the point is that there is a concept of *forbidden* naturally present, naturally developing, waiting for a word to be applied to it. Put in these terms it sounds a rather far-fetched hypothesis, but we have already seen evidence for it in earlier sections. When I adverted to empirical evidence that non-human primates have a natural sense of guilt, this is more or less what I meant. Naturally, if you raise a chimpanzee isolated in a cage it will have no such sense; but when it receives the cues of a "normal" socialization process then such a sense will develop – unlike, say, a recognition of oranges if it never encounters an orange.

On the assumption that my favored hypothesis about the "moral sense" is correct, it follows that the process by which humans form moral beliefs is an unreliable one, for they are disposed to do so regardless of the evidence to which they are exposed.[43] Suppose that the actual world contains real categorical requirements – the kind that would be necessary to render moral discourse true. In such a world humans will be disposed to make moral judgments (most generally, to believe that categorical requirements exist), for natural selection will make it so. Now imagine instead that the actual world contains no such requirements at all – nothing to make moral discourse true. In such a world humans will *still* be disposed to make these judgments (most generally, to believe that categorical requirements exist), just as they did in the first world, for natural selection will make it so.[44] What this shows is that the process that generates moral judgments exhibits an independence relation between judgment and truth, and these judgments are thus unjustified. If, therefore, we examine no other evidence, if we look only at the fact that humans make moral judgments, and endorse the hypothesis for which I have argued regarding the processes that yield these judgments, then we have no evidence one way or the other concerning the truth of the judgments. In such a situation we should, like good old-fashioned skeptics, withhold assent on the matter.

Robert Nozick gives some consideration to such thoughts in his *Philosophical Explanations*.[45] He points out that a rudimentary arithmetic ability is probably an evolved trait, but that hardly shows that mathematical beliefs are unjustified. Indeed, if elementary counting skills are the product of natural selection then they must have been useful to our ancestors, but being able to add two and two to make four is only going to be useful in a world where two plus two *does* sum to four. In other words, it is the *truth* of such beliefs that explains their usefulness. So the question is: does the truth of moral judgments similarly play a role in their usefulness? Unlike Nozick, I believe that the answer is "No." His argument for "Yes" is in a short passage:

The ethical behavior will serve inclusive fitness through serving or not harming others, through helping one's children and relatives, through acts that aid them in

---

[43] A failure to distinguish between "being exposed to evidence" and "receiving the appropriate environmental cues" might cause confusion here. One needs a certain upbringing in order for the disposition to make moral judgments to become manifest. The claim under scrutiny is that *once* those environmental cues are supplied, *then* a human will form moral beliefs irrespective of the evidence to which she is exposed.

[44] Michael Ruse puts forward a similar argument in *Taking Darwin Seriously*, p. 254. Ruse, however, makes the point in the course of deploying an Ockham's Razor argument against the moral realist, whereas my conclusion is that the judgment in question is unjustified.

[45] Nozick, *Philosophical Explanations*, pp. 342–8.

escaping predators, and so forth; that this behavior is helpful and not harmful is not unconnected to why (on most theorist's views) it is ethical. The ethical behavior will increase inclusive fitness through the very aspects that make it ethical, not as a side effect through features that only accidentally are connected with ethicality. (p. 346)

Can we imagine a creature finding it useful (in terms of reproductive fitness) to believe that two plus two equals four, in a world where it actually equals five? Clearly, there is something troubling about the counterfactual, for two twos *necessarily* sum to four. What about imagining a creature finding it useful to believe that, say, paying back loans is required, even though it is not required? Nozick's analogous objection will be that the counterfactual doesn't make sense because the connection between an action's being an episode of loan-repayment and its being a required action is non-contingent. But that's a far more controversial claim than the one concerning the necessity of arithmetic truths, and such a substantive piece of theorizing will need arguing for.

This is brought out more clearly when we note that Nozick hasn't addressed my "weaker" evolutionary hypothesis (from §6.1): the claim that what is "hardwired" is the general belief that moral requirements exist. When we imagine the world at which this belief is false – at which there are no moral requirements at all – and maintain that humans will nevertheless hold this belief for evolutionary reasons, Nozick will likewise need to claim that the thought experiment is incoherent, on the grounds that moral requirements necessarily exist. But such a substantive theoretical claim is far from self-evident.

Furthermore, if we change the example then we can see that Nozick's modal claim is dubious. Instead of cooperative activity, let us wonder about the human tendency to find incest morally repugnant. There is very good evidence that this is a hardwired response, and it is one which is easily explained in evolutionary terms (thus it is a good example of the "stronger" evolutionary hypothesis).[46] The evolutionary hypothesis will hold that humans have evolved to judge incest as morally forbidden, and I am arguing that, furthermore, the process that produces such judgments is an unreliable one, since humans would make the judgment whether or not incest is really morally prohibited. Nozick's argument will have to be that there is a necessary connection between ϕ's being an episode of

---

[46] See, for example, J. Shepher, *Incest* (New York: Academic, 1983); A. Maryanski and J. Turner, *The Social Cage* (Stanford: Stanford University Press, 1992), W. Arens, *The Original Sin* (Oxford: Oxford University Press, 1986).

incest and ϕ's being morally wrong. However, even if we dispense with overly general terms, and confine ourselves to, say, parent–child incest, the modal claim is terribly implausible. What exactly does Nozick (and "most theorists") think is morally wrong with incest? Unless he is to appeal, unattractively, to an unexplained "brute fact," presumably there will have to be an intermediate step in the argument – something like: Necessarily: if ϕ is an episode of parent–child incest then ϕ involves the traumatization of children; and necessarily: if ϕ involves the traumatization of children then ϕ is morally wrong. But the first conditional is surely false. (And it doesn't depend on my choice of intermediate step; choose anything you like that will make the second conditional seem plausible and the first will remain implausible.) We can easily imagine circumstances in which parent–child incest does not lead to childhood trauma. Such circumstances may be rare, or may even never actually obtain, but they are certainly *possible*. But to admit that much is for Nozick's argument to break down. If we indulge in the metaphor of asking what natural selection "cares about," then we might say that as far as incest-avoidance goes, natural selection does not care about childhood trauma – all it cares about is avoiding the increase of negative recessive genes in subsequent generations. The counterfactual argument will run as follows: imagine a circumstance in which parent–child incest does traumatize children: in such circumstances humans will naturally evolve to be disposed to judge incest forbidden. Now imagine a circumstance in which parent–child incest does not traumatize children: humans will *still* naturally evolve to be disposed to judge incest forbidden. Therefore such judgments are made independently of the truth. One might object that this only shows that judgments concerning incest are unjustified and that this says nothing about judgments concerning stealing, slavery, etc. But the point of the evolutionary hypothesis is to emphasize that moral judgments come from a naturally selected *faculty*: to show that that faculty sometimes systematically generates unjustified judgments is to show that the faculty is unreliable *simpliciter*.

Now that, one might think, is conclusion enough for the error theorist. However, the error theory that I have argued for in earlier chapters is not the "agnostic" variety – whereby we think that there is no evidence one way or the other sufficient for us to conclude whether or not moral judgments are true – rather, I aimed for the "atheistic" version, where we have good reason for *disbelieving* in morality. Can the evolutionary origin of morality provide grounds for the stronger conclusion?

6.5 UNJUSTIFIED MORAL JUDGMENTS *VS.* PROBABLY FALSE MORAL JUDGMENTS

In the original analog I used of John's paranoid suspicions of Sally, we were able to conclude (i) that John's judgments were unreliable and, given the circumstances of their genesis, should be neither believed nor disbelieved; but (ii) that given our independent knowledge of the unlikelihood that Sally was really out to get John, his belief is very probably false, and therefore should be disbelieved. So the question now is whether we can import into the moral case anything analogous to (ii). If we just completely ignore that fact that humans make moral judgments, what evidence do we have of there being inescapable demands upon our actions?

It seems to me that the answer to this question is "None." Imagine a world of intelligent creatures, living successfully and in most respects just like we do, but who employ no moral concepts at all. Perhaps their cooperative activities are, unlike ours, held together by egoism and a powerful Hobbesian sovereign. What phenomena might turn up in their world that provide evidence of "moral facts" obtaining? Suppose their sovereign dictator, in order to instill adequate fear of punishment, has a certain section of society marched off against their will to labor camps, subsequently to be exterminated. We, watching this through a telescope (as it were), would brand this dictator "morally depraved," and might say that this depravity was an important part of the explanation of his genocidal action.[47] But, given our ancestry, that's just what you'd expect us to think. The inhabitants of the imaginary world, given their presumably quite different ancestry, do not employ such explanations. It does not follow that they are phlegmatic victims, unable to object and unwilling to defend themselves. Perhaps they intensely dislike what is going on, and they are able to express this in dramatic and passionate ways. Perhaps they go to war against the dictator, and overthrow him for his actions. But at no point do they attempt to explain the genocide by reference to the *moral* status of the dictator. In order to explain those actions they appeal to his desires/intentions (to instill fear, etc.) and his beliefs (that genocide would be a means of

---

[47] The example of moral depravity explaining morally depraved actions comes from Nicholas Sturgeon's "Moral Explanations," in Copp and Zimmerman (eds.), *Morality, Reason and Truth*, pp. 49–78, though Sturgeon is talking about the real Hitler. In the background of much of my discussion here is the debate between Sturgeon and Harman. See Harman, *Nature of Morality*; idem, "Moral Explanations of Natural Facts – Can Moral Claims be Tested against Moral Reality?" in *The Spindel Conference: The Southern Journal of Philosophy*, supplementary volume 24 (1986), pp. 57–68; N. Sturgeon, "Harman on Moral Explanations of Natural Facts," also in *The Spindel Conference* (1986), pp. 69–78.

instilling fear, etc.). In order to explain and justify their own actions they appeal solely to egoistic considerations. Is there anything mistaken about their explanation? Is there some phenomenon, some aspect of the action, that is inadequately explained in such a way? The answer must be "No," for at no point need their explanation run aground, at no point need they encounter a phenomenon that they had not predicted.

But it is my contention that we can and must go further, and say that their explanation is *better* than ours. It is superior because it confines itself to (tolerably) unmysterious items: beliefs, intentions and desires. Our moral explanation, by contrast, makes appeal to something quite strange: moral depravity. A certain kind of moral naturalist may object: "There is nothing strange about moral depravity – it's just another name for items that the imaginary creatures are already willing to countenance: intentions to cause death and unhappiness for no good reason" (or something along those lines). To address this we must reiterate previous claims and lean on the arguments developed in earlier chapters of this book. It is insufficient to find some property, or cluster of properties, had by all, or nearly all, things to which we generally apply a label like "moral depravity," and then claim to have located the moral property. To be moral depraved (to use Nicholas Sturgeon's example) is not just a matter of intending to bring about death and unhappiness (or some such) – it is something which we *must not be*. Pretend that the imaginary dictator wanted to bring about death and unhappiness – would this have made his actions morally okay? No. Moral depravity, in other words, implies the soundness of categorical imperatives, and I have argued at length that such imperatives, applying to such things as refraining from stealing, promise-breaking, and (I'm afraid) genocide, are simply philosophically insupportable. The naturalist who hopes to sweep this authoritative aspect of morality under the carpet, and identify moral properties with "non-mysterious" natural properties, is like the desperate defender of phlogiston theory who says that he was talking about *oxygen* all along, but merely had wrongly claimed that oxygen was stored in bodies and released during combustion. He is (to quote Ian Hinckfuss) like one of "those theologians who . . . speak of themselves as Christians but interpret religious terms in such a way that, when properly understood, they turn out to believe nothing that a person ordinarily called an atheist would not believe."[48] Such moves are unacceptable. The chemist who speaks of "phlogiston" but attributes to it all the properties we associate

---

[48] Ian Hinckfuss, "The Moral Society: Its Structure and Effects," *Discussion Papers in Environmental Philosophy* (Canberra: Australian National University, 1987), p. 10.

with oxygen, the theologian who speaks of "God" but turns out just to be talking about, say, *love*, the naturalist who speaks of "moral depravity" but leaves out any notion of its authoritative "must-not-be-doneness" – all have simply changed the subject, and are not talking about phlogiston, God, or moral depravity at all.

We must conclude, then, that the evolutionary hypothesis presented at the outset of this chapter will not *independently* serve to show that moral judgments are probably false. At best it shows them to be unjustified, which is, of course, undermining enough. Even if this were all we could conclude, it may still suffice to lead us to reject moral thinking in certain circumstances. Suppose, for example, that there is some moral view that a person is inclined to doubt – perhaps she even recognizes that there is some evidence that counts against it – but suppose that she nevertheless believes the view on the basis of testimony from an "authority," or an authoritative group. If her deference to that authority is contingent upon the testimony issuing from a reliable source (and would it not be?), her discovery that the source is quite unjustified will undermine her belief – leaving her disposed not to withhold assent, but to *disbelieve* the view in question.

However, I have argued that if we supplement the evolutionary hypothesis with certain theses from previous chapters, we can conclude not merely that moral judgments are unjustified, but that they are *probably false*. This conclusion comes about through comparing the adequacy of two explanatory frameworks – a moral and non-moral one – and noting that the latter is superior in that it explains everything that the former does, but is simpler, more intelligible, testable, and, most importantly, avoids any mysterious items. That moral properties are mysterious is not something being simply assumed – the point of Chapters 2–5 was to argue it at length. The latter framework, then, is the one that is more likely to be true, and which ought to be believed.

Where does this leave us and our cherished conviction that the imaginary creatures, in explaining genocidal actions only in terms of beliefs and desires, are missing out on something terribly important: the *depravity* of the act? Surely this conviction demands explanation too? Let the imaginary creatures turn their telescopes upon us – what will they make of our moral convictions? At first they may find them extremely odd, perhaps they may even pause to wonder if perhaps we are seeing truths that they are not, and that these moral properties really are instantiated. But if their epistemic access extends back to our prehistoric development, they will find all the explanation they need there. Suppose the creatures contact us, and point out that we are wielding empty notions. We will object – we will tell them about something called "the genetic fallacy," we will point to sophisticated philosophical programs underway that hold out promise for making sense of categorical imperatives and external normative reasons ("any day now"). But, if the evolutionary hypothesis is correct, the very tendency to want to object along such lines is predictable too. The hypothesis is, *ex hypothesi*, counter-intuitive.

6.6 SOME EPISTEMOLOGICAL CONSIDERATIONS

There is a certain objection to my claim that the evolutionary origin of moral judgments corroborates their unjustifiability, which was previously neglected because we are now in a better position to deal with it. My claim was derived from the plausible but unexamined principle that a justified judgment is one that issues from a faculty or process that manifests sensitivity to the evidence. The objection might run that this is unduly restricted, and that there are other means by which a judgment might be justified. A prominent strategy for defending moral realism is to appeal to some form of coherentist epistemology, backed up, of course, with the thesis that moral judgments are an integral part of the coherent package. This may be augmented by a principle of epistemic conservatism – whereby we ought to hang on to the beliefs with which we find ourselves until such time as they are shown to be faulty – backed up with the thesis that we do find ourselves naturally with moral beliefs. I have no intention of embarking on a lengthy discussion of epistemology; what I shall do is grant the coherentist her framework, but suggest that moral judgments do not thereby attain justification – on the contrary.

A good example of the opponent in question is William Lycan, here summing up the view nicely:

[A]t any given time we find ourselves with some "spontaneous beliefs," beliefs that force themselves on us whether we will or no ... [O]ur retention and epistemic use of the spontaneous beliefs is justified by a ... principle of *conservatism* ... Of course, the warrant conferred by conservatism is initially very weak, and is overridden by almost any other evidential consideration; many spontaneous beliefs get knocked off or thrown out within nanoseconds, as hallucinations, misperceptions, inaccurate memories, superstitious forebodings, *déjà vu*, or whatever. But spontaneous beliefs that pass minimal consistency tests and that continue to fit without further anomaly into our overall body of belief become (what I have called) *tenable*, and enter more aggressively into our explanatory economy. The final test . . . is a matter of bootstrapping: if our overarching total theory can explain not only one of our spontaneous beliefs but how it is produced in us, and if the latter explanation involves the truth of the belief, then the belief is fully justified, perhaps to the point of counting as an item of knowledge. It is in this way that an initial spontaneous belief gets swept up into a coherent global explanatory structure. If there is circularity here, the circle is large, satisfying, and anchored in experience . . . [49]

I have no particular bone to pick with this methodology. What is doubtful is that moral judgments are at all likely to be "swept up" into our best overarching theory. All the considerations put forward in earlier chapters can be read as grounding this doubt. For example, it was argued that "moral facts" imply that a person may have reasons to act regardless of what desires and interests she brings to the deliberative process. But the upshot of previous arguments is that such a view of reasons *does not* fit into a wider coherent theory – we cannot make adequate sense of morality's authority.

In other words, pursuing a strategy of "wide reflective equilibrium" may lead to a wholesale exclusion of moral discourse just as smoothly as it may lead to a vindication. I have argued that once we see clearly the quasi-mystical commitments embodied by moral discourse, elimination is the more probable result. These undermining arguments can now be supplemented with the evolutionary hypothesis favored in this chapter. Assuming that that hypothesis stands up to empirical scrutiny, it will find a place in our "best overarching theory." This will have an enfeebling effect on the role of our "moral intuitions" in the mix, preventing them from "entering aggressively into our explanatory economy." Why so? Because the evolutionary hypothesis explains them away. It predicts that we *would* have such intuitions, even if they were false. A body of intuitions carries no independent weight in a coherentist play-off if already firmly established in that equilibrium is a theory that predicts that such intuitions will be held even if dramatically misguided.

Consider, further, Lycan's view that moral beliefs are "spontaneous." Up to a point, I have agreed. But "spontaneously arising" does not imply "unavoidable." This is important, since one might argue for moral intuitions having a robust role to play in the coherentist equilibrium on the

[49] Lycan, "Moral Facts and Moral Knowledge" (the passage is on the page marked "85," but pages 85 and 86 are erroneously reversed in my edition). See also Boyd, "How to Be a Moral Realist"; Brink, *Moral Realism*; Rawls, *A Theory of Justice* (Oxford: Clarendon Press, 1972); and N. Daniels, "Wide Reflective Equilibrium and Theory Acceptance in Ethics," *Journal of Philosophy* 76 (1979), pp. 256–82.

grounds that we are stuck with them, that we simply could not negotiate the world adequately if they were brought into question. For all my claims that moral beliefs arise naturally, I believe that there is a tendency rashly to overstate their *unavoidability*. Lycan asserts that "to produce a genuine freedom from moral intuitions, one needs a steady diet of hard drugs, or some other very powerful alienating force."[50] Peter Singer writes: "Even if in grim adherence to some skeptical philosophy we deliberately avoid all moral language, we will find it impossible to prevent ourselves inwardly classifying actions as right or wrong."[51] And Ruse suggests that nothing short of genetic engineering will impede our employment of moral judgments.[52] Ruse is correct if he means that the *disposition* to make moral judgments will require genetic alteration to eliminate, but if he means, as I suspect he does, that only genetic changes will stop us making moral judgments, then I am extremely doubtful.

There are many ways of canceling the manifestation of psychological traits, even those furnished by natural selection, if we see fit. As has been stressed, such traits are likely to be dispositions, requiring certain environmental cues – the kind that a small hunter-gatherer band might best provide – in order to manifest themselves. Change the environment, and you eliminate the manifestation of the disposition. (By "manifestation" I do not merely mean behavior, but include mental life.) For example, there is a convincing case to be made that mothers "spontaneously" bond with their young children, and that this trait has evolutionary origins. However, numerous examples of cases where such a bond fails to develop – due, presumably, to subtle and often unremarkable environmental influences – do not undermine the thesis that the bond is an evolved trait. Another example concerns certain xenophobic responses that humans all too often feel. Again, there is a plausible case to be made that a large dose of xenophobia improved reproductive fitness in ancestral humans, and that the trait is therefore a product of evolution. But with the appropriate education, role models, and cultural climate, all traces of the trait can be abolished. Of course, the trait *qua disposition* will remain, implying, perhaps, that a degree of ongoing vigilance in monitoring the socialization process in this respect will be necessary. But there is no need to assume that xenophobia will rear its head afresh with each generation. Horace chose an eloquent but misguided metaphor when he claimed: "Drive

[50] Lycan, "Moral Facts and Moral Knowledge," n. 29.
[51] Singer, *Expanding Circle*, p. ix.
[52] Ruse, *Taking Darwin Seriously*, p. 253.

Nature from your door with a pitchfork, and she will return again and again."[53]

The issue of whether a particular evolved psychological trait – such as the tendency to make moral judgments – could have all manifestation effectively quashed through altering environmental factors is an empirical hypothesis, subject to eventual testing. I am going to assume from now on that moral judgments can, at least in principle, be abolished from our psychological repertoire. It is important that the hypothetical person who makes no moral judgments is not caricatured as someone who "doesn't care." Perhaps Lycan is right that something along the lines of a diet of hard drugs is necessary to make a person utterly *indifferent* to all the pains and pleasures of those around her, but the question is whether a person need take such emotional reactions and present them, to herself and to others, as *moral* considerations. When faced with certain experiences, what presses upon one with apparently relentless ineluctability is a desire that *this not happen*; whether one chooses to bolster this to "It *ought* not happen; it *must* not happen" is entirely another matter. Certainly we have a tendency to do so, but I doubt very much that we unavoidably do so.

Arguing that moral judgments could be abolished is, obviously, a long way from arguing that they *should* be abolished. The question of whether we should abolish the discourse is a practical question, to be assessed according to a cost/benefit analysis of preference satisfactions. Suppose that such an analysis were to come out on the side of morality, revealing that moral discourse is extremely useful. One might think that this in itself would undermine the above claim that a coherentist methodology will exclude moral judgments, on the grounds that part of what gives an element weight in the coherentist equilibrium is its usefulness. The view that the usefulness of a judgment increases the likelihood of its being true actually has more to do with the pragmatist movement than its coherentist cousin. Since the distinction between a judgment's being useful and its being true is central to the remaining chapters of this book, let me briefly turn my sights on the pragmatist's attempt systematically to collapse it.

Again, it is not my intention to undertake a swift assault on the pragmatic theory of truth. Rather, I should point out that on no viable account of pragmatism is the equation "X is useful = X is true" accepted without a great deal of qualification, and once those qualifications are made the distinction on which my argument rests survives. Let us be clear what

---

[53] Horace, *Epistles* (Harmondsworth: Penguin, 1979), I, X, 24–5.

that distinction is, for it has only been mentioned in passing, but it is the center-piece of the next two chapters. I suggested the possibility that even after we decide that moral judgments are false (assuming we were to do so), the issue of what we ought to *do* with our moral discourse is still an open question. The natural thought is that we should just do our best to eliminate it, as we did with talk of witches and phlogiston. What the next two chapters investigate is the possibility that this natural thought is mistaken, and that we might be able to carry on using moral language in some manner, even allowing it to have an important role in our lives, while cognizant of its serious indefensibility. The grounds that would justify this continued use would be the benefits that we would gain in doing so.

This is where the pragmatist might be thought to make trouble. How can a discourse, a way of describing the world and our place in it, be *false*, and yet the continued employment of that language be pragmatically justified? The question is misguided, and no pragmatist worth her salt would have trouble seeing the answer. Consider: what is useful for me today may not be tomorrow, and may be never useful to you. Does it follow that it was true for me today but not tomorrow, and never true for you? Crazy theory if that's its consequence. Charles Peirce held that "truth" doesn't flit in and out of existence in this way, and nor is it agent-relative; rather, a judgment is considered true if and only if it is "indefeasible," in that we would at some point come to accept the judgment, and no further inquiry will lead us to revise this position.[54] The emphasis on a judgment's *surviving future inquiry* blocks the possibility of its truth changing over time, while the emphasis on what *we* come to accept – where "we" might mean humans – prevents the possibility of agent-relativity.

Bearing this in mind, let me lay a couple of preparatory building blocks for the next two chapters. The argument will have the conclusion that morality, though in error, is a justified practice in light of its usefulness. But it will not claim that moral discourse will be found useful on all evidential and rational improvements that we may undergo. I am content to argue that it may be useful to us now, and say nothing about what practical role it may have a thousand years hence. Second, even if we were to find employing moral discourse useful "forever after," it does not follow that we will find *believing* it useful. After all, believing something that (we are assuming) is known to be false sounds like the recipe for doxastic

---

[54] See, for example, Peirce's "How to Make Our Ideas Clear" [1868] in *Collected Papers*, vol. 5 (Cambridge, Mass.: Belknap Press of Harvard University Press, 1960), pp. 248–71.

disaster! The crucial question is "Can we gain the practical benefits that come from believing in morality without *believing* in morality?" Perhaps instead it could take on the status of a fiction, or a myth. That we employ a myth, for example, which fails to cohere with our wider beliefs does not suggest any particular practical problem; the employment of the myth may be useful in some manner – if only because we enjoy its narrative structure – but the myth does not thereby threaten to become true, even by the pragmatist's lights. If moral judgments likewise cease to be items of belief, then the pragmatist's challenge founders, for her theory doesn't apply to anything at all that we find useful. Vacuum cleaners are useful – perhaps they will remain useful at the end of all rational inquiry – but vacuum cleaners are not thereby true.

7

Fictionalism

7.0 IF THERE'S NOTHING THAT WE OUGHT TO DO, THEN WHAT OUGHT WE TO DO?

Let us suppose that the main conclusion of the previous chapters is correct: moral discourse consists largely of untrue assertions. Those arguments have primarily targeted deontological notions like *obligation* and *prohibition*. One might object that even if these arguments were faultless, all they show is that a certain proper subset of our moral discourse is flawed, but there is a rich and robust moral language that remains untouched. However, it is my contention that moral concepts are to a large degree holistically connected, such that a persuasive attack on categorical imperatives will, one way or another, count as a persuasive attack on a great deal more besides.

If there are no inescapable moral obligations, for instance, then there will be no inviolable claim rights (and *claim* rights are the central currency of ordinary rights-based moral discourse). Similarly, talk of virtues and vices generally implies the existence of obligations. Virtues are often thought of as character traits that one is obligated to cultivate. Or even if not that, a virtuous agent is taken to be one who is, *inter alia*, sensitive to, and acts in accordance with, her moral obligations. There may be accounts of the virtues that have neither of these implications, but that very fact indicates how distant they are from the notions as they are employed in common moral parlance.

Consider, thirdly, the idea of a morally good state of affairs. Obviously, if a morally good state of affairs is one that one is obligated to bring about, then *modus tollens* will do its work. If by "morally good state of affairs" we mean something weaker, then *modus tollens* may still do the work, but may require reiteration. Even if bringing about a morally good state of affairs is not obligatory, presumably it would be good to bring it about. So good states of affairs imply good actions. Ian Hinckfuss then argues as follows: "[I]f an act is morally good, then one has a moral right to perform that

175

act, and . . . if one has a moral right to do something, then everyone else has a moral obligation to allow one to do it."[1]

It is sometimes thought that a shift from talk of what one ought not do, to talk of what is unjust, or mean, or evil, etc. (what are sometimes called "thick" evaluative terms[2]) might side-step some problems. But what is *evil* if not something we ought not do or be? A "thick" evaluative term may have a comprehensible descriptive component, but it also (necessarily) has an evaluative component, and this evaluative component demands explanation here no less than it does for a "thin" evaluative term, like "good." My claim is not that all thick evaluative terms are suspect, but that those at the heart of *moral* discourse are. Nor am I claiming that the evaluative component of a thick moral term always directly concerns what one "must" or "must not" do, only that it generally implies the intelligibility of such strong prescriptions. Suppose, for example, that the evaluative component of the term "mean" amounts to something like "undesirable but morally permissible." From the concept of *morally permissibility*, with the addition of an unobjectionable negation operator, we can construct *moral obligation*: ϕing is obligatory iff refraining from ϕing is not permissible. Therefore an independent argument showing that moral obligation makes no sense also shows that moral permissibility makes no sense. (This would not be to claim that nothing is permissible, only that nothing is *morally* permissible.) Similarly, the practice of categorizing certain actions as "supererogatory" (desirable but not required) is sensible only against the background of a practice of categorizing other actions as "required."[3]

It is not necessary for me to claim that absolutely every piece of recognizably moral language implies the validity of categorical imperatives, only that a sufficient portion of them do, such that if we were to eliminate categorical imperatives and all that imply them from the discourse, whatever remained would no longer be recognizable as – could not play the role of – a *moral* discourse.[4] Any system of values that leaves out categorical

---

[1] Ian Hinckfuss, "The Moral Society: Its Structure and Effects," in *Discussion Papers in Environmental Philosophy* (Canberra: Australian National University, 1987), p. 5.

[2] See B. Williams, *Ethics and the Limits of Philosophy* (London: Fontana Press, 1985).

[3] Of course, even if nothing is required we might still truly say that some actions are "desirable but not required," just as one may point to a dog and say "It is a dog but not a unicorn." My claim is that the practice of employing the concept *supererogation* would be pointless if nothing is required.

[4] It should also be remembered that categorical imperatives may not be the only error-laden element of moral discourse. An error theorist need not find a single monolithic mistake committed by morality; it is enough if of the various elements of moral discourse,

imperatives will lack the authority that we expect of morality, and any set of prescriptions failing to underwrite this authority simply does not count as a "morality" at all. Moral discourse, in other words, is a house of cards, and the card at center bottom has "categorical imperative" written on it. So let us suppose that the previous chapters have succeeded in toppling the house of cards. The question that this and the following chapter addresses is "What should we now do?"

It might be thought that the question "If a moral error theory is the case, what should we do?" is self-undermining. And so it would be, if it were asking what we *morally* ought to do, but that is not what is being asked. It is just a straightforward, common-or-garden, *practical* "ought." In other words, the answer that the question invites will be a hypothetical imperative, and the arguments for a moral error theory have not threatened hypothetical imperatives. I do not want this issue to depend on any particular view of how we make such practical decisions. Let us just say that when morality is removed from the picture, what is practically called for is a matter of a cost-benefit analysis, where the costs and benefits can be understood liberally as preference satisfactions. (Two comments: first, I do not object if one favors talk of informed preferences as opposed to actual preferences; second, and more importantly, there is no assumption being made that these preferences are selfish in content.) By asking what *we* ought to do I am asking how a *group* of persons, who share a variety of broad interests, projects, ends – and who have come to the realization that morality is a bankrupt theory – might best carry on.

One might object that this, being a complex counterfactual question, is not something for which an answer should be undertaken from the armchair. And I quite agree that it would be foolhardy to assert an answer with any degree of assurance. This chapter centers on the more modest end of exploring what a neglected type of answer might look like. The business of arguing for that answer will be attempted in the next chapter, but I consider it a more speculative, and therefore secondary, task.

---

a sufficient number of them have their own problems. Even admitting, for example, that moral virtues do not imply categorical imperatives, one might argue nevertheless that virtue ethics is based on an empirically false view of character traits. See Gilbert Harman in "Moral Philosophy Meets Social Psychology: Virtue Ethics and the Fundamental Attribution Error," *Proceedings of the Aristotelian Society* 99 (1999), pp. 315–31. Even if there is no single error-laden element sufficient to sink moral discourse, a number of moderate flaws, which together add up to a serious problem, may be sufficient.

Suppose then that a group of persons have come to the uncomfortable conclusion that moral discourse, which they have been mindfully employing for centuries, is deeply flawed. Assuming that they take the evidence to be incontrovertible, then it would appear that the option of carrying on *believing* in moral discourse is closed. At the very least, carrying on believing in something the evidence of whose falsity they have seen and accepted would be irrational. And even if they *could* somehow talk themselves into carrying on with their old beliefs, they *should not*, for true beliefs are an extremely valuable commodity. Philosophers from antiquity have argued that truth has intrinsic value; indeed, the man who has a claim to having produced the earliest known use of the word "philosophy" in Greek – Heraclitus – tells us that "thinking well is the greatest excellence and wisdom: . . . perceiving things according to their nature."[5] I am not arguing anything so lofty, but rather am claiming that truth has *instrumental* value. This seems so obvious a claim that it probably isn't worth laboring; a few comments will suffice.

William James is frequently interpreted as equating *truth* with *utility*, but often his position sounds like the less ambitious and more plausible view that truth is useful: "The possession of truth, so far from being here an end in itself, is only a preliminary means towards other vital satisfactions."[6] James starts with an obvious example of how on a particular occasion a true belief is instrumentally superior to a false one: I am lost in the woods and seek a house; I come across a cow-path, form the belief that the cow-path will lead to a house, and act on the belief. If the belief is true I am saved; if not, my life may be lost. Now suppose that on a different occasion I am in the woods, but this time not lost and starving. Again I see a cow-path and form the belief that it leads to a house, but this time I have no interest in seeking a house, and therefore do not act on the belief. One may think that in the second case it makes no difference whether my belief is true or false. Perhaps I even have a whim to think myself miles from human habitation, in which case I would slightly prefer that I be mistaken. James disagrees. We never know whether and in what way a belief may be called upon to serve action, and, given this, it is better that it be true than false – "since almost any object may some day become temporarily important, the advantage of having a general stock of *extra* truths, of truths that shall

---

[5] This is fragment XXXII. The possible first use of "philosophy" is fragment IX. See C. H. Kahn, *The Art and Thought of Heraclitus* (Cambridge: Cambridge University Press, 1979), especially pp. 105 and 119–22.

[6] W. James, *Pragmatism: The Meaning of Truth* [1909] (Cambridge, Mass.: Harvard University Press, 1978), p. 98.

be true of merely possible situations, is obvious."[7] In the vast majority of cases having a true belief to act upon is more likely to bring satisfaction of desire than having a false belief on the matter, and given that we don't know in advance how and when we are going to employ a particular belief, the safest bet is to have the true one over the false one. This is not to say, of course, that the true one is always available and accessible, but when it is, we do well to have it.

A seemingly useful false belief, moreover, will require all manner of compensating false beliefs to make it fit with what else one knows. This is what is so hopeless about Plato's "medicine of deception": for the citizens of the republic sincerely to believe that their origin lay underground (to say nothing of being partly made of metal), they would need to interpret large amounts of the evidence of their senses in dramatically eccentric ways.[8] It is not merely that a stock of true beliefs is vastly more likely to be helpful than a stock of false ones, but that the *policy* of aiming for the truth, of having and trying to satisfy a general (*de dicto*) desire for the truth – what we might simply call "critical inquiry" – is the best doxastic policy around. Anything else, as Charles Peirce correctly insists, leads to "a rapid deterioration of intellectual vigor."[9] The conclusion, then, is that a group of moral error theorists should not believe in morality. This is not merely the claim that such a belief would be an epistemic error, but that it would be a *practical* error: in so far as their participation in critical inquiry (as opposed to Peirce's "pseudo-inquiry") is a pragmatically warranted practice, their belief and assertion of propositions the evidence of whose falsehood is available is likely to have negative repercussions.

Given this conclusion, what more is there to argue about? Doesn't it follow that moral error theorists should simply propose to do away with moral discourse – that they should consign it to the scrap heap of other bankrupt theories, along with phlogiston, demonic possession, and astrology? This step is a natural enough one to make. Nietzsche (if not an error theorist exactly, a vital ancestor) thought that if we were to be strong and honest,

---

[7] *Ibid.*

[8] In the Epilogue, I cast some doubt on how much *deception* was involved in Plato's "medicine."

[9] C. S. Peirce, *Collected Papers* (Cambridge, Mass.: Belknap Press of Harvard University Press, 1960), vol. 1, pp. 25–6. Susan Haack, in "Concern for Truth: What it Means, Why it Matters," *Annals of the New York Academy of Sciences* 775 (1996), p. 59, writes: "Intellectual integrity is instrumentally valuable, because, in the long run and on the whole, it advances inquiry; and successful inquiry is instrumentally valuable. Compared with other animals, we are not especially fleet or strong; our forte is a capacity to figure things out, hence to anticipate and avoid danger".

we would just cease to employ the faulty concepts; G. E. M Anscombe suggested that the "law conception" of morality that we inherited from Christianity and Kant should, in light of its flaws, "be jettisoned if this is psychologically possible";[10] and Simon Blackburn, without hesitation, assumes that if Mackie is correct "our old, infected moral concepts or ways of thought should be replaced."[11]

For all I know, "Jettison the discourse" is the correct answer, and it is not my intention to convince the reader otherwise. However, I do not think that it is the only candidate, and so it should not be accepted without debate. What we ought to *do* with our faulty moral discourse is a practical question, and if we are to weigh options sensibly, we must first investigate what benefits we might expect to forfeit if we were to abolish it. One moral error theorist, Ian Hinckfuss, argues that morality is not useful at all – on the contrary, it has brought little but harm, and the sooner we rid ourselves of its pernicious influence the better. He reminds us of the misery that moral beliefs have caused:

> the massacre of the moral Catholic highlanders by the moral Protestants at Culloden and its aftermath, the genocide of the peaceful and hospitable stone-age Tasmanians by people from moral Britain, the mutual slaughter of all those dutiful men on the Somme and on the Russian front in World War I, the morally sanctioned slaughter of World War II, especially in the area bombing of Hamburg, London, Coventry, Cologne, Dresden, Tokyo, Hiroshima and Nagasaki, and the subsequent slaughter in Korea, Vietnam, Northern Ireland and the Middle East – all this among people the great majority of whom wanted above all to be good and who did not want to be bad.[12]

I wonder, though, how much the specifically *moral* convictions should be blamed for such events, and suspect that the carnage would have occurred even without the backing of moral rationalizations. (In fairness to Hinckfuss, he immediately goes on to acknowledge this point.) But even if moral beliefs do bring harms, we need to ask whether they also bring compensating benefits. Would the harm be even greater without moral beliefs?

7.1 WHAT ARE THE BENEFITS OF MORAL BELIEFS?

It is the purpose of the next chapter to address this question in detail, but we should at least put on the table a sketch of an answer, so that we have some

[10] G. E. M. Anscombe, "Modern Moral Philosophy," *Philosophy* 33 (1958), p. 1.
[11] S. Blackburn, "Errors and the Phenomenology of Value," in his *Essays in Quasi-Realism* (Oxford: Oxford University Press, 1993), p. 149.
[12] Hinckfuss, "The Moral Society," p. 21.

understanding of the kinds of benefits that moral thinking brings. Morality, I will argue, functions to bolster self-control. It imbues certain desirable actions with a "must-be-doneness," which raises the likelihood of their being performed (likewise, *mutatis mutandis*, "must-not-be-doneness"). It goes without saying that if this "must-be-doneness" were attached to the wrong actions – undesirable ones – then it would be disastrous in practical terms.

Hinckfuss provides a depressing catalog of events that were perpetrated by people who – let us grant for the sake of argument – sincerely believed themselves to occupy the moral high ground. If he is to use this list as a way of showing how dreadful can be the consequences of moral belief (in the course of arguing for a moral error theory), he cannot mean that they are *morally* dreadful. If we are ever going to assess the usefulness of morality, we will need a way of "stepping out" of moral thinking, and the only way I know of doing that is to ask whether it is instrumentally profitable. So Hinckfuss must be taken as saying that events like the Victorian British genocide of native Tasmanians are (if a cold phrase can be excused) instrumentally suboptimal. My response to Hinckfuss's claim that moral beliefs have wrought such dramatic damage is that this just shows that people have had the wrong moral beliefs. Morality is a useful institution only if the sense of "must-be-doneness" is attached to the already useful actions.

But this way of addressing the issue cannot proceed until we get straight on the question of *to whom* the benefits are accruing or being denied. The Tasmanian genocide was obviously as desperate a misfortune as one can imagine *to the Tasmanians*. But might it nevertheless have been useful *for the British* to have the indigenous people "out of the way"? A vague thought is that when we are asking how useful morality is we're asking about how useful it is *to the society* as a whole. But it is far from clear what sense can be made of this notion, and, besides, it doesn't help us with our test case of the Tasmanian genocide, since this involves the collision of two separate societies. I prefer to hope that the question can be side-stepped by making the case that, across a wide range of situations, to harm another is to harm one's own interests. In the past few decades a body of understanding has built up concerning the instrumental justification of cooperative strategies among interacting agents with competing interests. (Some of this comes from evolutionary biologists, whose work was touched on in the previous chapter; further evidence will be discussed below.) For the present, I'll just state the case without argument.

To begin with, we should not think of the task as instrumentally justifying moral beliefs on a case-by-case basis – rather, I am satisfied to provide instrumental justification for "being a moral believer." This reflects the fact that we are creatures of habit and custom. One cannot, after a lifetime of atheism, suddenly think of a particular action, ϕ, as *commanded by Allah*, thereafter to return to one's secular beliefs, simply because it was useful on that singular occasion to think of ϕ as so-required. What requires justification is a policy. So what shall we say of the Victorian British? They held a policy of thinking that initiating violent hostility, in certain circumstances, was morally permissible. With regard to this particular "interaction," they forfeited the potentially greater gains of fostering a cooperative relationship. But it is insufficient to concentrate on the rewards of the single relationship, for there is also the vital matter of the player's *reputation* to take into account. By initiating hostility once, the British threatened the confidence of any number of other profitable partners. They lowered the chances of being sought out by others with offers of mutually useful ventures.[13] In this way it can be argued with some plausibility that the moral belief held by the British (that killing Tasmanians was permissible) was instrumentally disadvantageous *to them* as well as to the ill-fated Tasmanians. The moral judgment that initiating hostile actions is morally forbidden would, in the long run, have been useful all round.

This may sound like a heartless logic, but it is the result of purposely "stepping out" of moral thinking in order to assess its usefulness to an actor (in this case, a group), and selecting a particularly dramatic episode to make the point. It is not being argued that this cold egoism need figure in anyone's deliberations. On the contrary, if pursuing a cooperative strategy is instrumentally optimal, it may well be that the best means of regulating that strategy at the deliberative level is to cultivate a concern directly for one's fellows.

From these observations two quite different (indeed, conflicting) conclusions might be tempting. The first is that perhaps we have paved the way for a vindication of morality. After all, if we have arguments to the conclusion that people ought to cooperate (generally), and that this cooperation ought to be regulated by a direct concern for the welfare of others, then hasn't the moral error theory evaporated? Hasn't the argument just succeeded in undoing the earlier one urged in §3.2, the conclusion of which was that I could "discern no grounds for confidence concerning the thesis that self-interest and morality always coincide"? No, it hasn't.

[13] See R. H. Frank, *Passion Within Reason* (London: W. W. Norton & Company, 1988).

For a start, the above argument is conducted in contingent, "for-the-most-part" terms – were it really the case that the considered, fully informed preferences of the British would be best served by committing genocide (unlikely, but certainly possible), then they have no reason to refrain. Similarly, if a person's desires are not for self-interest, but perhaps for a fiery self-destruction in which she takes as many innocents with her as she can, then we can provide no reason for her to refrain. But these conclusions are at odds with moral thinking; we morally condemn genocide even if it is clearly self-serving; we morally condemn massacring innocents even when the killer renounces self-interest.

Furthermore, moral judgments are something more than judgments about an agent's long-term self-interest. Suppose that A has good reason to play fair with B, and has cultivated a sincere caring for B's welfare. But suppose that A breaks down and defects on the deal on one occasion, perhaps because of weakness of will. It will be reasonable for A to castigate herself, reasonable for B to complain, and reasonable for third parties to be annoyed (if they also care about B, and care about maintaining a matrix of cooperative relations). So it will be legitimate, all round, for people to judge: "A ought not to have done that." But none of this has supported the move to *moral* language. For what is the basis of the "ought" statement? What is the reason that A had to refrain from defecting? There are two possible answers, depending on how we would fill in the details of the example.

The first is that A's reason for refraining was that it was in her own interests to do so. But when B *morally* condemns A's action, he is not complaining that A harmed herself – he is complaining that A harmed *him*. When we morally condemn the British for the Tasmanian genocide it is certainly not because of the harm they inflicted upon themselves (what sense would there then be in punishing them?). But the framework we have offered of cooperative relations bound by long-term prudence does not warrant such judgments. The second possible reason that A had for refraining was that she cared for B. To be "a carer" was, we'll allow, in her self-interest, but this is not her motivating foundation. On the grounds of self-interest she has cultivated a habit of thinking in non-self-interested terms. If this were the case, then perhaps we can, after all, say that the reason she ought not to have harmed B was *because it harmed B*. This judgment, however, is a hostage to fortune. Had A *not* cared about B, then we could no longer provide this reason for her not harming him. Yet a *moral* judgment is not so counterfactually frail as this. Our moral condemnation of perpetrators of genocide is not based on self-harm, and nor does it depend upon their caring for their victims.

The second possible implication of the view that sincere cooperation is generally instrumentally justified is that we have paved the way not for the vindication of morality but for its effective elimination. After all, if we have arguments to the conclusion that people ought to cooperate (generally), and that this cooperation ought to be regulated by a direct concern for the welfare of others, then what need is there for moral thinking? Would not clear-headed instrumental thinking lead to the same results?

I believe that correct moral thinking and clear-headed instrumental reasoning generally *do* lead to the same conclusion, for to think otherwise is to accept that moral discourse is not instrumentally useful (and if it is not that, then in what sense is it useful at all?). Yet, in practice, moral thinking is not eliminable in favor of instrumental deliberation. The mere fact that I justifiably believe ϕing to be in my best interests simply does not ensure that I will ϕ. Humans are epistemically fallible creatures, and even when we are smart enough to see where lies the right answer, interfering factors like weakness of will, passion, accidie, etc., may provide obstacles to the right action being performed. A particular failing is, as Hobbes put it, the "perverse desire for present profit"[14] – something which Hume blamed for "all dissoluteness and disorder, repentance and misery,"[15] adding that a person should embrace "any expedient, by which he may impose a restraint upon himself, and guard against this weakness."[16] Moral thinking, I contend, is just such an expedient, in that it functions to bolster self-control against such practical irrationality. If a person believes ϕing to be required by an authority from which she cannot escape, if she imbues it with a "must-be-doneness," if she believes that in not ϕing she will not merely frustrate herself, but will become reprehensible and deserving of disapprobation – then she is more likely to perform the action. In this manner, moral beliefs can help us to act in an instrumentally rational manner.

This sketch will be expanded upon later; at this stage what matters is that we are aware that moral beliefs have played, and do play, a significant useful role. Hinckfuss is quite correct that tragedies are sometimes begotten, and

---

[14] Thomas Hobbes, *De Cive* [1642], chapter 3, section 27 (Oxford: Clarendon Press, 1983), p. 72.

[15] Hume, *Enquiry*, section 6 (1983), p. 55.

[16] Hume, *Treatise*, book 3, part 2, section 7 (1978), pp. 536–7. I have altered Hume's text from the first person singular.

exacerbated, by moral beliefs. My response has been that this shows how important it is that one gets the *right* moral beliefs. The right moral beliefs I understand to be the most useful ones. The objective of this section, in other words, has been to outline the case for claiming that having the right moral beliefs is instrumentally justified. Obviously, given earlier conclusions, I take this conclusion to be quite distinct from the question of whether moral beliefs are *evidentially* justified.

7.2 THE FICTIONALIST OPTION

Section 7.0 claimed that moral error theorists would be at a practical disadvantage if they carried on believing in morality. Section 7.1 has pointed out an important practical role that moral beliefs play. If both sets of arguments are cogent, then a moral error theorist finds herself in a pickle (perhaps wishing that she had never taken up philosophy in the first place): to keep her moral beliefs is likely to be detrimental to her interests, but so too will be their abolition. Now that the stage is set, we can move to the main object of this chapter, which is to explore a way of resolving the error theorist's predicament. Can the error theorist "carry on" with moral discourse in such a way that she (A) continues to gain the instrumental benefits of the discourse (or, at least, many of those benefits), but (B) does not accrue the costs of believing falsehood? I will argue in the positive, advancing a stance that may be adopted by the error theorist, which shall be called "fictionalism."

Let me stipulate that to take a fictionalist stance towards a discourse is to believe that the discourse entails or embodies a theory that is false (such that there is no error-free revisionary theory available), but to carry on employing the discourse, at least in many contexts, as if this were not the case, because it is *useful* to do so. The discourse in question may be terribly important to us – so much so that the pragmatic cost of eliminating it (in the way we eliminated phlogiston discourse) is greater than the cost of saying things which we know to fall short of truth. Therefore when we ask the question "Given a moral error theory, what ought we to do?" – a question which asks for the optimal option after costs and benefits are weighed – the fictionalist thinks that the correct answer is "Keep using the discourse, but do not believe it."

It must be stressed that fictionalism is not being proposed as a description of our actual moral discourse. I have argued that our actual moral judgments are uttered with assertoric force – that is, are expressive of beliefs – and that these beliefs are, for the large part, untrue. Fictionalism is, rather, an option for a stance we may adopt once we realize the error of our ways. (And by "we" I mean *users* of the discourse, not philosophers of a revisionary temperament.) It is not, therefore, being suggested that moral fictionalism is *true* – it is being put forward as a change that a group can make in its attitude towards a faulty discourse.

The kind of fictionalist stance that will be described is not intended to be confined to an attitude that we can take towards *morality*. Therefore, in order to avoid distraction, the moral question will be put aside for a while, in order to discuss fictionalism in general terms. Besides, the general and the particular discussions should be kept somewhat apart, since even if what is said concerning *moral* fictionalism turns out to be unconvincing, much of the general view may still have merit. So this chapter focuses first on fictionalism in general, describing a kind of positive attitude that an individual may take towards the theory that she knows to be false: the "fictive judgment." I propose that one might use a theory, think in terms of that theory, "immerse oneself in it," but so long as one remains disposed to deny it in one's most rigorous context of interrogation, one does not believe the theory. Thereafter I return to the case of *moral* fictionalism, but continue to limit discussion to describing what the theory would consist of. The matter of arguing for moral fictionalism is the job of the Chapter 8.

7.3 FICTIVE JUDGMENTS: VAIHINGER

An enthusiastic proponent of the fictionalist stance – for morality, as well as for infinity, freedom, absolute space, atoms, substance, abstract and general concepts, force, infinitesimals, and much more besides – was Hans Vaihinger.[17] I am not interested in his work *per se*, but it makes a useful point of departure. His views will be outlined, and, where they leave vital questions unanswered, developed.

Vaihinger distinguishes fictions from both presumptions and hypotheses. A presumption is something that is assumed when we lack certainty (one thinks of "presumed innocent until proven guilty"). A hypothesis is a suggestion that something is the case – or, as Vaihinger tends to put it, that something corresponds to reality. A hypothesis "seeks to be an adequate

---

[17] H. Vaihinger, *The Philosophy of "As If,"* trans. C. K. Ogden (London: Routledge & Kegan Paul Ltd., 1949). All textual page references to Vaihinger are to this book. The historical roots of fictionalism can be traced through Bentham, Adam Smith, Leibniz, Hobbes, William of Ockham, Maimonides, and back to the Skeptics.

expression of some reality still unknown" (p. 268), "it wants to be proved true, real, and an expression of reality" (p. 85). One may assert a hypothesis while being less than certain that it is true, and one may adopt a working hypothesis in such a circumstance (in which case the hypothesis will also be a presumption). By contrast, the judgment that something is a fiction – the fictive judgment – is "the acceptance of a statement or a fact although we are certain of the contrary" (p. 147). "The judgment is made with the consciousness of its non-validity" (p. 261).

These last quotes begin to highlight a source of complexity in fictionalism. Consider, for example, Ovid's frequently quoted passage: "The existence of gods is expedient: let us therefore assume it."[18] One might think that Ovid is exhorting us to indulge in a fictive judgment. However, it turns out that "assuming the existence of gods" requires only certain *actions*: "gifts of incense and wine on their antique hearths," etc. – in which case, it does not obviously involve a special sort of *judgment* or *attitude* at all. If this is all fictionalism amounted to, then it would not be terribly interesting. It would be no more problematic than is a petty example used by Vaihinger concerning the German Commercial Code of the time: goods that are not returned to the sender within a designated time were to be treated *as if* they had been authorized and accepted by the recipient (p. 35).

But many of the fictions that Vaihinger puts forward amount to more than treating something in a certain way; they require, in addition, that we *judge* that something is the case, that we *accept* that it is, while knowing that it is not. And it is here that problems arise. Put bluntly: if to make a fiction of p is to believe (judge, accept) that p while knowing that not-p, but to know that not-p is to believe that not-p, then to make a fiction of p is to believe that p while believing that not-p. The problem is compounded by Vaihinger's insistence that to overlook that one's fiction is a fiction – to believe that p while "forgetting" that one believes that not-p – is a vice to be avoided. "Full belief" in a fiction Vaihinger calls "logical optimism," and this is frowned upon, at least in "civilized man." Logical optimism "is harmless and innocent enough when found among primitive people, but it is a questionable attitude and becomes definitely dangerous and disastrous when encountered in men of a more advanced type ... Had primitive man already begun to doubt the objectivity of his logical forms he would never have become civilized. But if a thinker at a higher stage of civilization does not question this objectivity, he becomes a primitive man

---

[18] Ovid, "The Art of Love" book 1, 637, in P. Green (trans.), *The Erotic Poems* (Harmondsworth: Penguin, 1982), p. 186.

again and, in the worst sense of the word, an uncritical man" (p. 162). Later, in much the same vein, Vaihinger talks of fictions being mistaken for truths by "the less educated, childlike minds" which misconstrue them "in a literal, concrete and external sense" (p. 264).

These passages imply several things. First, in certain circumstances it may be more expedient to believe in a fiction while *not* knowing that it is a fiction than to accept it while knowing it to be a fiction (as with "primitive man"). Second, in some circumstances (those of "civilized man") the reverse is the case: it is dangerous – that is to say, practically suboptimal – to indulge in logical optimism; rather, one should accept one's fictions while knowing them to be fictions. We needn't dwell on to whom Vaihinger intended "primitive man" to refer; suffice it to say that it was not his readers. I point this out to clarify one kind of fictionalism that Vaihinger is *not* endorsing: that in which the philosophical or scientific cognoscenti know that some discourse is error-laden, but this knowledge is not widespread (either because it has been withheld for the sake of the greater good, or, as is more likely, because their journals and books just are not widely read). A circumstance in which most people believe something false and are unaware of this fact, but are in fact practically better off in this state of ignorance, does not involve "fictive judgments" and does not count as "fictionalism." One interesting point about Vaihinger's comments concerning "primitive and civilized man" is that the state of affairs just described *could* be the case, but it is contingently not so. The average person happens to satisfy whatever criteria Vaihinger has in mind that characterize "civilized man" – which is to say, it is recommended to the average person, on grounds of expediency, that she "accept" the fiction without mistaking it for an assertion of fact or a genuine hypothesis.

Let us now return attention to the curious kind of judgment that Vaihinger recommends for his reader – what is called "the fictive judgment." The fictive judgment has a positive and negative component – it is judged that A is B; simultaneously there is "a protest against the idea of its objective validity." "The judgment is made with the consciousness of its non-validity, but at the same time it is tacitly presupposed that this operation is permissible, useful and appropriate" (p. 261). When we make a fictive judgment that A is B, the "is" is an "abbreviation for an exceedingly complicated train of thought" (p. 264). Vaihinger pays disappointingly little attention to the nature of the curious kind of attitude – in particular, it is not clear whether he is recommending that one simultaneously believe that *p* and believe that not-*p*. In what follows, I will endeavor to avoid that conclusion. Let us say, rather, that to make a fiction of *p* is to "accept" *p* while disbelieving *p*.

This notion of "disbelieving acceptance" has been attacked by Hilary Putnam, taking Vaihinger as his explicit target, so we should disarm the criticism at the outset. Putnam's argument (a thread of his "indispensability argument") runs as follows:

[T]o ask whether statements are "true" cannot be separated from asking whether it is rational to accept those statements ... since it is rational to accept *p is true* just in case it is rational to accept *p*. But the end purpose of our whole "conceptual scheme" is just the prediction and control of experience ... The fictionalist concedes that the conceptual scheme of material objects (or whatever) leads to successful prediction (or as successful as we have been able to manage to date) and that it is as simple as we have been able to manage to date. But these are just the factors on which rational acceptance depends; so it is rational to accept our conceptual system, and rational to call the propositions that make it up "true".[19]

Putnam paints Vaihinger's fictionalism as the claim that if we have a well-confirmed theory T, with all internal virtues that one could ask for, but for which there is some possibility of its being disconfirmed, then we should "accept" T but not believe T. But, Putnam objects, the rational grounds of acceptance are the same as the rational grounds of belief ("at least in the sense in which one ever 'believes' a scientific theory – as an approximation to the truth which can probably be bettered"[20]), and therefore "disbelieving acceptance" is incoherent.

This is a caricature of Vaihinger. Vaihinger considers some of his fictions to be self-contradictory concepts. Presumably if T entails "*p* and not-*p*" then it is not going to have all the internal virtues. Nevertheless, Vaihinger thinks (and I agree with him), we may have grounds for accepting T. In other words, Putnam is using "acceptance" in a quite different way from Vaihinger. If we disambiguate, and use "acceptance" as Putnam intends it, then Vaihinger need disagree with nothing that Putnam claims concerning theory acceptance. In particular, the fictionalist need not endorse criteria for theory *belief* that are any more demanding than those held by Putnam; the fictionalist would merely prefer not to use the word "acceptance" there, since he has reserved it for a quite different attitude – something which Putnam has failed to notice. Putnam thinks that a fictionalist stance

[19] H. Putnam, *Philosophy of Logic* (New York: Harper & Row, 1971), pp. 68–9. Much the same point is raised by J. Newman, "The Fictionalist Analysis of Some Moral Concepts," *Metaphilosophy* 12 (1981), p. 54.
[20] Putnam, *Philosophy of Logic*, p. 73.

towards T is prompted by the absence of demonstrative proof that T is true, but this is simply a misreading.[21] I have not committed myself to the demanding epistemic criteria that Putnam tries to foist on the fictionalist: the arguments for a moral error theory from earlier chapters, for example, were designed to show that it is reasonable to disbelieve morality, but I am not so unblushing as to think that those arguments constituted demonstrative proof!

With this clarification made, let us investigate further this attitude of "disbelieving acceptance." In the following section I will attempt to make sense of fictive judgments in a way that does not involve the maker of the judgment in inconsistent beliefs, but this will require leaving Vaihinger behind.

7.4 FICTIVE JUDGMENTS: CRITICAL CONTEXTS

Consider Hume's philosophical distress at the conclusion of Book I of the *Treatise*, where his "reflections very refin'd and metaphysical" have left him in a state of skeptical angst – "in the most deplorable condition imaginable, inviron'd with the deepest darkness, and utterly depriv'd of the use of every member and faculty."[22] Hume is saved from his distress by the interference of "nature herself" – he dines, he plays a game of backgammon, he is convivial with his friends, and in doing so his philosophical torments evaporate. When he returns to his skeptical thoughts they seem cold and unengaging, and it is only with intellectual effort that he is able to feel their force again. Suppose that Hume's "refin'd reflections" lead him to endorse a skeptical thesis: "That there are other minds is no more probable than that there are not"; yet all his actions and thoughts while merrily playing

---

[21] Of course, Putnam does have a real opponent who may be called a "fictionalist," but it is not Vaihinger. The fictionalism Putnam has in mind is better represented by Pierre Duhem, or, more recently, Bas van Fraassen (see van Fraassen's response to Putnam: "Critical Notice: Hilary Putnam's *Philosophy of Logic,*" *Canadian Journal of Philosophy* 4 [1973–4], pp. 731–43). Such a position is essentially this: we can never have reason to believe that our scientific theories provide the truth – at best they provide empirically adequate descriptions – and therefore we ought not believe them, but we can provisionally accept them. The difference between this position and the one I am advocating on Vaihinger's behalf (and the reason I am not discussing Duhem and van Fraassen) might be summed up as follows: "agnostic" fictionalism says "I do not know whether T is true, but it is highly useful and therefore I shall accept it"; "atheistic" fictionalism says "I have sufficient reason for believing that T is false, but it is highly useful and therefore I shall accept it." I am arguing for the latter.

[22] Hume, *Treatise*, part 4, section 7 (1978), p. 269.

backgammon presuppose that he *is* interacting with other minds. Given that he cannot eliminate presuppositions of other minds from his thoughts and actions, does it follow that he disbelieves the skeptical thesis after all? No, it doesn't. When the positive existential proposition in question is put to him in interrogative form, when at his most undistracted, reflective and critical, then he will dissent from it (we'll assume). This, surely, is as good a test for a person's beliefs as one could hope for. Certainly, at least, it is a better test than what a person will assent to (dissent from) when distracted, unreflective and uncritical. (Note that I'm not claiming that this would be Hume's answer; it appears that when nature banishes his skeptical ruminations, she reasserts his *belief* in the doubted propositions. I am not here making any point about Hume's philosophical views, but merely alighting upon the situation he describes in order to illustrate a point.)

One might be tempted to hold that Hume believes *p* (the skeptical hypothesis) while he is in his study among his books, but disbelieves *p* as soon as he leaves and takes up with his friends. Though people *can* change their minds back and forth in this way, it seems a slightly desperate analysis of the present type of situation. One imagines that Hume, even when in the midst of playing backgammon, would answer in the negative if, out of the blue, he were suddenly posed a philosophical question that clearly presented itself as such (something like: "Do you *really* believe that the existence of other minds is probable?"). And it would be an odd view that held that an agent believes that *p* until the moment he is asked "In all seriousness: *p*?", at which point he immediately alters his belief to not-*p*.[23]

Part of what I mean by "undistracted" and "reflective" is that Hume is paying attention to his beliefs – when he dines and converses he still *has* the skeptical belief, but he is not attending to it. This is not to say that when one is in a "philosophical" frame of mind one is attending to *more* beliefs than at other times; rather, the kind of mechanisms that might distract one from beliefs relevant to the situation – mechanisms like akrasia, self-deception, mental apathy – are (ideally) "turned off." (Recall that Aristotle's solution to the problem of akrasia has it that the akratēs judges that refraining from *φ*ing is the best course of action, but his appetite for *φ*ing *distracts him* from that judgment.[24]) When one thinks "critically," moreover, one subjects one's attitudes to careful scrutiny: "Is my acceptance of *p* really

---

[23] A few exceptions aside. If "*p*?" is "Am I refraining from asking a question now?", then I suppose the odd pattern holds.

[24] See R. Demos, "Lying to Oneself," *Journal of Philosophy* 57 (1960), pp. 588–95.

justified?" One looks for connections and incoherencies amongst one's attitudes. Robust forms of skepticism are given serious consideration. All this will involve the agent in taking higher-order attitudes towards his first-order attitudes. A rough paradigm of this rigorous context is one that any reader is likely to be familiar with: the philosophy classroom. It's not that the philosophy classroom represents *everybody's* "most critical context"; my point is that what a person believes cannot be simply read off her actions, speech and thought – rather, the matter is determined by what she will say in a particular kind of context, of which "when doing philosophy" is offered as a familiar setting well towards one end of the continuum.

It is important to see that this distinction between more critical and less critical contexts is asymmetric. It's not merely that a person attends to *different* beliefs when doing philosophy than when, say, shopping; nor that she questions everyday thinking when doing philosophy, but equally questions philosophy when shopping. Critical thinking investigates and challenges the presuppositions of ordinary thinking in a way that ordinary thinking does not investigate and challenge the presuppositions of critical thinking. Critical thinking is characterized by a tendency to ask oneself questions like "Am I really justified in accepting that things like shops exist?" – whereas the frame of mind one is in when shopping is *not* characterized by asking "Am I justified in accepting that there is some doubt as to whether shops exist?" A simple way of making the distinction is to consider what a person will assent to (dissent from) when the question is introduced with appropriate cues to indicate that a rigorous and critical environment is being entered: "Seriously, all-things-considered . . . ," "Taking into account the possibility of skepticism . . . ," etc., ". . . *what do you really believe?*"

This notion of what a person is disposed to assent to if placed in a critical (etc.) context must not be read as involving any far-fetched counterfactual idealization. Who can judge what manner of peculiar things one would assent to if given *perfect* powers of reflection and critical thinking? A person's "most critical context" must be fixed in actuality – and the obvious means of achieving this grounding is to stipulate that he must sometimes (at a minimum, at least once) have *actually inhabited* that context, and therein either assented to, or dissented from, the thesis in question. In other words, it would be too bizarre to hold that an individual, who has never given the issue any careful thought whatsoever, but thinks and acts in accordance with theory T, does not really believe T simply because if he *were* to think carefully about it, he would deny it. But if we add that at some point he *has* adopted a critical perspective and therein sincerely denied T, and remains disposed to deny T were he again to adopt that perspective, then he disbelieves T, regardless of how he may think, act, and speak in less critical perspectives.

The position may be summarized by a sequence of questions. Consider any agent, S, and her relation to some thesis T. Is S disposed to assent to T on some occasions and dissent from T on other occasions? If "No" then S's attitude to T does not interest us; if "Yes," then continue. Let us call the contexts in which S is disposed to dissent from T "C1," and those in which she is disposed to assent to T "C2," and let us confine C1 and C2 to contexts that S has actually occupied at some point, and therein dissented from T and assented to T, respectively. Let us, further, summarize some of the above discussion with the premise: $\forall n \forall m$, Cn is more critical than Cm if and only if Cn involves scrutiny and questioning of the kinds of attitude held in Cm but not vice versa. Now we can ask: Is C1 more critical than C2? If "Yes," then S is making a fiction of T.

Certain aspects of that summary would certainly benefit from further clarification (what is involved in "assenting" and "dissenting"? what is it to "scrutinize and question"?), but more important discussion beckons. Three points are worth highlighting before carrying on. First, if S is making a fiction of T, it will not necessarily be obvious from observing her everyday discourse and practice. It may even be unobvious to S in everyday contexts. Nevertheless, since she is, all along, disposed to deny T in a more rigorous context, she does not really believe it. Since her being so disposed may not be readily apparent, we might be ignorant of this disposition and therefore unhesitatingly credit her with a belief in T. She might even credit herself with the belief if she is not thinking carefully about the matter.

Second, it is important not to make too much of the fact that I used Hume's skeptical misery to illustrate the point. Hume's "skeptical solution" to his own skeptical doubt is that Nature *makes us* "yield to these illusions."[25] A dubious aspect of this solution is that it is quite unclear how Nature's compulsion provides any kind of *warrant*. Yet Hume appears to hold that it does: after demonstrating that inductive reasoning is unjustified, for instance, he goes on to distinguish good from bad instances of

<hr/>

[25] Hume, *Treatise*, book 1, part 4, section 7 (1978), p. 267. See also the *Dialogues Concerning Natural Religion* [1779]: "To whatever length any one may push his speculative principles of scepticism, he must act, I own, and live, and converse like other men; and for this conduct he is not obliged to give any other reason than the absolute necessity he lies under of so doing" (part 1 [Oxford: Clarendon Press, 1935], p. 165).

such reasoning – belief in miracles on the basis of testimony, for example, is unwarranted. In the previous chapter I stated my assumption that the making of moral judgments is not "forced" upon us by our nature (though the disposition to do so may be). A fictive moral judgment is something that a person in some manner *chooses*, and doing so may be justified on pragmatic grounds. Thus the moral fictionalism under consideration eschews Hume's rhetoric of compulsion, and in so doing avoids the problem of reinstating warrant for the practice.

Third, it ought to be clear that the class of potential fictive judgments is broad and varied. At one extreme there are fictive judgments that we certainly do make, such as when we spend half an hour reading a fairy story, saying things like "Once upon a time there lived a dragon." We do not really believe that there ever were dragons, since were someone to force a switch to a more critical context with a question like "You don't really believe that, do you?" we would answer "Of course not." Nevertheless, if unbothered by silly questions, we can indulge ourselves in such a fiction. At the other extreme is the more fully immersing kind of fictive judgment for which our disbelief will only be admitted in a very critical context, such as a philosophy classroom. It is not obvious that we typically make such judgments at all, but I see no reason why we could not. The thesis under consideration, then, is that we could make a fiction of morality – one which will engage our emotions, guide our actions, influence our decisions, and, in short, bring the pragmatic benefits of morality that we might expect – all without belief.

7.5 FICTIONALISM AND MAKE-BELIEVE

The previous paragraph noted a connection between the kind of fictive stance that I am suggesting for morality and the kind of attitude we take towards fictional stories. It will be useful to explore this connection further because both, in my opinion, center on the nature of make-believe. In the process I also want to dispel any worries that making fictive judgments need involve self-deception or irrationality.

Morality is not a fiction in the way that, say, the Sherlock Holmes stories are a fiction. The Holmes stories were created *as* a fiction; moreover, they consist of a limited number of propositions to which a person can take an attitude such as belief, or disbelief, or something more complicated (belief coupled with a fictional operator, for example). Morality, by contrast, does not have an author – certainly not one who created it *as* a fiction, and nor does it have a defined body of propositions. As to the latter question – that of the *content* of "the story of morality" – I have in mind that it need consist primarily of a few general existential claims such as the following: "There are obligations and prohibitions: things that we ought to do, and things we ought not do, regardless of whether it suits us or furthers our interests," "People have basic rights, regardless of whether any institution recognizes those rights," "People have character traits – such as courage or dishonesty – which explain their actions and by which actions may be appraised," "Wrong-doers deserve punishment," etc. We should also include some particular claims, such as "Torturing babies to pass the time is always wrong," which will provide some minimal constraints on the content of the obligations, rights, etc. The important thing to note is that at the "core" of morality is a cluster of key notions like *obligation, right, virtue*, etc., and to accept morality is to accept this conceptual framework. It does not follow that two moral fictionalists can come to agree over a particular case – whether a second-trimester abortion is permissible, for example – simply by consulting the "story of morality," in the way that two Holmes fans may consult the canonical texts in order to settle a dispute about Watson's war wound. The fiction of morality is in many ways "open," but I suggest that by containing relations among its posits (between obligations and rights, for example), and some general constraints (such as "Painful consequences are relevant to right action"), it contains rough internal rules of disputation.

With these significant differences between moral fictionalism and literary fictions noted, we can, nevertheless, draw profitable comparisons. It has been argued that the notion of *make-believe* lies at the heart of our responses to fictions, and this, I think, transfers to the fictionalist stance.

Consider the Holmes stories, and the various attitudes one may take towards them. We have all heard of American tourists who turn up at Baker Street wanting to see where the Victorian detective – the *real* Victorian detective – lived. Such people are simply unaware of the facts – they believe a fiction, but not knowingly; they have not made a fictive judgment. Now imagine a second person who at "some level" knows that Holmes is a fiction, but for whatever pathological reason we care to think of, has come seemingly sincerely to believe in Holmes's existence. Even when asked in all seriousness whether Holmes existed, this character answers in the affirmative, and perhaps only sessions of psychotherapy will bring him to admit the lie he lives. This is a self-deceived person; he has embarked on a self-induced course of error-acceptance. A third Holmes fan takes great pleasure in pretending that the stories are veridical. She visits the London sights that Holmes is said to have visited; she says, "If Holmes saw Moriarty *here*, and then lost track of him *there*, then he must have followed him down *this* street"; she pictures Holmes being there. For the space of the day, perhaps, she gives in to the fiction and "forgets" all about Conan Doyle. She may even become slightly annoyed at the mention of the writer in the course of her London sightseeing, since it spoils the atmosphere that she is creating. To call this character "self-deceived" is unfair, since she can, at any time, readopt the critical perspective from which she knows very well that it's all fiction. When she gives in to the fiction she knows what she is doing – she is drifting away from what she knows to be the truth because doing so indulges an enjoyable diversion. Only the third character satisfies the requirements for having made a fictive judgment, though it is a mild and frivolous one.

The moral fictionalist is in important respects like this third Holmes fan. He is not self-deceived, since it is within his grasp to enter the "critical mode" should he care to – it does not take a course of psychotherapy to get him to admit the flaws of morality. When the context of discussion shifts towards the more rigorous, philosophical end of the spectrum – when the person is asked about what he *really* believes – then the maker of the fictive judgment can, but the victim of self-deception cannot, move with the context.

Certain authors have presented an account of self-deception which stops short of describing the agent as believing *p* and believing not-*p*; instead the subject of self-deception believes that not-*p* but "thinks" and acts as if *p*.[26] This is similar to the account of the fictive judgment that I favor. As an account of *self-deception* this kind of thesis has been criticized as "too unparadoxical" to be adequate.[27] Perhaps the criticism is fair – it is not my

[26] See especially K. Bach, "An Analysis of Self-Deception," *Philosophy and Phenomenological Research* 41 (1981), pp. 351–70. According to Bach, "thinking that p" is neither necessary nor sufficient for believing that *p*. If one believes that *p* but desires not-*p*, one may be self-deceived so long as one does not think what one believes. The mechanisms by which one may accomplish this "inattention" are rationalization, evasion and jamming, each described by Bach in detail. However, since Bach's intention is specifically to describe *self-deception*, and since the fictive judgment has little to do with self-deception, many of his points, though interesting, are oblique to my purposes. See also N. Hellman, "Bach on Self-Deception," *Philosophy and Phenomenological Research* 44 (1983), pp. 113–20; and K. Bach, "More on Self-Deception: Reply to Hellman," *Philosophy and Phenomenological Research* 45 (1985), pp. 611–14.

[27] The unwieldy phrase comes from S. Darwall's "Self-Deception, Autonomy and Moral Constitution," in B. P. McLaughlin and A. O. Rorty (eds.), *Perspectives on Self-Deception* (London: University of California Press, 1988), pp. 407–30.

concern to adjudicate. The point is that even if "too unparadoxical" to capture the pre-theoretical desiderata of *self-deception*, this kind of analysis may serve perfectly well as a description of the agent participating in a fictive judgment.

What is going on in our minds when we participate in make-believe? The correct answer, I believe, is "thoughts."[28] When a child make-believes that the upturned table is a ship, she is *thinking* the proposition "The table is a ship" (with all its associated imagery), or perhaps simply "This is a ship," without believing that proposition. The proposition is, of course, false, but we could not on that account accuse the child of any error. It is also worth noting that "mere thoughts" can engage our emotions. If one sits vividly thinking about one's house burning down and all one's worldly belongings with it – not believing it, nor even believing it particularly likely – that may be sufficient to prompt anxiety or fear. This, I take it, is what happens when we engage emotionally with fiction – when we feel fear at horror movies or sadness at novels. Some people have been troubled at the idea that we have emotional responses to fiction, and have even gone so far as to deny this apparently obvious truth.[29] Others have claimed that although we do have emotional responses to fiction, all such emotions are irrational, comparable to phobias.[30] I have argued against both such views in detail elsewhere, so here will state my view bluntly.[31] Thoughts, as was noted above, often produce emotions – indeed, I would claim that thoughts (like beliefs) can be partly constitutive of emotions. Thoughts are often under our control in a way that beliefs are not: although one cannot just *believe* that Napoleon won Waterloo (not even if offered a million dollars to do so), one can certainly entertain the thought – can make-believe – that he won Waterloo, pretty much whenever one wants to. It

[28] See P. Lamarque, "How Can We Fear and Pity Fictions?" *British Journal of Aesthetics* 21 (1981), pp. 291–304; Noël Carroll, *Philosophy of Horror* (New York: Routledge, 1990), pp. 24–6.

[29] See A. Kenny, *Action, Emotion and the Will* (London: Routledge and Kegan Paul, 1964), p. 49; M. Budd, *Music and the Emotions* (London: Routledge and Kegan Paul, 1985), p. 128. The view is frequently attributed to Kendall Walton – "Fearing Fictions," *Journal of Philosophy* 75 (1978), pp. 5–27, *Mimesis and Make-Believe* (Cambridge, Mass.: Harvard University Press, 1990) – but he appears to reject it in "Spelunking, Simulation, and Slime," in M. Hjort and S. Laver (eds.), *Emotion and the Arts* (Oxford: Oxford University Press, 1997), pp. 37–49.

[30] See in particular Colin Radford, "How Can We Be Moved by the Fate of Anna Karenina?" *Proceedings of the Aristotelian Society* supplementary volume 49 (1975), pp. 67–80, and the veritable industry that this article begot.

[31] See R. Joyce, "Rational Fear of Monsters," *British Journal of Aesthetics* 40 (2000), pp. 209–24.

seems that entertaining thoughts of Anna Karenina or Dracula are as much actions as entertaining guests for dinner.[32] (And if entertaining thoughts is not always like this, it is frequently, which is all my case requires.) As actions, episodes of make-believe must be assessed for rationality according to the instrumentalist principle that was laid down in earlier chapters. In the case of literary fictions, there are desirable ends of pleasure and instruction that we may hope to gain through engagement with them, and any action we perform that we are justified in believing will conduce to such ends is, *ceteris paribus*, rational. Participation in make-believe, and the having of the associated emotions, may therefore be rationally defensible; in the case of literary fiction it usually is. I would employ the same model for moral fictionalism: if we are justified in believing that a moral fictive judgment will prompt an emotional reaction (no matter how mild), and we are justified in believing that this reaction may lead to desirable ends (say, by influencing our motivations against the temptations of defecting), then it is, *ceteris paribus*, perfectly rational for us to make that fictive judgment.

The object of make-believe that is prompting emotions may even be something impossible: the child may pretend that the candlestick walks and talks (while remaining a candlestick); the Holmes fan may pretend that the stories are true, despite containing contradictory references to the position of Watson's war wound; one might pretend that water is XYZ though it is necessarily H_2O; and so on. I do not have a theory to offer concerning the semantics of impossible thoughts, but I am reasonably confident that we have them. Consider the plot of the familiar Socratic dialog: after lengthy discussion Socrates dismantles the way his interlocutors are using a common term, such as "justice" or "piety." Often the conclusion is entirely negative, such that by the end we are supposed to admit that we do not really know what we mean by these terms at all – perhaps Socrates has even revealed contradictions in his rival's account. Yet it would be an extreme view that concluded, retrospectively, that none of the parties involved had ever had any beliefs of the form "X is just" or "Y is pious." And if one can believe something then one can make-believe it.

---

[32] In this I am in broad agreement with the work of Harry Frankfurt, who argues that on certain occasions we are "active" with respect to our desires (when we "identify with them"): "Turning one's mind in a certain direction, or deliberating systematically about a problem, are activities in which a person himself engages" – "Identification and Externality," in A. O. Rorty (ed.), *The Identities of Persons* (Berkeley: University of California Press, 1976), p. 240.

7.6 FICTIONALISM AND METAETHICS

Let me sum up where we have gotten to. To make a fiction of some thesis T is to be disposed to assent to T in certain circumstances without believing T. This covers acts of story-telling and engaging with literary fiction in general: both activities involve an act of make-believe, which is to be understood as having the thought of T. Thoughts of T may prompt emotions. Regarding literary fictions, moreover, it is reasonable to argue that the emotions that they inspire in us are not an accidental by-product, but often the very reason that we bother with them. In other words, we gain a benefit from engaging emotively with literary fictions. I am making the same claim for moral fictionalism, reiterating the qualification that it is not being asserted that our moral discourse is actually like this, but that it could be moved in that direction if we deemed it practically expedient to do so. Suppose we were to do so. What should be said, from a metaethical perspective, about such a discourse expressive of fictive judgments?

Again, it is useful first to consider the more familiar case of dealing with literary fictions. When our third Holmes fan looks at a street in, say, Beckenham, and claims "Holmes was here," what shall we say about this utterance? She doesn't *believe* that Holmes was here; she is pretending. Nor, I maintain, is she *asserting* that Holmes was here – rather, she is pretending to assert.[33] Some people have argued that sentences concerning fiction, such as "Holmes went to Beckenham," ought to be interpreted as containing a tacit story-operator, such that they maybe treated as true assertions; thus the sentence becomes "According to the Conan Doyle stories, Holmes went to Beckenham," which is true.[34] It is important to distinguish two different things that we can do with a fictional story: we can talk about the story ("In Conan Doyle's story, Holmes goes to

---

[33] In saying this I am disagreeing with, among others, Gregory Currie, *The Nature of Fiction* (Cambridge: Cambridge University Press, 1990), in preference for the view of J. R. Searle, "The Logical Status of Fictional Discourse," in his *Expression and Meaning* (Cambridge: Cambridge University Press, 1979), pp. 58–75. For others apparently in Searle's camp, see R. Ohmann, "Speech Acts and the Definition of Literature," *Philosophy and Rhetoric* 4 (1971), pp. 1–19; R. M. Gale, "The Fictive Use of Language," *Philosophy* 46 (1971), pp. 324–39; M. M. Eaton, "Liars, Ranters, and Dramatic Speakers," in B. R. Tilghman (ed.), *Language and Aesthetics* (Lawrence: University Press of Kansas, 1973), pp. 43–63; M. C. Beardsley, "Aesthetic Intentions and Fictive Illocutions," in P. Hernadi (ed.), *What Is Literature?* (Bloomington: Indiana University Press, 1978), pp. 161–77. It must be noted, however, that all the important points of this chapter will go through, with adjustments, even if Currie is right and Searle is wrong.

[34] See, for example, D. Lewis in "Truth in Fiction," *American Philosophical Quarterly* 15 (1978), p. 38.

Beckenham"), or we can *tell* the story ("Holmes went to Beckenham"). In the former case we are asserting something, but in the latter we are not – we are pretending to be a person who has access to a realm of facts which we are reporting. Sometimes, no doubt, the former proposition can be expressed elliptically using the latter sentence, but it would be a mistake to interpret the latter sentence as *generally* elliptical, for it makes no sense of the times when it is used as a piece of pretense, in the act of *telling* the story, for instance. Our Holmes fan, when she says "Holmes was here" is not saying anything equivalent to "According to the Conan Doyle stories, Holmes was here," otherwise in what sense is she *pretending*?[35]

One possible form of moral fictionalism would hold that when we say things like "Stealing is morally wrong" we are really saying something equivalent to "According to the story of morality, stealing is wrong." Gideon Rosen puts forward this type of fictionalism with respect to *modal* discourse.[36] He thinks that modal discourse has problematic existential commitments, which disappear when a "story operator" ("According to the story of possible worlds . . . ") is prefixed. A distinctive feature of this view is that modal discourse remains assertoric, but those assertions are about a fiction.

This is not the kind of view that I am proposing for moral discourse. The fictionalism that I prefer sees moral discourse as ceasing to be assertoric altogether. As such, the proposed moral fictionalism avoids a problem that besets Rosen's modal version: if the translation scheme endorses "*P* iff according to the fiction of *X*s, *P*" as a means of avoiding ontological commitment to *X*s, but *according to the fiction of Xs there exist Xs*, then the fictionalism has failed to avoid exactly what it was designed to avoid.[37] Since, presumably, morality is in a similar manner "self-endorsing," then any reductionist moral fictionalism would fall foul of the same obstacle.

The important upshot of my kind of fictionalism is that, were it adopted, moral discourse would cease to be assertoric, and would therefore be something towards which we ought to be *noncognitivists*. Since it is not being

[35] For a similar point made, see Walton, "Fearing Fictions," p. 20.
[36] G. Rosen, "Modal Fictionalism," *Mind* 99 (1990), pp. 327–54.
[37] See D. Nolan and J. O'Leary-Hawthorne, "Reflexive Fictionalisms," *Analysis* 56 (1996), pp. 23–32; G. Rosen, "A Problem of Fictionalism about Possible Worlds," *Analysis* 53 (1993), pp. 71–81; S. Brock, "Modal Fictionalism: A Response to Rosen," *Mind* 102 (1993), pp. 147–50. Another kind of problem besetting reductionist fictionalism (but not my version) is presented in G. Vision's "Fiction and Fictionalist Reductions," *Pacific Philosophical Quarterly* 74 (1993), pp. 150–74.

claimed that fictionalism is true of our actual moral discourse, the proposal is not that noncognitivism is true of our actual moral discourse. Rather, fictionalism amounts to the claim that noncognitivism might *become* true, if we were to alter our attitude towards moral discourse. (This is an important difference with more familiar forms of noncognitivism, such a Simon Blackburn's.[38]) Sir Philip Sidney (who knew a thing or two about fiction) summed up the point in grand manner: "the Poet, he nothing affirmes, and therefore never lyeth . . . though he recount things not true, yet because hee telleth them not for true, he lyeth not."[39] The moral fictionalist is like Sidney's poet: because he "nothing affirmes," he could not be accused of *making a mistake*, regardless of the false sentences and faulty concepts that he employs.

Traditional noncognitivism states that when one says "ϕ is morally good" one is expressing a certain kind of approval towards ϕ – saying something along the lines of "ϕ: hurrah!" – thus ". . . is morally good" is only syntactically a predicate, but semantically functions to indicate that a certain desire-state or emotion is present. By contrast, the kind of fictionalist noncognitivism offered here holds that ". . . is morally good" *is* a logical predicate – it does function to pick out a property (though it may not succeed) – but we may utter "ϕ is morally good" without assertoric force: not as an expression of a belief, but an expression of a thought. For this reason, the kind of noncognitivism I am suggesting does not involve a "translation" of moral sentences (analogous to "ϕ: hurrah!"). One might be tempted, for example, to hold that a noncognitivism centered on make-believe is committed to "ϕ is morally good" meaning something along

[38] See Simon Blackburn, *Spreading the Word* (Oxford: Oxford University Press, 1984) and *Essays in Quasi-Realism*. Blackburn's "quasi-realist project" is the attempt to earn the right of realist talk (of moral facts, moral knowledge, truth, etc.) for a discourse that in fact expresses desires or emotions; the quasi-realist is a philosopher who explicates moral discourse in such a way that the ordinary users of that discourse turn out not to be committing mistakes after all. By contrast, moral fictionalism begins with a moral error theory: the view that there is no way for philosophers to reconstruct, explicate, or reconceive of actual moral discourse in such a way that actual users of the discourse are not, after all, committing fundamental errors about the nature of the world. Fictionalism offers an avoidance of error only when it involves an actual change that takes place in the users of the language. Those who continue to use the discourse as it is presently used – who continue to assert untrue things – are not thereby "rescued" from their blunders. If someone sincerely believes that, say, Napoleon won Waterloo, then I cannot, from the vantage of my armchair, reconceive of her doxastic practice in a fictionalist light, thereby rendering her "Waterloo discourse" unproblematic.
[39] Sir Philip Sidney, *Apologie for Poetrie* [1580s] (Westminster: A. Constable and Co. Ltd., 1901), p. 52.

the lines of "Let's pretend that ϕ is morally good" – which is worded like a command or suggestion. But this is quite misguided. By comparison, if I am participating in a game of make-believe with some children – pretending to be a bear, perhaps – then I might crawl around on the floor, growling and saying things like "I am going to eat you!", "I am a bear!", etc. I am not asserting that I am a bear, I am pretending to assert that I'm a bear. More specifically, I am pretending to be a (talking) bear asserting something about myself – that is why I make the utterance in a gruff voice. Someone crawling round, growling, and enjoining "Let's pretend that I am a bear!" is not playing the game very well. He might as well say (in an ordinary voice) "Let's pretend that I am a bear and that I am saying this in a gruff voice." There is no reason, given the fictional-ist noncognitivism that I am describing, for "translating" the basic moral utterance into some other wording or linguistic structure. The content re-mains the same (warts and all) – what changes is the force with which it is uttered.

Suppose someone who has been a sincere believer in morality becomes convinced of the error of his ways. Naturally, we would expect that he should cease to have moral beliefs. One might also think that any moral utterances that he might subsequently make – along the lines of, say, "Stealing is wrong" – would not be assertions, since they would not be expressive of beliefs. However, there is a complication here that must be settled before ending.

Consider lying. Lying is a species of assertion where the speaker utters a proposition that she does not believe. Does this show that assertion is *not* the expression of belief? No, for the simple reason that one can express a belief that one does not have. This is no more perplexing than the idea that when one apologizes one expresses regret, and can do so without actually feeling regretful; or the idea that one's saying "Thank you" succeeds in expressing gratitude even when one feels none. These ideas are untroubling because the notion of "expression" involved does not denote a relation between the speaker's mental states and his utterances, but rather indicates a linguistic convention held by a community of speakers. If a speaker utters the words "Sorry for breaking the window" in the appropriate context (where he has broken the window or acts as an authorized representative of those who have done so, where others might be justifiably annoyed at the window having been broken, where those others are present and listening, etc.) then he succeeds in the speech act of *expressing regret*. If it is discovered that he feels no regret at all, then it will not be denied that he apologized, but will be claimed that he did so insincerely.[40] The same thing goes for assertion: whether one asserts is not merely a matter of whether one believes the proposition uttered, but depends upon a framework of linguistic conventions within which one's utterance occurs. Thus one can express a belief that one does not hold. With these thoughts in mind, let us return to the fictionalist.

With a case of literary make-believe – say, story-telling – there is a well-entrenched set of linguistic and non-linguistic conventions which indicate that a non-belief-expressing context is being entered into. The obvious one is prefixing a sequence of sentences with "Once upon a time . . . ," though others less obvious will suffice. Something similar may be charitably attributed to Sidney's claim that the poet "nothing affirmes": in ordinary circumstances everyone knows when a poem is being recited, and knows not to treat utterances therein as assertions. Here, then, is another important disanalogy between moral fictionalism and our engagement with literary fictions. Suppose Fred comes to disbelieve morality, but wishes, for whatever reason, to carry on using its language. It cannot be casually said that he makes no error because he is not expressing beliefs. Suppose everyone around Fred sincerely believes in morality, and has no reason to suspect that Fred is different. Fred is, in other words, a "lone fictionalist." If his moral utterances are made within a framework of conventions according to which they *are* belief-expressing (never mind that he lacks the beliefs in question), then are they not assertions after all? Of course, there will be general conventions which may be exploited by Fred to indicate a withdrawal of assertoric force: he might prefix his moral utterances with something analogous to "Once upon a time," or put them in the subjunctive mood, or utter them in an overtly sarcastic tone of voice. But suppose he doesn't do any of these. Are his utterances assertions? I don't think so. I'm inclined to say that in such a case the conventional understanding between speaker and audience has broken down to such a degree that Fred's speech acts are, in Austin's terms, "misfiring" – Fred has, in a sense, ceased to speak.

I suppose that we might, in such circumstances, be noncognitivists of a sort about Fred's moral discourse, for it consists of sentences in the indicative mood that are not assertions. But this is hardly a satisfying conclusion. After all, the idea is supposed to be that continuing with an unasserted moral discourse might be a pragmatically good idea, but the costs of encouraging a fractured and miscommunicating society are likely to be severe.

[40] See J. L. Austin, *How to do Things with Words* (Oxford: Oxford University Press, 1962); and R. Joyce, "Apologizing," *Public Affairs Quarterly* 13 (1999), pp. 159–73.

For this reason, there can be no honest "lone fictionalist" – not unless he is willing to exploit standard public devices to indicate that his utterances are not to be taken as expressions of belief. If he employs no such devices, then he is either failing to communicate or he is lying. This observation forces us to be more precise about what fictionalism consists in. I have described it as an attitude that we may adopt towards a faulty theory, which may be advisable in practical terms. It is important now that the plurality of the "we" be taken seriously. If it is to be viable it must be an attitude that a *group* may take towards a hitherto believed theory.

I do not think that this requires that every member of that group be disposed to deny the theory in his or her most critical context. It would suffice that a sufficient number of members of the group are so disposed – enough to constitute there being a convention that entering into *this* topic involves a withdrawal of assertoric force. It is also possible that if the employment of a discourse involves a degree of "deference to experts," then such a convention may be considered to be present so long as those agreed to be "experts" have the fictionalist attitude. Unfortunately, at this stage I do not feel confident about discussing in more precise terms how the conventions governing illocutionary acts are established and maintained.[41] The point is, though, that we do have such conventions, and a group of speakers could choose to exploit extant conventions, or develop new ones, such that an understanding develops that when one enters into moral discourse one is performing a linguistic activity the sentences of which will not (generally) be endorsed as true in very critical environments, and therefore do not count as belief-expressing. (If I may be permitted an unsubstantiated empirical remark: it seems to me that the account just described might well capture a reasonably widespread attitude towards religion that developed in the twentieth century.[42])

7.7 CONCLUSION

I believe that a coherent position has been sketched out. Sections 7.3 and 7.4 described a kind of positive attitude that we might take towards a

---

[41] See Austin, *How to do Things with Words*, p. 26, who writes: "There must exist an accepted conventional procedure having a certain conventional effect, the procedure to include the uttering of certain words by certain persons in certain circumstances". See also Searle, *Expression and Meaning*.

[42] See Robin Le Poidevin, "Is God a Fiction?" in *Arguing for Atheism* (New York: Routledge, 1996), pp. 107–23; Don Cupitt, *Taking Leave of God* (London: SCM Press, 1980).

theory which does not involve believing it. Sections 7.5 and 7.6 developed this idea via a fruitful comparison with our engagement with literary fictions, claiming that this engagement centers on entertaining thoughts (noting that thoughts may produce emotions), and that the conventions surrounding literary fictive discourse render it non-assertoric. It is quite clear that no such conventions render our actual moral discourse non-assertoric, but it has never been my claim that it is so. The idea is, first, that if an individual comes to believe in a moral error theory, she may, nevertheless, continue to employ morality as a fiction. She may appeal to it in her day-to-day life as much as she pleases, but so long as she remains disposed to deny it in her most rigorous court of inquiry, she does not believe it. Second, I moved the discussion from focusing on the individual to considering a community of persons a sufficient number of whom take such an attitude. If in such a community it is apparent that this is the predominant attitude, then there are good grounds for saying that their moral utterances are non-assertoric: they express thoughts rather than beliefs. Thus any practical losses that accrue from having false beliefs, from cultivating a policy in which false beliefs are likely, or from encouraging others to form false beliefs – all may be avoided. Far from encouraging shabby or deleterious doxastic habits, fictionalism grows naturally from a particular sensitivity to, and abhorrence of, false beliefs.

This is a description of what a possible fictionalism would look like, but if it is to be of anything other than academic interest, something needs to be said of the claim that it might be *a good idea* for us to adopt such a position with a faulty theory. Why, in particular, would we want to take this attitude specifically to *morality*? More pointedly: I outlined an argument that morality is a useful thing for the (typical) individual – but doesn't this usefulness depend upon its being *believed*? In the next chapter I will attempt to argue "No": morality can continue to furnish significant benefit, both at a societal and an individual level, even when it has the role of a fiction.

8

Moral fictionalism

8.0 THE VALUE OF MORAL BELIEFS

In the previous chapter, in order to motivate the fictionalist case, it was necessary to outline an argument that morality is instrumentally useful (§7.1). The first objective of this chapter is to expand on that sketch, hoping to make it more compelling. When I say that "morality" is useful, we can initially assume that what is under consideration are moral *beliefs*. The strategy will then be to argue that the benefits brought by moral beliefs can survive the shift to fictionalism: the attitude of *acceptance* can bring the same sorts of benefit. If this is not true, then the fictionalist case collapses. For a while, then, let us forget about fictionalism, and discuss again the function of moral beliefs.

One might be excused for thinking that the thesis that morality is useful has already been argued for in Chapter 6. However, the hypothesis that morality is an evolved tendency does not, in and of itself, show that it is a useful trait for individuals or for groups. Adaptations are useful to genes – specifically, whatever gene has the trait as its phenotypic effect. For instance, if the environment were reliably such that an individual's sacrificing his life would thereby ensure the maturation of several of his offspring, then such a sacrificing trait would, *ceteris paribus*, improve reproductive fitness. But it would in no way be useful *to the individual* to have that trait, and it is individuals that we are interested in. Nevertheless, we might suppose that in the general course of things the interests of the gene and the interests of the individual bearing those genes run together. In Chapter 6 the enhancement of reproductive fitness brought by morality was understood in the simple (perhaps simplistic) terms of the Prisoner's Dilemma, and that reasoning transfers to the individual.

Agents in a Hobbesian state of nature satisfy the requirements of a Prisoner's Dilemma (PD) matrix.[1]

---

[1] Nearly everyone agrees with this. For the contrary view, however, see A. Alexandra,

A

	cooperate	defect
cooperate	8 / 8	10 / 1
defect	1 / 10	3 / 3

Rational players in a one-off game apparently should both defect. Hobbes's "solution" for such poorly performing defectors is that they should agree to have a sovereign power overseeing all interactions, penalizing defections and rewarding cooperation. "Solution" is in scare quotes to ward off misunderstanding. Hobbes doesn't show that it is rational to cooperate in a situation which satisfies the PD matrix. Rather, the presence of the sovereign in effect increases the pay-off for cooperation (rewards) and decreases the pay-off for defection (punishments). In other words, the sovereign is a means of avoiding getting into PD situations. It's a "solution" in so far as it shows how one can do better than three per interaction with one's fellows, but it doesn't show how one can do better than three per game *in a PD situation.*

The sovereign enforces cooperative behavior, but doesn't require that the participants "be moral" – where this has something to do with altruistic motivation, with doing one's duty from a sense of duty, with cultivating certain personality traits, etc. This is brought out by the familiar complaint against the Hobbesian "solution," that it doesn't have an answer to the "Foole" or Hume's "sensible knave" – the agent who, on some occasions, sees that he may secretly defect and avoid the wrath of the sovereign. Were Plato's Gyges to turn up with a reliable ring of invisibility and ask "Why should I not kill and steal?" Hobbes has no answer.[2]

"Should Hobbes's State of Nature be Represented as a Prisoner's Dilemma?" *Southern Journal of Philosophy* 30 (1992), pp. 1–16.

[2] See D. Gauthier, "Three against Justice: The Foole, the Sensible Knave, and the Lydian Shepherd," *Midwest Studies in Philosophy* 7 (1982), pp. 11–29; idem, *Morals by Agreement* (Oxford: Clarendon Press, 1986), pp. 160–63; and D. A. DeBruin, "Can One Justify Morality to Fooles?" *Canadian Journal of Philosophy* 25 (1995), pp. 1–31. A moral skeptic might answer the question posed by DeBruin's title: "Yes, *only* to Fooles." (The joke is Paul Benacerraf's.)

In fact, everybody in the civil society may well *be* a sensible knave – the only question is how frequently they can practice their knavery. Hobbes's response is to give the sovereign maximal powers of observation, limiting the opportunities for knavery as much as is practically feasible. It's in each individual's interests that the sovereign be as powerful as possible. Even though this means that an individual, William, foregoes the gains of an occasional piece of knavery, he also avoids being the victim of knavery, and gains the peace of mind of not having to be constantly vigilant lest his neighbors have noticed that the sovereign's back is turned. When being exploited may amount to having his throat cut (thereby losing all gains from all future games), then it is preferable to forego the opportunity of exploiting in order to avoid the possibility of being exploited. Of course, *ideally* William would like the sovereign to have unfailing awareness when it comes to his neighbors and inattentiveness when it comes to *him*, but that kind of differentiation is not possible to select. Such infeasible fantasies aside, William will do best if he has a sovereign with unfaltering attentiveness. But is such an omniscient sovereign a realistic possibility? Surely, as a matter of fact, there will be numerous opportunities for "getting away with it." Of course, so long as the sovereign *roughly* enforces the law, and so long as William avoids getting his throat cut by other sensible knaves, then chances are he's better off than he would be in a state of nature, but he would be better off still if there were a means of guaranteeing an ideal, incorruptible, omniscient sovereign.

Think of morality as a kind of internalized sovereign. If all parties are under the impression that cooperating is "just the right thing to do," that it is a kind of behavior that one has an "inescapable obligation" to perform, then when PD situations loom they may be avoided. Situations that satisfy the PD matrix for agents with no independent interest in cooperating (who will therefore, if rational, end up all defecting), will not satisfy the PD matrix for agents with a standing preference to cooperate; the latter agents may therefore reap the rewards of mutual cooperation. Hobbes's sovereign is a means of avoiding getting into PD situations, but if two people notice that the sovereign's back is turned, that the costs and benefits of the sovereign's penalties and rewards have been subtracted from the equation, then they are back satisfying the PD matrix again, and, if it's a one-off game, will immediately defect. If, however, each possesses a reliable internalized preference for cooperation, then they will avoid such situations. Morality, according to this way of thinking, functions as a defection tax.

It is not merely that an "internalized sovereign" avoids the inevitable epistemic shortfallings of a real authority. The rewards and punishments doled out by Hobbes's sovereign are concrete, whereas those provided by an internalized counterpart are less tangible – perhaps nothing more than the feelings of guilt and self-pride. One might think that the former would prompt more resolute motivations, but psychology experiments have repeatedly shown that the reverse is true.[3] Across a range of situations, the offering of a physical reward for performing an act actually tends to lower the effectiveness of one's performance. Concrete rewards lead to the devaluing of the action being rewarded, and the threat of punishment prompts stress that interferes with performance of complex activities. One is far more likely to be motivated to perform a task, and perform it well, when the rewards and punishments are self-generated.

Since it is well known that in *iterated* PD games it is rational to adopt a cooperative strategy, a natural question is whether a sovereign – be it internal or external – is needed for repeated games.[4] However, the real world faces a problem that no strategy in a PD tournament faces: the *secret defector* – the character who defects without anyone knowing, or, at least, without anyone knowing that it was *he*. The practical cost of the secret defector is serious: not merely the minimal pay-off that he forces upon his opponent, but the sense of vulnerability and mistrust that he creates and reinforces throughout society. But why should the secret defector care about that? Why should he cultivate an internalized sovereign? Hume would argue that the secret defector also risks harming himself. He speaks of knaves "betrayed by their own maxims; and while they purpose to cheat with moderation and secrecy, a tempting incident occurs, nature is frail, and they give into the snare; whence they can never extricate themselves, without a total loss of reputation, and the forfeiture of all trust and confidence with mankind."[5] Had the knave an internalized sovereign – were he to imbue cooperative actions with a "to-be-pursuedness," to think of defection as *forbidden*, etc., such that he would not be tempted towards knavery even when nobody is watching (were he, in other words, to be a knave no more) – then he would never run the risk of such massive forfeiture.

---

[3] See Stuart Sutherland, *Irrationality: The Enemy Within* (London: Penguin Books, 1994), pp. 105–24. I am indebted to Sutherland's book for pointing me towards a number of the empirical psychology studies which are referred to in the present chapter.

[4] See Axelrod, *Evolution of Cooperation*. It is worth noting, incidentally, that when Hinckfuss argues that we could all get on very well without morality, it is Axelrod's work to which he looks. My discussion here will reveal why I think Hinckfuss is mistaken.

[5] *Enquiry*, conclusion (1983), p. 82.

It is worth reviewing Hume's answer to a sensible knave more carefully, for I believe that it is roughly correct. First, the knave misses out on benefits that by their very nature cannot be gained through defection: "Inward peace of mind, consciousness of integrity, a satisfactory review of [his] own conduct" – advantages which are constituted by a disposition not to cheat one's fellows.[6] Moreover, the knave will lose these benefits for comparatively trivial gains ("the feverish, empty amusements of luxury and expence"). That we care about such social advantages Hume puts down to Nature. In that respect, his answer is only to the *ordinary* sensible knave. Were intelligent aliens to land on Earth and commence slaughtering humans, there could be no appeal to their "inward peace of mind" and their "consciousness of integrity," since there would be no reason to assume that they cared about such things.

Hume's second strategy is to point out that secret defectors are unlikely to be epistemically infallible, and therefore they risk being caught, which has dramatic costs ("forfeiture of all trust and confidence with mankind"). Thirdly, secret defectors, since they have on their minds the possibility of secret defection whenever they are certain of evading detection, are likely to be tempted to cheat in situations where the chances of evading detection are less than certain, thus, again, risking severe punishment. As before, these are only good answers for ordinary, ordinarily situated people; the bearer of the ring of Gyges would remain, quite reasonably, unconvinced. (This is why earlier I criticized Hume's answer as having "inevitable limits.")

But what do these answers mean to the ordinary person who contemplates secret defection? They give her good instrumental reasons for acting in a cooperative manner, for behaving herself, for refraining from cheating her fellows even when it appears that she might be able to get away with it. On the face of it, they don't appear to give her any reason to cultivate *moral beliefs* (assuming that such cultivation were even possible). On the contrary, such reasoning promises to lay the foundation for a cooperative society that has done away with moral thinking altogether: the knave-no-more regulates her actions, plays a part in a successful cooperative society, all according to an enlightened self-interest. It would appear then, that what started out as a discussion of the instrumental role of moral beliefs has, if anything, revealed their redundancy.[7]

---

[6] *Ibid.*

[7] Cf. M. Zimmerman, "The 'Is-Ought': An Unnecessary Dualism," *Mind* 71 (1962), pp. 53–61.

But I do not think that this is so. It is not that Hume is mistaken: his answers would be good if we lived in a world populated entirely by humans enjoying perfect rationality. But we do not live in such a world, and nor are we likely to, and in the world of less-than-ideal humans *moral* beliefs play an important instrumental role. Let me explain.

For all our rational prowess and successful empirical methods, it took us a long time to recognize even basic human goods, like leafy green vegetables. Even once the information is available, it does not get transmitted very reliably throughout the population. And, importantly, even when an individual is perfectly aware where her interests lie, weakness of will can interfere and cause suboptimal choices to be made: the sincere belief that one must eat plenty of vegetables and avoid fatty foods all too frequently fails to result in the appropriate response. The correct analysis of weakness of will is a controversial matter, but nobody denies that there is something wrong with the akratic agent. The akratēs believes that ϕing is best, but when the point of action comes, she intentionally refrains from ϕing. Either her beliefs are in a state of unreliable flux (in which case, at the time of action, she has changed her mind about what she most values), or there is a lack of coherence between her beliefs about what is best and her actions (in which case, her action might well be called "irrational").

Eating vegetables may seem like a rather frivolous illustration, so let us have a more dramatic one. When there is a fire in a crowded theater, many more lives will be saved if everyone stays calm and heads for the exits in an orderly manner. Yet this is rarely what happens, and the panic that generally ensues reduces everyone's chances of survival. Instrumental rationality may prescribe a course of action that one's very life depends upon, and yet people frequently find themselves unable to comply. (Interestingly, it is well documented that the chances of a crowd panicking will be greatly lowered if an assertive authoritative person takes charge.[8] This observation sits comfortably with my contention that the role of morality is to act as a kind of "internalized authority.")

So suppose a person has a firm and justified belief that she will, all things considered, be more likely to achieve happiness if she deals fairly and honestly with her comrades, and that the best dividends for her are to be gained through pursuing a cooperative strategy. Does it follow that she *will* cooperate fairly? The existence of weakness of will – however we wish to explicate it – shows that the answer is "No." There may be a temptation

[8] See D. J. Schneider, *Social Psychology* (Reading, MA: Addison-Wesley, 1976), pp. 298–305.

to defect secretly when she thinks she can get away with it. The akratic agent will, therefore – regardless of how much knowledge of the self-harm of defection with which we credit her – occasionally surrender to temptation, either overriding that knowledge or temporarily re-evaluating its content. Since no agent that we need bother ourselves with is epistemically infallible, nobody will be entirely reliable in distinguishing the situations in which she is likely to be spotted from those in which she is likely to escape detection. Our agent will, therefore, sometimes get caught in the act. In defecting she will have injured her neighbor, leaving him with minimal pay-off. In being *caught* defecting, she will have prompted the defection of others – which is to say, she will be punished. One possible consequence will be the sparking of a round of mutual defections, in which everybody suffers. (And it is worth noting that tit-for-tat strategies, once engaged in mutual defection, have no means of re-establishing cooperation.[9]) A more certain consequence will be the origination or reinforcement of a sense of mistrust and uncertainty.

For this reason I would underline the reference to *temptation* in Hume's answer to the sensible knave. Merely to believe of some action "This is the one that is in my long-term best interests" simply doesn't do the job. Most of us know this from personal experience, but there is abundant empirical evidence available for the dubious.[10] The pursuit of what we value is frequently subverted by the temptation for what we desire. (For the value/desire distinction, see §3.6.) The belief that the valued action is in our long-term self-interest needs to be supplemented and reinforced. If one has a tendency to think of the valued action in terms of something that "just must be done," that is somehow required regardless of whether it suits you, then one is much less likely to yield to the temptation of refraining. The stronger the terms in which the value of the action, or its sense of "requirement," is conceived, the less likelihood there is that

---

[9] See Axelrod, *Evolution of Cooperation*, p. 138; M. A. Nowak, R. M. May and K. Sigmund, "The Arithmetics of Mutual Help," *Scientific American* 272 (1995), pp. 50–5.

[10] See, for example, G. Ainslie, "Impulsiveness and Impulse Control," *Psychological Bulletin* 82 (1975), pp. 463–96; T. Schelling, "The Intimate Contest for Self-Command," *The Public Interest* 60 (1980), pp. 94–118; *idem*, "Self-Command in Practice, in Policy, and in a Theory of Rational Choice," *American Economic Review: Papers and Proceedings* 74 (1984), pp. 1–11; R. Hernstein, "Self-Control as Response Strength," in C. M. Bradshaw, E. Szabadi, and C. F. Lowe (eds.), *Quantification of Steady-State Operant Behavior* (Amsterdam: North Holland Biomedical Press, 1981), pp. 3–20; J. Elster, *Ulysses and the Sirens* (Cambridge: Cambridge University Press, 1984), *idem*, "Weakness of Will and the Free-Rider Problem," *Economics and Philosophy* 1 (1985), pp. 231–65.

akrasia will win out. This, I believe, is an important instrumental value of moral beliefs: they are a bulwark against the temptations of short-term profit.

When agents calculate costs and benefits, then the possibility of temporarily "fiddling" the subjective values in order to rationalize a defection is always a possibility. Why would an agent do such an irrational thing? Because the short-term profit is tangible and present, whereas the long-term profit is distant and faint. If an agent is thinking only in terms of hypothetical imperatives – thinking that he ought to ϕ because doing so will, in the long run, satisfy his desire for X – then there is room for temptation to enter in the form of rationalization: "Well, how much do I *really* want X, anyway?" The lure of immediate profit may interfere with the agent's ability to deliberate properly so as to obtain a valuable delayed benefit. However, if he is thinking that ϕing simply *must* be performed, then the possibilities for rationalization diminish. Someone armed with moral beliefs thinks of cooperation as categorically required, and the distinctive value of categorical imperatives is that they silence calculation. Moreover, one's ability to calculate effectively is subject to a range of other interfering factors. This point was well made by Chester Bowles, the American Under Secretary of State in the early 1960s. He writes:

Anyone ... who has strong convictions about the rights and wrongs of public morality ... has a very great advantage in times of strain, since his instincts on what to do are clear and immediate ... [By comparison, someone lacking] such a framework of moral conviction ... adds up the pluses and minuses of any question and comes up with a conclusion. Under normal circumstances, this pragmatic approach should successfully bring him out on the right side of the question.

What worries me are the conclusions that such an individual may reach when he is tired, angry, frustrated, or emotionally affected.[11]

We have an argument, then, for why having moral beliefs is instrumentally valuable. Saying that they act to combat akrasia may make them sound rather trivial, but I suspect that this is the product of decades of philosophers discussing akrasia in terms of not brushing one's teeth, or having an extra serving of chocolate bombe. One is equally subject to temptation when it comes to the possibility of breaking an inconvenient promise, and the content of that promise may be as consequential as you

---

[11] Bowles's diary is quoted by Peter Singer, *Expanding Circle*, p. 162.

wish to imagine it. Besides, it is not being claimed that this is the *only* value of morality, but it will suffice for our purposes.

8.1 MORALITY AS FICTION

Now let us wheel fictionalism back into the picture, and recall the account of "acceptance" that was submitted in the previous chapter. The all-important question is whether the kinds of benefits that have been just described can be obtained with a fictive attitude towards morality. I admit that the hypothesis has a certain initial implausibility about it; however, I also believe that, with care, the case can be made.

It is important to recognize that it is not my intention to argue that making a fiction of morality would provide *all* the benefits that a believed morality brings. Three scenarios need to be compared. First, where moral discourse has been abandoned altogether, and is mentioned only as we now refer to historical oddities like a vitalistic life force. Call this "abolitionism." Second, where moral claims are (somehow) believed, despite the fact that evidence of the falsity of such beliefs are glaring. Third, where it is adopted as a fiction. My argument in favor of fictionalism requires only that the third option will be pragmatically preferable to either of the others. I suppose that there is a fourth option to consider – namely, where the evidence that makes a moral error theory compelling is somehow "hushed up," so that most people gain the benefits of sincere moral beliefs without this in any way clashing with evidence that they have been exposed to. We might call this option (reminiscent of "Government House Utilitarianism"[12]) "propagandism." But I doubt that propagandism will be pragmatically optimal for much the same reason that I expressed for doubting the second option (see §7.0). No policy that encourages the belief in falsehoods, or the promulgation of false beliefs in others, will be practically stable in the long run. Here I agree with Richard Garner, commenting on Plato's state policy of deception: "If the members of any society should come to believe Socrates' fable, *or any similarly fabricated radical fiction*, the result would be a very confused group of people, unsure of what to believe, and unable to trust their normal belief-producing mechanisms. It is not wise to risk having a society of epistemological wrecks in order to achieve some

---

[12] See, for example, Henry Sidgwick's *The Methods of Ethics* (Indianapolis: Hackett Publishing Company, 1981), especially pp. 489–92. For criticism, see B. Williams, "A Critique of Utilitarianism," in J. J. C. Smart and B. Williams (eds.), *Utilitarianism: For and Against* (Cambridge University Press, 1973), pp. 135–40.

projected good through massive deception."[13] The two serious options to compare, then, are the first and third: abolitionism versus fictionalism. So long as fictionalism reliably wins that comparative cost-benefit analysis, then it is the preferable strategy. It is not required that it supplies *all* the benefits that would be provided by a sincerely believed morality.

I argued that the instrumental value of moral beliefs lies in their combating of weakness of will, their blocking of the temporary revaluing of outcomes that is characteristic of short-sighted rationalizations, their silencing of certain kinds of calculation. And it is my contention that these desiderata can be satisfied, to some extent, even if the moral claims are not believed.

Consider again the question of how to combat weakness of will. Suppose I am determined to exercise regularly, after a lifetime of lethargy, but find myself succumbing to temptation. An effective strategy will be for me to lay down a strong and authoritative rule: I must do (say) fifty sit-ups every day, no less. I am attempting to form a habit, and habits are formed – and, for the doggedly weak of will, maintained – by strictness and overcompensation. Perhaps in truth it doesn't much matter that I do fifty sit-ups every day, so long as I do more-or-less fifty on most days. But by allowing myself the occasional lapse, by giving myself permission *sometimes* to stray from the routine, I pave the way for akratic sabotage of my calculations – I threaten even my doing more-or-less fifty sit-ups on most days. I do better if I encourage myself to think in terms of fifty daily sit-ups as a non-negotiable value.

However, to believe sincerely that fifty daily sit-ups are needed in order for me to achieve my end of health is to have a false belief (we'll assume), the holding of which will require other compensating false beliefs. If it is true that *more-or-less* fifty sit-ups *nearly* every day is sufficient for health, then that is what I ought to believe. On the other hand, to *pay attention* to this belief exposes me to self-subversion – a slippery slope to inactivity. This is precisely a case where my best interests are served by rehearsing thoughts that are false, and that I know are false, in order to fend off my own weaknesses. But in order to get the benefit from this strategy there is no necessity that I *believe* the thoughts, or attempt to justify them as true when placed in a philosophically critical context. While doing my sit-ups I think "Must do fifty!" but if, at some other time, you ask me whether I really *must* do fifty, then I will say "No, sometimes forty would suffice."

[13] R. Garner, "Are Convenient Fictions Harmful to Your Health?" *Philosophy East and West* 43 (1993), pp. 87–106.

Human motivation is often supported better by mental images than by careful calculation. Hume uses the example of a drunkard "who has seen his companion die of a debauch, and dreads a like accident for himself: But as the memory of it decays away by degrees, his former security returns, and the danger seems less certain and real."[14] Hume's point is that we put weight on near and recent evidence, though there is no justification for our doing so. We can imagine the drunkard being presented with impressive statistics on the probabilities of alcoholics suffering an unpleasant end, but remaining quite unmoved; yet one friend dies, and he becomes a teetotaler (at least for a while). It's not that he disbelieved the statistics, and the death of the friend need not alter his beliefs about how likely he is to suffer a similar fate, but the "tangibility" of the one death encourages, in Hume's words, "a superior influence on the judgment, as well as on the passions."[15]

If the drunkard has decided that his long-term interests are best served by abstinence, what strategy should he pursue to that end? He should read the statistics, yes, but – perhaps even more importantly – he should attempt to keep the image of his dying friend vivid. Yet he does still better if he can relate that image to his own plight; if he thinks: "If I drink, that's what will happen to me." Now that proposition is false. What is true is something like "If I drink, then there's a 10 per cent chance [say] of this happening to me." But *that* thought looks dangerous. He does better with the stronger: "If I drink, then this *will* happen to me." Yet does he, need he, *believe* this? No: he need not believe it in order for it to affect his actions in the desirable way, and, moreover, he *ought not* believe it because it is false.

We must not be distracted by the fact that I have chosen one relatively trivial example of exercising, and another concerning what is (arguably) an addictive behavior. Whenever moral decisions are made by an individual, such that the possibility of "immoral" behavior is a temptation, then such regulative images can play a very useful role. The range of actions includes the likes of stealing, promise-breaking, sexual harassment, nepotism, unfair dealing, violence, and any deadly sin you care to think of. Akrasia may be

---

[14] Hume, *Treatise*, book 1, part 3, section 8 (1978), p. 144.
[15] *Ibid.*, pp. 143–4. Hume's point, which is completely plausible anyway, receives empirical backing from a large-scale survey conducted on doctors' attitudes towards smoking. Smoking has dropped most dramatically in chest physicians and radiologists – those who have been exposed to the effects of the activity – while other types of doctor, though no doubt aware of the statistics, are much less moved. See E. Borgida and R. E. Nisbett, "The Differential Impact of Abstract vs. Concrete Information on Decisions," *Journal of Applied Social Psychology* 7 (1977), pp. 258–71.

fended off to some degree by the tempted subject picturing as vividly as she can herself punished and vilified. But the focus on chastisement may also lead her to reflect more carefully on the possibilities of evading it. She does better if such images are supplemented by the thought that the action in question is just *wrong* – that even if she managed to evade punishment she would still be punishment-deserving, guilty, reprehensible. These thoughts will be bolstered if they are expressed publicly: a tendency to say things like "Stealing is a morally terrible thing," etc.[16]

One might complain that the mere "holding of images" is all very well, but surely for the tempted person sincerely to *believe* that in stealing she would become morally reprehensible would be far more effective in regulating honest behavior and seeing off akrasia. And that is probably true. But the possibility of sincere moral belief is no longer the relevant comparison class. We are comparing fictionalism with abolitionism, asking whether moral thoughts and moral language could continue to have a useful role once moral *belief* is no longer an option. My argument is that maintaining the moral discourse in the manner described would at least be a reliable improvement on straight thinking (and straight talk) about one's long-term preference satisfactions.

To those who would object that a mere fiction could not have any significant impact on one's decisions, let me provide three disparate examples (among many) of seemingly trivial aspects of a person's mental life making a notable difference to their actions. The first example is from gambling. In the game of blackjack, players can frequently be persuaded to take a kind of side bet called "insurance," which, on average, they will (pretty obviously) lose money on. Yet in one study it was observed that more than 12 per cent of players always insure. It is hypothesized that this irrational behavior is induced simply by labeling the losing bet "insurance" (a truism of which advertisers have long been aware).[17] The second example concerns people playing Prisoner's Dilemma games. If, prior to playing the game, a person has been exposed to a touching radio story concerning an act of sacrifice, such as the donation of a kidney for transplant, then he will be far more likely to adopt a cooperative strategy than a person who

---

[16] For empirical evidence that public avowals strengthen resolve, see C. Kiesler, P. Mathog, P. Pool, and R. Howenstein, "Commitment and the Boomerang Effect," in C. Kiesler (ed.), *The Psychology of Commitment* (New York: Academic Press, 1971), pp. 74–85.

[17] See W. A. Wagenaar, *Paradoxes of Gambling Behavior* (Hove: Lawrence Erlbaum Associates, 1988). For the curious: "insurance" is offered when a player's first card is an ace. She can then stake up to half her original stake on the dealer getting a blackjack. If he does, then she wins double her stake; otherwise she loses it.

has instead listened to a story about an act of violence. We can assume that these stories did not alter the players' beliefs, but had noticeable influence nonetheless.[18] Pairs of people playing iterated PD games will also be much more likely to develop a cooperative strategy if the information concerning how the other acted in the previous round is conveyed by a written note passed through a slot, as opposed to one of two small lights being activated, despite the fact that the content of the information is the same by either means.[19] My third example comes from experiments on an individual's willingness to supply another person with a powerful electric shock. (The subject believed himself to be taking part in a quite different kind of test, regarding which shocking the other person was an element; of course, the person being "shocked" was only acting.) All sorts of seemingly inconsequential factors will increase the likelihood of the person being willing to administer dangerously high shocks – a simple one being if you put him or her in a white lab coat.[20]

Examples like these show how easily influenced humans are, concerning important decisions, by apparently trifling factors: how an action is labeled, what story has just been on the radio, whether information is handwritten, what one is wearing. In light of such considerations, the idea that a fictional stance towards morality may continue to have a positive practical impact on our lives loses some of its *prima facie* implausibility.

Let me say more about what "taking the fictive stance towards morality" may consist in. Whereas for Hume's drunkard the regulative "image" may be something that he conjures briefly when confronted with a glass of vodka, the analogous "moral thoughts" may be well-rooted habits of thinking that are overturned only when the person enters a very critical context of discussion, such as a conversation on metaethics. And the fact that the person *is* so-disposed to deny the truth of moral claims in such an environment may not be something that she is typically aware of. Indeed, to *be* aware of that fact is, to some degree, already to be operating towards the more critical end of the spectrum. Part of being "immersed"

---

[18] H. A. Hornstein, E. LaKind, E. Frankel, and S. Manne, "Effects of Knowledge about Remote Social Events on Prosocial Behavior, Social Conception, and Mood," *Journal of Personality and Social Psychology* 32 (1975), pp. 1038–46.

[19] M. E. Enzle, R. D. Hansen, and C. A. Lowe, "Humanizing the Mixed-Motive Paradigm: Methodological Implications from Attribution Theory," *Simulation and Games* 6 (1975), pp. 151–65.

[20] P. G. Zimbardo, "The Human Choice: Individuation, Reason and Order versus Deindividuation, Impulse and Chaos," in W. J. Arnold and D. Levine (eds.), *Nebraska Symposium on Motivation* (Lincoln, Nebr.: University of Nebraska Press, 1970), pp. 237–307.

in a theory is thinking that being immersed in the theory is appropriate – which is to say, not paying attention to the fact that one is "immersed in a theory" at all. So the "moral images" in question may well *seem* to the subject as very much the same as beliefs. The difference between a thought and a belief here is not a phenomenological one; it is a matter of a disposition to dissent.

This reminder should also serve to counter a potential worry that the fictionalism presented is relevant to only a small range of moral decisions: where an individual has to make an on-the-spot decision which akrasia could potentially disrupt. If employing the fiction of morality is to be a habit (and it will certainly be more useful if that is the case), then its employment will extend beyond "temptation situations" to contexts where weakness of will may not be a factor. Consider, for example, the situation of the ethics committee of a hospital trying to work out the optimal and ethical means of allocating funds. Is it feasible that weakness of will is looming over these proceedings? Personally, I don't find it at all implausible to claim that combating the temptations of short-term profit is important even there. But even if that were not so – even if akrasia is somehow excluded by the fact that it is a group of interacting persons making a careful collective decision under no time constraints – it may still be useful to each individual if she thinks in moral terms since this will support and encourage her tendency of doing so in personal "temptation situations." If this "tendency" were something that one could flick on and off at will then it would be of no use; in order to work it must be a "life strategy." Recall that we are not trying to justify moral thinking on a case-by-case basis, but rather trying to provide instrumental justification for "being a moral thinker." Thus when the member of the hospital ethics committee decries a course of action as "unethical" then she is acting upon (one might say "acting out") her habit of ethical thinking. Having such a habit is in her best interests. (No one is saying, of course, that this thought figures in her deliberations.)

Suppose that members of the hospital ethics committee are moral fictionalists; in other words, there is some more critical context – say, the philosophy classroom – wherein they are disposed to assent to moral skepticism. (This, of course, sounds decidedly odd, because fictionalism is not a familiar phenomenon, and our present expectations are that members of ethics committees will be sincere moral believers.) An important point to stress is that even if this were true, it would not follow that the deliberations of the committee are *uncritical*. On the contrary, options are discussed with immense care, consequences are given full consideration, and a great deal of reflective skill may be brought to bear. My point is simply that this context may nevertheless not be the *most* critical available. Recall that in the previous sentence "critical" indicates a kind of asymmetric questioning, not the amount of "brain power" that is involved. The less critical context may involve more deliberative sophistication, attention to a greater number of factors, and – in some sense of the word – a more serious attitude. By analogy, one may, qua philosopher, be resolutely skeptical of the existence of numbers (and thus skeptical of the relations that hold among them), without this in any way intefering with the sophisticated arithmetical abilities brought to bear when calculating one's tax return. Or a person may, after philosophical reflection, believe that our everyday conceptions of *color* embody a fundamental error, to such a degree that she comes to endorse an error theory of color. Yet there is no reason why the very same person might not be a skilled impressionist painter – an activity requiring acute abilities of visual discernment and appreciation. The level of "critical thinking" required to motivate either philosophical stance – skepticism about numbers or colors – may be in many ways elementary compared with the skills of numeracy or painting.

Of course, there is every possibility that the context of the hospital ethics committee *is* each member's most critical context. Assume that it is. In this context they are disposed either to affirm or deny moral concepts. If the former, then these people are sincere moral believers, and so their status is not of interest to this discussion. What if the latter? This would mean that the deliberations of the committee eschew moral talk altogether, in which case, I suppose, we should hardly continue to call it "an *ethics* committee." But what's important to stress is that even in this case it just wouldn't follow that the committee would immediately start sanctioning secret drug trials, operations without proper consent, surreptitious acts of euthanasia, and the like – not, at least, if they were deliberating well. Anyone who thinks otherwise has not absorbed the understanding of rational cooperative strategies that has been achieved in the last few decades of game theory and evolutionary psychology. For ordinarily situated, ordinary humans, harming innocents is still a bad idea, for Hobbesian and Humean reasons. The hospital "*non*-ethics committee" should, in ordinary circumstances, come to the same decisions as the ethics committee. My point has been that to deliberate in terms of Hobbesian and Humean reasons – to *attend to* the fact that proscriptions against harming others apply only to ordinarily situated humans – is likely often to be a poor strategy.

Whether a typical ethical hospital committee is a context wherein deliberating explicitly in terms of Hobbesian and Humean reasons is likely to lead to inferior decisions – or whether doing so in that context may lead, indirectly, to inferior decisions being made elsewhere in the lives of those concerned – I don't pretend to know. But I would reiterate the point made above, that all the argument requires is that there are *some* contexts in which employing a moral concept (that one is disposed to deny on another occasion) is a useful strategy. If my opponent can think of a range of cases where adopting morality as a fiction seems incompatible with the amount of reflective deliberation appropriate to those situations, so be it. I have been exploring the possibility that the fiction may have practical use throughout our lives, to be overturned only in, say, the philosophy classroom, but it shouldn't be forgotten that an interesting thesis has been established even if the employment of the fiction turns out to be useful only in a more restricted range of contexts.

8.2 THE RETURN OF GYGES AND THE SENSIBLE KNAVE

We started out with the question "If there is nothing we morally ought to do, then what ought we to do?" and now an answer has been offered: "Continue with moral discourse as a fiction." Section 8.1 has been concerned with arguing that this may be a better answer than "Jettison the discourse." However, the answer is best thought of as a piece of advice, and, like most pieces of advice, it might not be the best advice for everybody. Advice generally comes in the form of a hypothetical imperative, relying for its legitimacy on the addressee having a certain desire. It ceases to be good advice for somebody who lacks the desire in question, or who has a different and superior means of satisfying the desire.

For instance, I do not think for a moment that Plato's Lydian shepherd must have a reason for taking the fictionalist stance towards morality. He is a very unusually situated person, and what is good advice for an ordinary person will not be good advice for him. It might be objected that if I'm permitted to sweep Gyges aside in such a cavalier manner, then so too may my opponent from earlier chapters who is trying to uphold moral realism (as a system of hypothetical imperatives): why cannot the defender of morality just claim that Gyges is so unusual that moral prescriptions do not apply to him? But moral prescriptions *are* applied to him! That was the point of my argument for an error theory: we unhesitatingly morally condemn the shepherd for his killing and raping, yet, upon any reasonable account of practical reasons, we have no business doing so. Moral imperatives are not like pieces of advice. (Indeed, it was to make exactly this point that Glaucon produced the example in order to challenge Socrates.) This is not to deny the claim that moral imperatives will, for ordinarily situated persons, point in the same direction as good practical advice. This latter claim I have endorsed. But the general convergence of the practically instrumental and the moral provides no basis for moral realism. Some have argued, for example, that since long-term selfish judgments turn out to favor cooperation, promise-keeping, etc., such judgments just *are* moral judgments (or, at least, moral judgments are a proper subset of judgments of "enlightened self-interest"). But this strategy unravels when we consider the instances where there can be no serious case made that an agent's ends *are* served by cooperation, coupled with the observation that moral discourse may still adamantly condemn him – such as the situation of Gyges.

But what is the strength of moral fictionalism if it does not apply to Gyges? First, let us note that such a limitation on the project was inevitable. When it comes to answering the question "Why ought I adopt morality, even as a fiction?" it cannot be argued that one *must* adopt the moral fiction – where the "must" is read as a categorical imperative. The unsatisfiable desideratum of "inescapability" is an important part of the error; could it be provided at this point in the proceedings, as a way of *demanding* that one immerse oneself in a fiction, then we would never have gotten this far: morality would not demand the error theoretic stance after all, and so fictionalism would be misplaced.

The strength of the advice that recommends moral fictionalism is no more and no less than this: it will be in the long-term best interests of ordinarily situated persons with normal human desires. (I do not pretend to have established the truth of this claim with any assurance, but rather to have proposed considerations in its favor.) If faced with a Gyges in our midst, or merely someone who has had an unusual socialization process to the extent that her desires are aberrant (she is quite lacking in human sympathy, for example), then from the fact that we could not reasonably exhort them to adopt the fictive stance towards morality it does not follow that we must calmly accept any mischief or violence that they perpetrate. We may decide to imprison them (if we manage to catch Gyges), or inflict whatever retribution seems appropriate. By "we" I mean the hypothetical community that has adopted the fiction of morality. We will claim of such miscreants that they are morally mistaken, we will wield categorical imperatives and make external reasons claims, and if we punish them we may consider the retribution to be morally deserved. In describing the situation in such terms we would be participating in a fiction. "Monstrous fiction," one might complain, "that licenses *real* punishment." But it is not our participation in the fiction that is responsible for our doling out punishment, for what would the abolitionist do if faced with an uncaring villain? Exactly the same. If a villain is harming us and our projects, then we must do something about it. It need make no difference to the severity of the punishment whether we describe the situation in terms of our needs and desires or in terms of the violation of our moral rights.

What, by comparison, of the sensible knave? The original sensible knave was a selfish agent who wondered why he should follow moral advice like "Be nice to your fellows." He believed that the best way of satisfying his selfishness was to be seen to be nice, and perhaps encourage genuine niceness in others, but to be as nasty as he pleased when (A) it was to his advantage, and (B) he could get away with it. Now the sensible knave is being offered new advice: "Adopt morality as a fiction." Can he reason in the same manner as before, to the same Machiavellian conclusion? If I am correct in claiming that the advice *is* good advice for the average person, and we assume that the sensible knave is an average person, then it will be good advice for the average sensible knave. (If he is not "average," but has eccentric desires or a ring of invisibility, then what I have said about Gyges will also apply to him.) If he encourages the fictionalist stance in others, but only pretends to cultivate it in himself, then he is simply not being effectively selfish. The whole point of the moral fictive stance is that it is a strategy for staving off inevitable human fallibilities in instrumental deliberation. Without the stance, the knave will be vulnerable – he will make mistakes; he will rationalize to himself poor decisions; he might get what he immediately desires, but not what he values; he will defect on deals and he will pay the price.

8.3 ODYSSEUS AND THE SIRENS

One might object that if the everyday calculations of our interests are so vulnerable to weakness of will, then why won't the fictionalist's decision to adopt morality as a fiction be equally vulnerable? The answer is that the decision to adopt morality as a fiction is not an ongoing calculation that one makes over and over. It is not being suggested that someone enters a shop, is tempted to steal, decides to adopt morality as a fiction, and doing so bolsters her prudent though faltering decision not to steal. Rather, the resolution to accept the moral point of view is something that occurred in the person's past, and is now an accustomed way of thinking – it is what Jon Elster calls a "precommitment."[21] Its role is that when entering a shop the possibility of stealing doesn't even enter one's mind. One is reminded of Odysseus' decision to have himself bound to the mast of his ship so as not to give in to the song of the sirens. The circumstance in which he made that decision was one in which he was free of temptation, but he was shrewd enough to anticipate the overthrow of control.

Exactly what the real-life equivalent of saying "Tie me to the mast" is – exactly *how* the habit of taking the moral fictive stance gets formed – is not something regarding which I have well-defined views. Habits get formed in all sorts of ways. The whole idea of there being a "decision" to adopt the fiction is something of a philosopher's artifice. Rather, it is more likely that a person is raised by her parents to accept moral prescriptions, initially, as items of belief. (Just you try explaining the Prisoner's Dilemma and tit-for-tat strategies to a four-year-old!) Thus thinking of certain types of action as "right" and others as "wrong" becomes natural and ingrained. And it is only later, when a broader and more sophisticated understanding is possible, that the person sees how philosophically troubling are the concepts of *moral right* and *moral wrong* (and, therefore, all that they imply them). At that point she may decide that really there is no such thing – she becomes a moral error theorist – but these patterns of thought are now so deeply embedded that in everyday life she carries on employing them, and is happy to do so – she becomes a moral fictionalist.

It might be thought that the previous paragraph contains the seeds of its own undermining. I claimed that the decision to adopt morality as a fiction is not subject to weakness of will because it is a habit that one forms, and not a day-to-day decision. But if it is so easy to say that about the decision to adopt the moral fiction, then why can't one say it about the decision, say, to act cooperatively? After all, the fictive stance was practically justified on the grounds that it combats weakness of will. But if we now have a different piece of general advice about how to fend off akrasia – ("Form well-entrenched habits of acting, such that the thought of acting otherwise doesn't enter your mind") – then hasn't moral fictionalism become obsolete?

---

[21] Elster, *Ulysses and the Sirens*, p. 37.

No, it hasn't. We need to compare three agents, all of whom, we can imagine, walk into a shop where the possibility of stealing an item arises. We will assume that for all three agents stealing would be a practical mistake. Agent 1 is the prudential calculator. He thinks about his chances of getting caught, he thinks about his epistemic fallibility when it comes to calculating his chances of getting caught (perhaps he remembers Hume's advice from the closing paragraphs of *An Enquiry Concerning the Principles of Morals*), and he decides, quite correctly, that the best course of action is to refrain. Agent 2 is the moral fictionalist. She has adopted morality as a fiction, and has a solid habit of thinking of stealing in terms of "must-not-be-doneness." Were you to sit her down in a philosophy classroom, then she would admit to agreeing with most of what Mackie says; nevertheless, when she is out shopping such thoughts are far-off. Stealing doesn't cross her mind. Agent 3 doesn't think in moral terms at all; perhaps he, too, agrees with Mackie. Nevertheless, he has a stable habit of acting in an honest manner. That's just how he was brought up. Stealing doesn't cross his mind, either.

Agent 1, I have already argued, is most likely to steal. The question we are now facing is "Why would agent 2 be more resolute than agent 3?" Well, on this occasion she may not be, but she has an advantage across a range of situations. Why? Because when the possibility of stealing does enter her mind (not necessarily while she is shopping, but perhaps when watching a documentary about shop-lifting), agent 2 has something to tell herself about why she does not steal. She doesn't steal because it is morally wrong. She feels justified, and is able to articulate that justification to herself and others. What, by comparison, is agent 3 to say? "Well, I just don't want to steal; it never enters my mind." But perhaps when he finds that this is all that he has to say on the matter, he may begin to have doubts as to how convincing a "justification" it is. Suppose both agents 2 and 3, on separate occasions, enter the shop with their mutual friend, the Foole. The Foole is filling his pockets with goods while the proprietor's back is turned, and urging his companion to the same: "Come on! Why not?" Agent 2 has something definite to say to the Foole. Agent 3 may founder for a convincing reply. Of course, agent 3 can always fall back on an appeal to the long-term disadvantages of knavery, but then he is just becoming like agent 1.

Furthermore, agent 2 can appeal to a justificatory framework according to which law-breakers are subject to severe penalty. Again, clear-headed instrumental thinking will come to the same conclusion: it is important that those who defect on deals suffer the "moralistic aggression" of the community. Further, it is important that those who do not adequately express this condemnation of defectors are themselves disapproved of (though not necessarily so severely as the original culprit).[22] But which will more reliably ensure that the right response is given: instrumental deliberation that comes to the conclusion "Now I must express disapproval towards this wrongdoer," or a habit of thinking of the wrongdoer as, literally, a *wrongdoer*? Only the second involves a full-blooded notion of the criminal *deserving* punishment. The former, by contrast, sees punishment as "called for" in order to maintain social stability. If one sees a criminal as deserving punishment, then, I submit, one will be more motivated to enforce that reprimand. By the same token, if one sees oneself as *deserving* punishment for stealing (as opposed to seeing oneself as *risking* punishment), then that will harden one's resolve not to.

What of agent 3 in this respect? I have described him in rather thin terms as having a raw habit of not stealing; the important thing is that he does not "moralize" that habit. So if he were to break the habit on some occasion, it is not clear he would feel anything other than surprise at having done so. Moreover, agent 3's reliable habit of refraining from stealing does not provide him with any particular reason to condemn others who do steal (nor to condemn those who fail to condemn thieves). Agent 2's habit of moral thinking, by comparison, *is* a disposition to think in terms of having reasons, and seeing others as having reasons.

It may be complained that agent 3 has been described in insufficient terms. Would it make a difference if his "habit" were not merely one of refraining from stealing, but rather one of feeling sympathetic towards others, of caring for their welfare – an emotion which banishes the thought of stealing? This will provide him with a general interest in seeing stealing refrained from, so he will in some sense be willing generally to condemn thieves. It may also provide him with an emotion other than mere surprise were he to break down and steal something: he will feel disappointment. However, *guilt* still does not enter his worldview. Were he (exceptionally) to steal, he would not see himself as *deserving* of punishment, nor would he so judge any other thief. His habit makes him dislike stealing for the harm it does, but it need not counsel retributive action, nor any action at all once the harm is done. Even if agent 3's sympathy for the harmed

---

[22] See R. Axelrod, "An Evolutionary Approach to Norms," *American Political Science Review* 80 (1986), pp. 1095–111.

victim manifests itself as a desire to see some reparation delivered, there need be nothing in his feeling that demands that the reparation be fair, nor that it is the wrongdoer who must foot the bill. Perhaps his sympathy is such that the observation of a harm done just "makes him" want to see the perpetrator punished (even if it is himself). However, once his anger at the crime has worn off, then the force that was behind any motivation to see punishment carried out will also evaporate.

I am not arguing that agents 1 and 3 are completely hopeless, or that they could not be trusted in shops! All that is being claimed is that agent 2 has an edge when it comes to combating temptation: in her everyday life the possibilities of breaking promises, stealing, etc., tend not to enter her calculations, and when they do she has something firm, vivid, and non-negotiable with which to oppose them. For those who think that I have been too hard on agent 3, let me allow that his habit of sympathy, backed up by an awareness of the instrumental importance of fair play and punishment, will permit him to operate successfully in a matrix of cooperative ventures. All that my argument requires is that if he had an active moral conscience − even if that conscience is a matter of fictive acceptance − then he would do better still. The best-situated agent is probably one who combines all three types that have been under discussion. That fact suffices to establish the conclusion that an agent who has made a fiction of morality is better placed than one who has abolished all thought of it from his mind.

"But" (I hear my opponent object) "agent 2 doesn't really *believe* that stealing is wrong! What's to prevent her entering 'critical mode' while in the shop, suddenly remembering that morality is a load of rubbish, and cramming her pockets?!" It is true that when she is in "critical mode" she expresses her disbelief that stealing is morally wrong, and there is no particular reason why she might not confront that disbelief while shopping. But if she is thinking clearly she also knows that fair-dealing is instrumentally best. In other words, she, too, can fall back on the calculations that keep agent 1 on the straight and narrow (all going well), and in "critical mode" that is what she will do. Of course, nothing guarantees that she will not steal. She may succumb. But people with moral *beliefs* yield to the temptation to sin, too. Perhaps in a world with no moral beliefs people will succumb more often. However, it is a background assumption of this and the previous chapter that the price of encouraging false beliefs, especially in the face of disconfirming evidence, is too grave a matter to make a fourth kind of agent – she who doesn't steal because she *believes* that it is morally wrong – an expedient option.

8.4 A MODEST CONCLUSION

Let me finish by reiterating the modest intentions of this chapter. Concerning fictionalism in general I am satisfied that a possible position has been carved out. But as to the question of whether *moral* discourse (or any familiar discourse) should be placed within that space, I am less convinced. I do not pretend to have firmly established the case that taking the fictive stance towards morality will definitely bring pragmatic gains. It is an empirical matter, and I have only put forward some considerations in favor of the hypothesis, not a mature theory. If the reader thinks that the picture I have painted leaves morality with a rather feeble role, then so be it. Personally, I do not think that a strategy for combating weakness of will, for helping us to achieve our own long-term best interests, is insignificant; but, in any case, my argument doesn't depend upon the fictive stance providing an *enormous* practical gain: if the returns are reliably just slightly higher than those of its competitors, then the case for moral fictionalism is made.

I also do not wish to give the impression that in my opinion combating weakness of will is the *only* benefit brought by morality. It is the feature that I have focused on here, but there may be others. I claimed above that moral thinking provides a strong foundation for "moralistic aggression" towards defectors, which is a different kind of advantage. A distinctively moral framework may also provide something of a shared experience of value which binds a community together. Why is it, after all, so important to us that we *condemn* the uncaring killer, as opposed merely to jailing him? Isn't it primarily an exercise in fortifying the links among the condemners, something that a non-moral response to crime, no matter how vigorous, could not accomplish? Perhaps, further, the appeal to an authority that lies outside our chosen ends, that cannot be articulated but has a powerful "felt" quality, may satisfy some need for an essentially mysterious element underpinning human affairs. (I consider this a little further in the Epilogue.)

A further benefit that morality may bring stems from the fact that it is, whether we like it or not, a familiar and widespread way of understanding our relations to each other, and therefore to abolish it entirely may bring anxiety and confusion. An epistemic conservative may find in this fact a reason to *believe* in morality, but (as I argued in §6.6) whatever *prima facie* case might thus be made, once we get past the first appearances and consider how moral facts fit with our broader understanding of the world, we will find insuperable difficulties. But the fact that we ought (by the coherentist's own standards) to give up on moral beliefs does not avoid the consequence that doing so may be difficult. The fictive stance may be a useful means of alleviating the disturbance of that upheaval.

We can consider this first at the level of the individual. Humans don't enter this world as fully rational, reflective thinkers. From the selfish and short-sighted condition of childhood we must somehow get to a state where we can properly appreciate the benefits of cooperation, and (even more difficult) where we can appreciate the benefits of *sincere* cooperation (that is to say, cooperation without the disposition to defect if one can get away with it). Having moral *beliefs* – judging cooperation to be "just the right thing to do" – promises to be an effective pedagogical tool in developing the appropriate set of attitudes. The point is Aristotelian in spirit: we start off lacking virtue, and the road to obtaining it involves taking already virtuous agents as role models, treating what for them are merely "rough guidelines" as if they were strict rules of conduct. The claim I am considering is similar, though it does not pertain to rule-following versus particularism. Rather, just as the novice cannot comprehend the subtleties of "moral perception" but requires rules to follow (Aristotle thinks), so too the novice cannot easily appreciate the benefits of developing a preference for sincere cooperation, and so needs authoritative, "no-questions-asked" reasons. By believing in this authority and performing these actions the child can start to appreciate the benefits of sincere cooperation (she begins to see that "inward peace of mind and consciousness of integrity" are better than "worthless toys and gewgaws"). But when the time comes for more critical thinking, then the belief in "moral authority" must be questioned along with everything else, and if the thinker is astute and open-minded, then (I believe) she should find reason to disbelieve these "truths." This person still has reason to value sincere cooperation, but the transition through the moral crisis to the point where she can appreciate her reasons may be rocky. To discover that one has had false beliefs about important matters is difficult; the response "Well, if these actions aren't *objectively required* then I have no reason to perform them" is a natural enough reaction. This is one place where taking a fictionalist stance may be important. The agent continues to use the language of morals, continues with her familiar patterns of thinking, but allows herself to express disbelief in it all when she is placed in highly critical contexts. Eventually she may be able to eliminate the moral concepts from her thoughts and language altogether, and be motivated instead by instrumental beliefs and fellow-feeling, but the moral way of thinking has the advantage of familiarity and of habit, and therefore can serve as an interim stance.

And, highly speculative though this all is, fictionalism as a transitional measure may be a good idea on the societal level, too: for a group that comes to realize the defective nature of a hitherto believed framework. For what it's worth, the idea of fictions as transitional devices sits comfortably with much of what Vaihinger claims. He says that his fictions are "provisional representations which at some future time are to make room for better and more natural systems" (*The Philosophy of "As If"*, p. 19), and later he quotes with approval a scientist's description of the atom as "a transitional idea whose provisional character is obvious . . . an exceedingly useful interim-concept" (p. 71). Recall Vaihinger's (offensively labeled) distinction between "primitive man" and "civilized man." For the former, taking the fictive stance would be a practical disaster; it is recommended only to the latter. But there is a hint now of a "future person," who has done away entirely with her fictions. Nevertheless, *we* are at the transitional phase, where we need the familiarity of our fictions and need the benefits of hard-nosed critical thinking. To permit moral beliefs undermines our much-needed disposition to believe only in things well supported by the evidence; on the other hand, to eliminate such precious concepts entirely from our lives may throw us into a cultural crisis characterized by distress and defection. The future may be a utopia where such fictions are unnecessary, but, Vaihinger would say, our society is far from utopian: we are still in the process of dragging ourselves from the shadow of superstition and primitivism, and are in need of many of our old beliefs to take on the role of myths.

Talking of the future development of "our society" in such an airy fashion is, of course, rather preposterous. I indulge in it only to highlight the point that the fictive stance may bring benefits at one time that it would not at another. But the major considerations that have been volunteered in this chapter have argued for an ongoing role for morality: so long as we live in a world of imperfect rationality and epistemological fallibility, morality has a place.

These are all empirical guesses, and I am the first to admit that they could turn out to be mistaken. Perhaps, despite all that has been claimed, we could get by perfectly well if we abolished moral discourse entirely.

I am quite prepared to accept such a conclusion, but think it important that all other options first be thoroughly explored. It is important not merely to the moral error theorist but to his opponents too, for the latter judge the battle to be worth fighting in part because of worries about what might *happen* if a moral error theory were to become widely accepted as true. There is a vague but deep-rooted concern that moral skepticism might corrupt the youth, or, more generally, leave people believing that "everything is permissible," with potentially destructive effect. A moral error theory is, as I remarked in the preface, seen not merely as counter-intuitive, but as genuinely threatening. If this concern is shown to be unjustified – as the possibility of moral fictionalism suggests it may be – then perhaps the motivation for resisting a moral error theory is in need of re-examination.

Epilogue: Debunking myths

Myths are narratives; they tell of the exploits of heroes, of supernatural events, of other worlds, of primordial love affairs and of symbolic deaths. When I talk of morality as a myth I do not intend to use the word literally, since morality, as we now conceive of it, lacks any such literary structure. But nor do I intend to use the word in its familiar quasi-metaphorical mode, to mean simply a widely held belief that is false ("the myth of the noble savage"). Perhaps, then, "myth" is an ill-chosen term, but it is employed because I believe there is room for a fruitful connection to be made between the fictionalist attitude towards a false theory and a culture's attitude towards its myths.

A naive view of myths takes them to be inadequate hypotheses, attempting to explain natural phenomena. According to such a view, a culture would not distinguish its myths from any of its other descriptions of the world, and, indeed, would not recognize them as "myths" at all. Such a view has long been discredited. Bronislaw Malinowski, in his groundbreaking field studies of the Trobriand Islanders early in the twentieth century, found the natives using three classes of narrative. The first consists of grotesque, bawdy tales, often involving supernatural events, which are told entirely for entertainment and are not believed for a moment. These he called "folk tales." The second class may be called "historical legends," relating deeds of past chiefs, heroes, battles and shipwrecks. Though containing a large dose of exaggeration and embellishment, these tales are taken to be true accounts of past events. The third class is what the natives called *lili'u*, which Malinowski translates as "myths." These stories tell of a world different to the present one: where people have supernatural powers, humans emerge from the ground, animals change into people, flying canoes speed through the air, where islands are fished from the ocean. These narratives "are not taken as items of ordinary knowledge. They are regarded by the people as sacred."[1] "These stories do not live by idle interest; they are not narrated as historical accounts of ordinary facts. They are to the natives a statement of a higher and more important truth, of a primeval reality, which is still regarded as the pattern and foundation of present-day life."[2] Although not items of "ordinary knowledge," *lili'u*, Malinowski reports, are believed to be true. What is interesting is that they are "special" beliefs, epistemically *sui generis*, and are known by the people to be so: the Trobriand Islanders acknowledge that a class of narrative counts as "myth" without this in any way undermining the practical importance of these stories – on the contrary, the practical import of these stories lies precisely in their distinct mythical status.

At the heart of Malinowski's work is the claim that what defines the class of myths is not their fabulous content, but the distinctive role that they play in the functioning of the society. That function is not to explain, nor entertain, but to "strengthen tradition," to provide a mandate for social arrangements: myth "expresses, enhances and codifies belief; it safeguards and enforces morality; it vouches for the efficiency of ritual and contains practical rules for the guidance of man."[3] Ivan Strenski compares this to the myth of Adam and Eve, which, though not considered literally true (generally), has "functioned in the past, among other things, to charter the institutions of wearing clothes, bearing children in pain, or working by the 'sweat of our brows.' "[4] If myth is to be understood in this way, then the details of content become almost arbitrary. One Trobriand myth tells of how witchcraft was brought to the people by a flying crab – but does it really matter that it was a crab, or would the myth function just as effectively if it were a flying spider?

Malinowski's functionalism is no longer in vogue, and he was certainly mistaken in thinking that *all* myths function to underwrite social institutions (indeed, I should say that any monolithic theory of "*the* function of myth" is bound to be mistaken), but his emphasis on the social context of myths, on their pragmatic purposes, remains important. For Malinowski, myths receive all the justification they need from their practical consequences, and though they are undoubtedly false if construed

---

[1] B. Malinowski, "The Foundations of Faith and Morals" [1935], reprinted in *Malinowski and the Work of Myth* (Princeton: Princeton University Press, 1992), p. 139.
[2] *Ibid.*, p. 141.
[3] B. Malinowski, *Myth in Primitive Psychology* (London: Kegan Paul, 1926), p. 23.
[4] Malinowski, *Malinowski and the Work of Myth*, p. xvii.

literally, he would claim that to focus on their falsehood is to miss the point.[5] Of the myths embodied in Christianity he writes that even the non-believer "must at least recognize them as indispensable pragmatic figments without which civilization cannot exist."[6] The position appears to be that mythical (and religious) belief is instrumentally justified but not evidentially justified.

How tenable this view is depends on whether we're talking about an inhabitant of the Trobriand archipelago in 1920, or whether we're talking about, say, a twenty-first-century Trobriand Islander who has attended university. Consider another Trobriand myth that involves a flying canoe.[7] The story is false, but was it, from the point of view of the 1920s native, evidentially unjustified? Perhaps not. Given the islander's parochial and limited understanding of the world, it was (arguably) consistent with the available evidence that canoes might fly in certain circumstances. It is true that they had never observed a canoe to fly, but authoritative figures, in whom they were taught to place their trust, spoke confidently of such things. But my interest lies in the modern educated islander. For she has, we'll imagine, been exposed to ample evidence that canoes cannot fly (not unless equipped with wings and an engine), such that for her the mythical belief is certainly evidentially unjustified. Might it nevertheless be, as Malinowski seems to think, an instrumentally justified belief? I doubt it. For reasons discussed in Chapter 7, an evidentially unjustified belief is exceedingly unlikely to be instrumentally beneficial in the long term. The upshot of those arguments, which is worth reiterating in response to Malinowski's view, is that things the evidence of whose falsehood is accessible *ought not to be believed*. To take a closer-to-home example: in the eighteenth century it was (perhaps) not unreasonable to take the Adam and Eve story as literally true, in the absence of any superior theory of human origins. But given what we now know of human evolution, to continue to take the story at face value would be deeply foolish. Myth as a believed narrative (even when the belief is, in some manner, known to

---

[5] It might be noted that this claim, which is the main one I am struggling to make in this discussion of myths, should also be accepted by the structural analyst (the discussion of whose theory I am purposely avoiding). For example, Lévi-Strauss influentially argues that the function of myths is to "mediate" contradictions via structural relationships. Myths, according to this account, may not serve as pragmatic *charters*, but since they do serve as problem-solving mechanisms their justification must still be in terms of their usefulness.
[6] Malinowski, *Malinowski and the Work of Myth*, p. 172.
[7] See B. Malinowski, *Argonauts of the Western Pacific* (London: Routledge and Kegan Paul, 1922), pp. 311–16.

Epilogue: Debunking myths

be of a special sort) may operate as a "sociological warrant" for historical societies, but it cannot function in that way for us. This is not to claim that myths have no important role for us. The point I'm making is that we must not *believe* them. This "must" does not merely reflect doxastic normativity – it is a piece of sound practical advice.

But is Malinowski even correct that the *lili'u* are items of belief? The mere fact that people may describe their attitude towards them as "belief" is far from clinching, since if embracing them were a form of well-entrenched make-believe, say, then a willingness to claim that the stories are true, and that one believes them, may well be a component of that make-believe. Joseph Campbell argues that myth, as it functions in "primitive" cultures, is dominated by an act of make-believe. A case in point is the central role of the *mask* in many rituals surrounding mythic activity:

The mask is revered as an apparition of the mythical being that it represents, yet everyone knows that a man made the mask, and that a man is wearing it. The one wearing it, furthermore, is identified with the god during the time of the ritual of which the mask is a part. He does not merely represent the god: he *is* the god. The literal fact that the apparition is composed of (a) a mask, (b) its reference to a mythical being, and (c) a man, is dismissed from the mind, and the presentation is allowed to work without correction upon the sentiments of both the beholder and the actor. In other words, there has been a shift of view from the logic of the normal secular sphere, where things are understood to be distinct from each other, to a theatrical or play sphere, where they are accepted for what they are *experienced* as being, and the logic is that of "make-believe" – "as if."[8]

Even Malinowski acknowledges that the "belief" with which he credits the Melanesians is suspect, for he recognizes that a person's apparently firm beliefs in a mythical afterlife sit uncomfortably with unwavering attempts to avoid death at any cost:

[The native's] intense fear of death, his strong desire to postpone it, and his deep sorrow at the departure of beloved relatives belie the optimistic creed and the easy reach of the beyond which is inherent in native customs, ideas, and ritual. After death has occurred, or at a time when death is threatening, there is no mistaking the dim division of shaking faith.[9]

---

[8] J. Campbell, "The Historical Development of Mythology," in H. A. Murray (ed.), *Myth and Mythmaking* (Boston: Beacon Press, 1960), pp. 33–4. See also R. R. Marett, *The Threshold of Religion* (London: Methuen, 1914); J. Huizinga, *Homo Ludens: A Study of the Play-element in Culture* (London: Routledge & Kegan Paul Ltd., 1949); F. Salamone, "Religion as Play," *Journal of Religion in Africa* 7 (1975), pp. 201–11; E. Norbeck, "Religion and Human Play," in A. Bharati (ed.), *The Realm of the Extra-Human: Agents and Audiences* (The Hague: Mouton, 1976), pp. 95–104.
[9] Malinowski, *Myth in Primitive Psychology*, pp. 105–6.

235

Let us hypothesize, with Campbell, that the attitude taken towards myth is not one of belief. It is highly doubtful that this hypothesis is true as a universal claim, but it is sufficient for our interests if it accurately describes some mythic attitudes and ritualistic activities, for then it serves as a precedent of an institution of central cultural importance, one that provides incentives for decisions and a mandate for action, which is characterized by an attitude better described as "make-believe" than "belief." The connection to moral discourse may well be more than a "precedent," though I do not have space to explore a more substantive relation. Axel Hägerström, arguing for a moral error theory in the early part of the twentieth century, traced our modern moral and legal conceptual framework back to its Classical Roman roots, wherein the ultimate grounding for notions like *desert, property rights*, etc., lay in the magical forces of superstition.[10] Yet, interestingly, Hägerström is not arguing for abolitionism, for he thinks that the secure operation of a cooperating society depends upon these fictions. The question of whether we should, in light of his findings, continue to *believe* in our legal fictions is not something he addresses.

If myths are not items of belief, then the question of their evidential justification does not arise. Myth becomes a *practice*, and practices are justified in terms of whether they serve their purpose. It follows that the act of debunking myths must consist of showing them to be pragmatically futile, or out-moded, or inert. Showing them to be false is beside the point. The person who exposes the logical flaws or empirical implausibility of a myth is not like a scientist offering a superior theory – she is better classed as a "spoilsport," like a member of the audience who talks loudly during a play. Campbell speculates that "the guardian figures that stand at either side of the entrances to holy places: lions, bulls, or fearsome warriors with uplifted weapons" function to keep out the "spoilsports and positivists" who must be kept aloof.[11]

[10] A. Hägerström, *Inquiries Into the Nature of Law and Morals*, ed. K.Olivecrona, trans. C. D. Broad (Stockholm: Almqvist & Wiksell, 1953). "This insuperable difficulty in finding the facts which correspond to our ideas of . . . rights forces us to suppose that there are no such facts and that we are here concerned with ideas which have nothing to do with reality . . . [W]e mean, both by rights of property and rightful claims, actual forces, which exist quite apart from our natural powers; forces which belong to another world than that of nature, and which legislation or other forms of law-giving merely liberate . . . We feel that here there are mysterious forces in the background from which we can derive support." Much of Hägerström's writings pre-dates Broad's translation by some decades. See also J. Passmore, "Hägerström's Philosophy of Law," *Philosophy* 36 (1961), pp. 143–60, and C. D. Broad, "Hägerström's Account of Sense of Duty and Certain Allied Experiences," *Philosophy* 26 (1951), pp. 99–113.
[11] Campbell, "The Historical Development," p. 40.

One such spoilsport was Euhemerus, whose lost work from the fourth century BC exposed the Greek gods as deified men: Zeus, for example, was a historical Cretan king, who, with a few centuries of exaggeration and idealization, became apotheosized.[12] In a surviving work from much the same period, Palaephatus attempts to purge the Greek myths of all fabulous elements (though he leaves the gods alone).[13] He complains, for instance, that centaurs couldn't possibly exist, if only because of digestive complications! – instead, the whole legend must derive from some young horsemen who succeeded in killing bulls with javelins, and who subsequently became known as "the centaurs" (from *kent-*, "to prick," and *tauros*, "bull"). Others – Prodicus of Ceos, Herodotus, Thucydides, Diodorus Siculus, Ennius[14] – all, at one time or another, gave similar explanations, but only Euhemerus made it into the English language in the form of the word "euhemerism."

It has been claimed that the objective of such writers was not to debunk, but rather to clear away the incredible parts of a misunderstood or wildly exaggerated story, so as to leave a plausible historical account worthy of belief.[15] But if Palaephatus succeeds in leaving us with a believable account of some horsemen, he also leaves us with a story that is utterly uninteresting. And if Euhemerus convinced his audience that "Zeus" ultimately denotes a Cretan king, why would they continue to build temples to him? These writers were clearly motivated to correct people's false beliefs in the literal narrative. (Palaephatus repeatedly scolds anyone who believes in such things as centaurs as being "childish," and "a fool.") But in separating the wheat from the chaff in this manner they also destroy the function of these stories. A narrative about a magical hero living in a past golden age may serve as a moral precedent for contemporary mores (returning to Malinowski), in a way that a true narrative about a historical king who won a war cannot.

The Greeks must have believed their myths, else Euhemerus *et al.* would not have bothered with their efforts. (Nobody would write a lengthy

---

[12] See Diodorus Siculus, book 6 (London: William Heinemann Ltd., 1939).
[13] Palaephatus, *On Unbelievable Tales*, trans. J. Stern (Wauconda, Ill.: Bolchazy-Carducci, 1996).
[14] We can add Hecataeus of Miletus, Acusilaus of Argos, Pherecydes of Athens, Hellenicus of Lesbos, Herodorus of Heracleaia, Dionysus Scyobrachion (see Stern (trans.), *Unbelievable Tales*, pp. 11 and 13). Plutarch's program of "purifying myth by reason," from a few centuries later, should also be mentioned.
[15] See, for example, Stern (trans.), *Unbelievable Tales*, pp. 8–9 (who claims this only of Palaephatus).

treatise revealing that Emma Bovary never lived.) But perhaps they hadn't always done so. It is natural to think of the Greeks starting out in a state of sincere belief (in which Euhemerus found them), and moving in time through doubt and fragmentation, and thence to disbelief. But one may instead conjecture that the "starting position" was as described by Campbell: where a myth is not experienced as a description of past history or natural phenomena, but as "a highly played game" in which belief and disbelief are temporarily put aside.[16] And perhaps it was only later in cultural history, when the original dynamism of the myth had already deteriorated, that the story as a historical narrative, as an item to be believed, came to dominate.

The question of how a culture responds when it becomes clear that an important believed narrative is false is one I find very interesting. One type of response would be to accept the falsehood of the literal details of the narrative but attempt its rescue by finding in it "allegorical truths." This move is structurally similar to what Palaephatus tried to accomplish. He poured scorn on anyone who took the myths at face value, but thought that they were distortions of a genuine historical truth which was worthy of belief. The "allegoricist" also denies the veridicality of the face value of myths, but thinks that they nevertheless deliver truths in symbolic form. The difference is that the latter will insist that the truths embodied in the myth are of profound importance, whereas Palaephatus has no grounds for claiming that anyone need bother themselves with the stories any more, unless she happens to have a historical curiosity.

Reading myth as allegory begins with Thales, who saw the story of Demeter and Persephone as "really" being about the cycle of winter and summer. The Stoics systematically decoded myths in this way, as did nearly all medieval and Renaissance writers (e.g., Francis Bacon's interpreting the claws of the Sphinx as the axioms and arguments of science, penetrating and grasping the mind[17]), and allegoricism reached a crescendo of implausible theorizing in the late nineteenth century. It is possible that seeing myths as moral allegories was also Plato's attitude. The well-known "myth of the metals" from the *Republic* is often interpreted as a "noble lie" – that is, as an item put forward for belief by the citizenry. However, Janet Smith argues that *gennaion pseudos* is better rendered as "noble fiction."[18] The

---

[16] Campbell, "The Historical Development," p. 43.

[17] Francis Bacon, *De Sapientia Veterum* [1609], *Works*, vol. 6 (London: Longmans & Co., 1890), pp. 755–7.

[18] J. Smith, "Plato's Myths as 'Likely Accounts', Worthy of Belief," *Apeiron* 19 (1985), pp. 24–42. Smith's view is rather more complex than I have space to discuss. She goes on

important distinction here, it seems to me, is the one made by Sir Philip Sidney, quoted in §7.6, between stories that are "affirmed" (told as true) and those that are not. If the myths of the *Republic* are fictions rather than lies, then it is possible that Plato never intended for the populace to believe them – they are, after all, so preposterous in content that a public that believed them could hardly be one that prized intelligence. But as an established *allegory* the myth may nevertheless convey vital truths about brotherhood, selflessness, etc. The myth is false, but it imparts truths. (For what it's worth, this interpretation makes sense of Plato's seemingly inconstant attitude towards myths: some myths reveal truths, and should therefore be accepted; others fail to convey truths, and are therefore pernicious.)

However, it may be argued that when a myth comes to be seen as an allegory it has already lost its potency. To see the ritual mask as a mask – that is, as a representation – is, Campbell would claim, to be one whose presence the "guardians of the temple" are designed to exclude. Ernst Cassirer made the same point, describing myth as "tautegorical," not allegorical: "the 'image' does not represent the 'thing'; it *is* the thing."[19] Faced with a euhemerist, adherents of a culturally important myth do themselves and their myth no favors if they attempt the "It's-just-an-allegory" defense. Considering a myth to be allegorical is a phase in the slow death of the myth. It reveals that the myth no longer plays a robust social role, for it is an admission that the narrative is dispensable in favor of straight talk. Such adherents equally do themselves no credit if they attempt to defend the literal truth of a preposterous story. So why defend the myth at all? Why not just let it drop and walk away, or treat it thereafter as merely a piece of entertaining fiction? But if the narrative is one that has performed a cluster of important cultural tasks – if it is being treated not merely as a piece of history, but, as Malinowski would put it, as a "pragmatic charter," as something which regulates conduct, or, as Lévi-Strauss would prefer, as a problem-solving mechanism[20] – then any attempt at debunking

to argue that many of Plato's "myths" *are* intended to be believed, if only provisionally, in so far as they are *eikotes logoi*: accounts likely to be true. However, it is not clear to me whether she intends this conclusion – presented with respect to the myths of the *Timaeus* and *Phaedrus* – to apply to the *Republic*'s myth of the metals, which, by her own admission, is surely too outlandish to be taken seriously.

[19] Ernst Cassirer, *The Philosophy of Symbolic Forms*, vol. 2: *Mythical Thought* (New Haven: Yale University Press, 1955), p. 38.

[20] Claude Lévi-Strauss, *The Savage Mind* (Chicago: University of Chicago Press, 1966); *idem, Mythologiques* (Paris: Plon, 1964–8).

will be stoutly resisted. Often, to expect a culture simply to drop its myths – when these myths are pulling their weight in the social order – is to expect it to become, literally, a new culture – and that is asking a lot.

I venture to suggest that the best defense against the euhemerist is to declare that the myth has nothing to do with *truth*, and, derivatively, nothing to do with belief. The adherents of the myth should just declare the mythoclast a spoilsport who is missing the point. But if they want to be ingenuous in this defense, then they had better get clear among themselves that they are *not* believing it. And this, of course, reveals a weakness at the heart of fictionalism, which we have already encountered. When appealing to myths is a well-defined practice – as in the Trobriand *lili'u*, for example – then all participants are aware that they are "special" ("sacred," is Malinowski's preferred term). All parties know that the telling of a *lili'u* is a serious and distinct kind of appeal, and they are not likely to mistake it for the telling of a fairy tale or for the communication of "ordinary" information. But if a culture diversifies and fragments, or mis-comprehends its own traditions, or for whatever reasons impoverishes its own categories of assent to the extent that the only recognized kind of important positive attitude is *belief*, then this understanding may be lost. Fictionalism is predicated on the assumption that encouraging a habit of false belief has inevitable deleterious consequences. Its fragility is that a fiction that is presented as being of central practical weight, as something demanding allegiance, is likely to be read by the careless as something demanding belief.

In such a circumstance the euhemerist can be seen as playing an important role, for he warns his audience that the narratives are not true, and admonishes anyone who has fallen into the easy (and therefore tempting) habit of belief. He combats the vice of credulity. Euhemerus and Palaephatus, as far as we know, were not social reformers, and no doubt despite their arguments many continued to believe in Zeus and centaurs. Hume, another great debunker, was resigned to the fact that whatever he might say about miracles, however sound his arguments, "the deluded multitude" would continue to believe in them[21] (69 per cent of Americans, according to a *Time* magazine poll). Hume's intended audience is primarily *the philosopher* who makes no effort to quell erroneous reasoning, for little can

---

[21] D. Hume, *An Enquiry Concerning Human Understanding* [1748], section 10 (Cambridge: Hackett Publishing Company, 1977), p. 87.

be done about the fact that "the gazing populace receive greedily, without examination, whatever soothes superstition, and promotes wonder."[22] The euhemerist writes for the same audience: for those philosophers who are defending the myth as true – for they, at least, ought to know better.

[22] *Ibid.*

Select bibliography

Altham, J., "The Legacy of Emotivism," in G. Macdonald and C. Wright (eds.), *Fact, Science and Morality* (Oxford: Basil Blackwell, 1986), pp. 275–88

Anscombe, G. E. M., "Modern Moral Philosophy," *Philosophy* 33 (1958), pp. 1–19

Austin, J. L., *How to do Things with Words* (Oxford: Oxford University Press, 1962)

Ayer, A. J., *Language, Truth and Logic* [1936] (Harmondsworth: Penguin, 1971)

Baier, K., "Rationality, Reason, and the Good," in D. Copp and D. Zimmerman (eds.), *Morality, Reason and Truth* (Totowa, NJ: Rowman & Allanheld, 1984), pp. 193–211

Bentham, J., "Essay on Logic," in *Collected Works*, vol. 8 (Edinburgh: William Tait, 1843)

Blackburn, S., *Spreading the Word* (Oxford: Oxford University Press, 1984)
Essays in Quasi-Realism (Oxford: Oxford University Press, 1993)

Brandt, R., *A Theory of the Right and the Good* (Oxford: Clarendon Press, 1979)

Brink, D., "Moral Realism and the Skeptical Arguments from Disagreement and Queerness," *Australasian Journal of Philosophy* 62 (1984), pp. 111–25
"Externalist Moral Realism," in *The Spindel Conference: The Southern Journal of Philosophy*, supplementary volume 24 (1986), pp. 23–41
Moral Realism and the Foundations of Ethics (Cambridge: Cambridge University Press, 1989)

Campbell, J., "The Historical Development of Mythology," in H. A. Murray (ed.), *Myth and Mythmaking* (Boston: Beacon Press, 1960), pp. 19–45

Cassirer, E., *The Philosophy of Symbolic Forms*, vol. 2: *Mythical Thought* (New Haven: Yale University Press, 1955)

Carnap, R., *Philosophy and Logical Syntax* (London: Kegan Paul, Trench, Trubner & Co. Ltd., 1935)
Meaning and Necessity (Chicago: University of Chicago Press, 1956)

Coe, C. and Rosenblum, L., "Male Dominance in the Bonnet Macaque: A Malleable Relationship," in P. Barchas and S. Mendoza (eds.), *Social Cohesion* (Westport, Conn.: Greenwood, 1984), pp. 31–64

Darwin, C., *The Descent of Man* [1871] (Princeton: Princeton University Press, 1981)
The Expression of the Emotions in Man and Animals (London: John Murray, 1873)

Elster, J., *Ulysses and the Sirens* (Cambridge: Cambridge University Press, 1984)

Falk, W. D., "'Ought' and Motivation," *Proceedings of the Aristotelian Society* 48 (1948), pp. 492–510

Select bibliography

Firth, R., "Ethical Absolutism and the Ideal Observer," *Philosophy and Phenomenological Research* 12 (1952), pp. 317–45

Foot, P., "Morality as a System of Hypothetical Imperatives," *Philosophical Review* 81 (1972), pp. 305–16

Frank, R. H., *Passion Within Reason* (London: W. W. Norton & Company, 1988)

Frankena, W. K., *Ethics* (Englewood Cliffs, NJ: Prentice-Hall, Inc., 1973)

Frankfurt, H., "Freedom of the Will and the Concept of a Person," in G. Watson (ed.), *Free Will* (Oxford: Oxford University Press, 1982), pp. 81–95

Garner, R. T., "On the Genuine Queerness of Moral Properties and Facts," *Australasian Journal of Philosophy* 68 (1990), pp. 137–46

"Are Convenient Fictions Harmful to Your Health?" *Philosophy East and West* 43 (1993), pp. 87–106

Geach, P. T., "Ascriptivism," *Philosophical Review* 69 (1960), pp. 221–25

"Assertion," *Philosophical Review* 74 (1965), pp. 449–65

Glassen, P., "The Cognitivity of Moral Judgments," *Mind* 68 (1959), pp. 57–72

Hägerström, A., *Inquiries Into the Nature of Law and Morals*, ed. K. Olivecrona, trans. C. D. Broad (Stockholm: Almqvist & Wiksell, 1953)

Hampton, J., *The Authority of Reason* (Cambridge: Cambridge University Press, 1998)

Harman, G., "Moral Relativism Defended," *Philosophical Review* 84 (1975), pp. 3–22

"Is There a Single True Morality?" in D. Copp and D. Zimmerman (eds.), *Morality, Reason and Truth* (New Jersey: Rowman & Allanheld, 1984), pp. 27–48

Hinckfuss, I., "The Moral Society: Its Structure and Effects," *Discussion Papers in Environmental Philosophy* (Canberra: Australian National University, 1987)

Hume, D., *A Treatise of Human Nature* [1739], ed. L. A. Selby-Bigge (Oxford: Clarendon Press, 1978)

An Enquiry Concerning Human Understanding [1748] (Cambridge: Hackett Publishing Company, 1977)

An Enquiry Concerning the Principles of Morals [1751] (Cambridge: Hackett Publishing Company, 1983)

James, W., *Pragmatism: The Meaning of Truth* [1909] (Cambridge, Mass.: Harvard University Press, 1978)

Joyce, R., "Rational Fear of Monsters," *British Journal of Aesthetics* 40 (2000), pp. 209–24

"Noncognitivism, Motivation, and Assertion" (forthcoming)

"Apologizing," *Public Affairs Quarterly* 13 (1999), pp. 159–73

Kant, I., *Groundwork to the Metaphysics of Morals* [1783], trans. H. J. Paton (London: Hutchinson, 1985)

Korsgaard, C., "Skepticism About Practical Reason," *Journal of Philosophy* 83 (1986), pp. 5–25

The Sources of Normativity (Cambridge: Cambridge University Press, 1996)

Lewis, D., "How to Define Theoretical Terms," *Journal of Philosophy* 67 (1970), pp. 427–46

"Dispositional Theories of Value," *Proceedings of the Aristotelian Society*, supplementary volume 72 (1989), pp. 113–37

Lycan, W., "Moral Facts and Moral Knowledge," in *The Spindel Conference: The Southern Journal of Philosophy*, supplementary volume 24 (1986), pp. 79–94

Mackie, J. L., *Ethics: Inventing Right and Wrong* (New York: Penguin Books, 1977)
  The Miracle of Theism (Oxford: Clarendon Press, 1982)

Malinowski, B., *Argonauts of the Western Pacific* (London: Routledge and Kegan Paul, 1922)
  Myth in Primitive Psychology (London: Kegan Paul, 1926)
  "The Foundations of Faith and Morals" [1935], in *Malinowski and the Work of Myth* (Princeton: Princeton University Press, 1992), pp. 131–72

McDowell, J., "Are Moral Requirements Hypothetical Imperatives?" *Proceedings of the Aristotelian Society*, supplementary volume 52 (1978), pp. 13–29

Mill, J. S., *Utilitarianism* [1863] (Cambridge: Hackett Publishing Company, 1979)

Millgram, E., "Williams' Argument Against External Reasons," *Noûs* (1996), pp. 197–220

Milo, R., "Moral Indifference," *The Monist* 64 (1981), pp. 373–93

Moore, G. E., *Principia Ethica* [1903] (Cambridge: Cambridge University Press, 1948)

Nishida, T., "Review of Recent Findings on Mahale Chimpanzees," in R. W. Wrangham, W. C. McGrew, F. de Waal and P. G. Heltne (eds.), *Chimpanzee Cultures* (Cambridge, Mass.: Harvard University Press, 1994), pp. 373–96

Nozick, R., *Philosophical Explanations* (Oxford: Clarendon Press, 1981)

Peirce, C. S., *Collected Papers* (Cambridge, Mass.: Belknap Press of Harvard University Press, 1960)

Putnam, H., *Philosophy of Logic* (New York: Harper & Row, 1971)

Quine, W. V., *Methods of Logic* (London: Routledge & Kegan Paul, 1952)
  Theories and Things (Cambridge, Mass.: Harvard University Press, 1981)

Railton, P., "Moral Realism," *Philosophical Review* 95 (1986), pp. 163–207

Ramsey, F., *Philosophical Papers* (Cambridge: Cambridge University Press, 1990)

Richards, R., "A Defense of Evolutionary Ethics," *Biology and Philosophy* 1 (1986), pp. 265–93

Rosen, G., "Modal Fictionalism," *Mind* 99 (1990), pp. 327–54

Rottschaefer, W. A. and Martinsen, D., "Really Taking Darwin Seriously: An Alternative to Michael Ruse's Darwinian Metaethics," *Biology and Philosophy* 5 (1990), pp. 149–73

Ruse, M., *Taking Darwin Seriously* (Oxford: Basil Blackwell, 1986)

Russell, B., *Collected Papers* (London: George Allen & Unwin, 1983)

Sade, Marquis de, *The Complete Justine, Philosophy in the Bedroom, and other Writings*, trans. and ed. R. Seaver and A. Wainhouse (New York: Grove Press, 1965)
  The Misfortunes of Virtue, and other Early Tales, trans. D. Coward (Oxford: Oxford University Press, 1992)

Scanlon, T., *What We Owe Each Other* (London: The Belknap Press of Harvard University Press, 1998)

Select bibliography

Smith, J., "Plato's Myths as 'Likely Accounts', Worthy of Belief," *Apeiron* 19 (1985), pp. 24–42

Smith, M., *The Moral Problem* (Oxford: Blackwell, 1994)

"Internal Reasons," *Philosophy and Phenomenological Research* 55 (1995), pp. 109–31

"Objectivity and Moral Realism: On the Significance of the Phenomenology of Moral Experience," in J. Haldane and C. Wright (eds.), *Reality, Representation and Projection* (New York: Oxford University Press, 1993), pp. 235–55

"In Defense of *The Moral Problem*," *Ethics* 108 (1997), pp. 84–119

Sober, E., *The Philosophy of Biology* (San Francisco: Westview Press, 1993)

Stevenson, C. L., "The Emotive Meaning of Ethical Terms," *Mind* 46 (1937), pp. 14–31

Ethics and Language (New Haven: Yale University Press, 1944)

Strawson, P. F., "On Referring," in A. Flew (ed.), *Essays in Conceptual Analysis* (London: MacMillan & Co. Ltd., 1956), pp. 21–52

Sturgeon, N., "Moral Explanations," in D. Copp and D. Zimmerman (eds.), *Morality, Reason and Truth* (Totowa, NJ: Rowman & Allanheld, 1984), pp. 49–78

Sutherland, S., *Irrationality: The Enemy Within* (London: Penguin Books, 1994)

Vaihinger, H., *The Philosophy of "As If,"* trans. C. K. Ogden (London: Routledge & Kegan Paul Ltd., 1949)

de Waal, F., *Good Natured: The Origins of Right and Wrong in Humans and Other Animals* (London: Harvard University Press, 1996)

Chimpanzee Politics (Baltimore: Johns Hopkins University Press, 1982)

Wiggins, D., "Categorical Requirements: Kant and Hume on the Idea of Duty," in R. Hursthouse, G. Lawrence, and W. Quinn (eds.), *Virtues and Reasons* (Oxford: Clarendon Press, 1995), pp. 279–330

Williams, B., *Moral Luck* (Cambridge: Cambridge University Press, 1981)

Wittgenstein, L., *Philosophical Investigations* (Oxford: Basil Blackwell, 1963)

"Lecture on Ethics," *Philosophical Review* 74 (1965), pp. 3–12

246

Index

247

Index

For EU product safety concerns, contact us at Calle de José Abascal, 56–1°,
28003 Madrid, Spain or eugpsr@cambridge.org.

www.ingramcontent.com/pod-product-compliance
Ingram Content Group UK Ltd.
Pitfield, Milton Keynes, MK11 3LW, UK
UKHW010342140625
459647UK00010B/762